Mayank Chhaya has been a journalist for the past 25 years, during which period he has reported extensively on India, Pakistan, Sri Lanka and the United States. He is a commentator on South Asian affairs for the New Delhi-based Indo-Asian News Service, and also runs the news and current affairs website www.dailysub.com. He lives in Chicago.

t

DALAI LAMA

*The Revealing Life Story
and His Struggle for Tibet*

An Authorized Biography

■

MAYANK CHHAYA

I.B. TAURIS

LONDON · NEW YORK

Published in 2008 by I.B.Tauris & Co Ltd
6 Salem Road, London W2 4BU
175 Fifth Avenue, New York NY 10010
www.ibtauris.com

First published by Doubleday,
a division of Random House, Inc.
Copyright © 2007, 2008, Mayank Chhaya

ISBN: 978 1 84511 763 4

A full CIP record for this book is available from the British Library

Printed and bound in Great Britain by
Biddles Ltd.

To

KESUMI,

my wife and hopefully my friend

JASHN AND HAYAA,

our son and daughter

CONTENTS

PREFACE TO THE
PAPERBACK EDITION

In the last decade and a half the 14th Dalai Lama has increasingly looked like a peripatetic advocate of compassion and peace who may or may not be espousing a specific cause. Since 1989, when he won the Nobel Peace Prize, his message has become progressively disengaged from a specific geopolitical entity, namely Tibet. There are people who may not even immediately associate the Dalai Lama with the broader question of Tibet's occupation by China.

However, the violent protests by Tibetans in Lhasa and elsewhere to coincide with the 49th anniversary of the March 10,

1959 uprising came as a grim reminder that the 73-year-old Buddhist monk's primary context is Tibet and his immediate concern is the future of its people. To the extent that this biography comes out soon after Lhasa exploded into a rage that was probably boiling for close to 20 years, it would hopefully help readers understand the issues and conflicts that define not just Tibet but the Dalai Lama himself. It would also help understand his motivations and how he is in an extraordinary position of being a monk sitting at the heart of one of the world's last great conflicts.

The Sino-Tibetan conflict is an old one, old enough for people to forget its relevance and its consequences. It is particularly so when the predominating party to the dispute, China, has stunned the world with its incredible economic progress in the last 30 years and effectively papered over any angularities of its existence. That is why the March, 2008 Tibetan protests and their ferocity served a historic purpose in helping refocus the world's attention to the core issues of the conflict. In a movement reminiscent of the political rebellion against Myanmar's military junta in late 2007, Buddhist monks took to the streets in Lhasa apparently to mark the anniversary of the 1959 uprising. They could not have chosen a more provocative time.

Determined to showcase the best of all things Chinese in the run-up to the Games, Beijing was not about to tolerate a few hundred militant monks bent upon spoiling the party. The Chinese reaction was swift and, by all accounts, harsh. Despite a near total information blackout, stories of many Tibetan deaths—some sources put it close to 100 in the first four days—and widespread injuries came out. What the subsequent protests did was to drop the question of Tibet right in the middle of an international community which treats the cause with far less urgency than it deserves.

The violent protests, which triggered several smaller ones worldwide, highlighted many competing forces at play in the Tibetan dispute at once. They illustrated that societal fractures in Lhasa and elsewhere in Tibet run far deeper than not just what China would have the world believe but also what it had convinced itself about. In equal measure, they revealed the extent of frustration that ordinary Tibetans, both inside and outside Tibet, feel about the Dalai Lama's steadfastly pacifist, non-violent "middle way" approach. At the more operational, practical level, quite ironically it showed how an innately peaceful people under occupation would do well to occasionally vent some fury if only to keep their cause relevant and current.

While researching for the book the author got a glimpse into how the younger generation of Tibetans does not share the Dalai Lama's commitment to non-violence at any cost. The book touches upon the possibility that ordinary Tibetans would run out of patience for the Dalai Lama's pacifist approach and instead choose a path that he is so instinctively against. His lifelong training as a Buddhist monk requires him to pursue the path of non-violence no matter how provocative the challenges and how demanding the circumstances. That commitment was severely tested by the latest protests as ordinary Tibetans appealed to him not to stop them. By his own admission he had the same sense of foreboding about the crisis as he had during the March 10, 1959 uprising. He said according to a Chinese military document between March 1959 and September 1960, 87,000 were people killed. In charting the trajectory of the Dalai Lama's life since he was declared to be the reincarnation of the 13th Dalai Lama the biography attempts to explain the historic forces that shaped his personality and philosophy. It is as much a chronicle of what happened in the past five decades as it is a reasonable speculation about what the future holds for the six-century old institution of the Dalai Lama.

It is fascinating that even in examining whether the latest round of protests makes the Dalai Lama's role redundant, one cannot help but focus predominantly on his person as well what he stands for. Inevitably the protests have thrown up the question about whether he commands the same level of respect and following that he has traditionally enjoyed. He attributes the fact that there are those who are very critical of his approach to a culture of democracy that he has fostered within the exiled Tibetan community since the early 1960s. The biography dwells on his efforts to democratize an institution which has often been accused of encouraging serfdom.

What is forgotten by those who rush to announce the demise of the Dalai Lama's institution is that even after nearly five decades of his absence from his homeland, Tibetans would still not mind being rounded up by the Chinese police for displaying his portrait in their homes. More than anybody else the Dalai Lama has recognized and institutionalized reforms in order to make the Tibetan governing structure more in line with modernity than it has been. He frequently describes himself as leading a "semi-retired" life and signaled that his role in any future dispensation would be limited at best.

Being a Dalai Lama is not a role that he chose of his own volition. It was chosen for him at an age where he was in no position to make any informed judgment other than which candy to eat. From that perspective, the Dalai Lama has continuously fashioned himself for roles which he may not necessarily have liked to perform. For instance, his role as a champion of non-violence and compassion is natural to him but that often puts him in direct conflict with many of his own constituents.

It was widely expected that Beijing would stamp out the spiraling protests with urgency mixed with ruthlessness, especially because it is desperate to ensure a smooth conduct of the Olympic Games. However, what it was unlikely to accomplish is to put a firm lid on the searing heat generated by the uprising.

From all available accounts out of Tibet coupled with the tone of the Dalai Lama's reaction, it became clear that a decisive phase may have been reached in the nearly six-decade old Sino-Tibetan stand-off. This is particularly surprising because there were no recognizable signs pointing in the direction of such an assertive expression of disaffection. Although the six million Tibetans are singularly ill equipped to take on the mighty Chinese establishment, the timing of the protests was fraught with history and had the potential to fundamentally alter the equation.

In so much as the goal of the protestors was to draw the world's attention to their plight, it was met with manifest success as the story dominated global headlines for days and, in a sense, forced China on the defensive. Now whether a defensive China is a more amenable China is an open question. If history is any guide China does not like being pushed into any negotiating position, particularly when it comes to nationalities such as Tibetan which it views as subservient to the larger Chinese identity. This much was proved by the strong reaction from Chinese Premier Wen Jiabao. He said rioters used "extremely cruel" methods to undermine the Games.

"We have ample evidence to prove that the riots were organized, premeditated, masterminded and incited by the Dalai clique," Wen said in his first press conference after being elected to a second five-year term by national legislators.

"This has all the more revealed that the clique's consistent claims of not pursuing independence but peaceful dialogue are deceitful lies," he said.

While the Dalai Lama has been used to being branded as a "splittist" and "propagandist" by the Chinese since his exile to India in 1959, the level of violence affected him enough to announce that if the violent protests continued to spiral he would step down as the head of the government-in-exile in McLeod Ganj, India. It was a sincere offer but more than that it was an expression of how much he disapproves of any means other than peaceful to address the issue.

He has acknowledged that his "middle way" has not borne concrete results but has still remained completely wedded to it. The Dalai Lama stepping down as the head of the government-in-exile really means nothing in practical terms because he will remain the spiritual leader and in that capacity he will continue to preside over the destinies of the Tibetan people. Under the Tibetan traditions Dalai Lamas do not resign. They just reincarnate.

At the time of the book's printing it is unclear what the eventual outcome of the protests will be. What is clear, though, is that they have served the purpose of reawakening the world's concern about Tibet and the role the Dalai Lama plays in resolving the dispute. With Tibet back as an outstanding issue and the world calling for its peaceful resolution, this biography will bring to those unfamiliar with what is at dispute some sense of history as well as some sense of what its main protagonist is all about.

Mayank Chhaya
March 2008

DALAI LAMA

■

INTRODUCTION

The Fourteenth Dalai Lama and Tibet were the most mysterious part of my childhood apocrypha. Everything about the man and his land was fabulous—mystical stories of reincarnation unfolding in fog-laden valleys of frozen mountains at the height of 13,000-plus feet. Tonsured monks in ochre robes contrasted against the white snow-covered landscape of the Himalayas appeared so stunningly picturesque to me that I did not care if such a world could really exist. It did not matter whether the stories were true or not as long as they were captivating. There were pretty good chances that both Tibet and the Dalai Lama existed, but in my Indian childhood in the early 1960s they seemed to belong more to magical folklore than reality. In a country where the real and the magical constantly fuse and metamorphose into each other, what difference did it make whether this world actually existed? In any event, for a child who was not even ten years old, the magical seemed infinitely more engaging than the real.

That view changed every time the winter came and the Dalai Lama's existence became all too real when hundreds of his portraits and pictures adorned the sidewalks of my town along with piles of brightly colored sweaters that Tibetan refugees came to sell. At least it was true that there were Tibetan people. It appeared quite possible that after all someone called the Dalai Lama did indeed exist. I remember having asked a Tibetan woman who the "grown-up babylike figure in the picture" was. "That is His Holiness. He is the living Buddha," she replied. I neither understood "His Holiness" nor "the living Buddha." I knew of only one Buddha, who had been dead for some 2,500 years. The question that troubled me was if Gautama Buddha had died so long ago how come he was still living? It took me another decade and a half to unravel that mystery.

Since I grew up in a country where renunciates and ascetics crowd the landscape, yet another monk was unlikely to attract my attention. This was particularly true of the one who lived some thousand miles away in the pre-Himalayan Dhauladhar mountain range in northwest India. In the 1960s and '70s the Dalai Lama was featured in local Indian newspapers frequently, especially after the country's disastrous war with China in 1962. There were some delightfully misinformed people in my neighborhood who seriously believed that India could avenge its humiliating defeat at the hands of China using the Dalai Lama's Tantric powers, which ordinary people took to mean some sort of black magic or occult practices. In their neat, if completely flawed, formulation, the

Dalai Lama, forced to flee Tibet amid grave threats to his life by the invading Chinese army barely three years earlier, would be thirsting to settle scores with them. And could there be a more potent weapon for a reincarnate Buddhist monk than black magic?

In 1967, a full five years after the war between India and China, one of my neighbors gathered unsuspecting and impressionable children like myself and conjured up an image of the Dalai Lama going into a deep trance and unleashing destructive energy against the People's Liberation Army. Since he came from the land of Mount Kailash, the putative hub of the Hindu god Shiva, the raconteur told us that the Dalai Lama had three eyes, one right in the middle of his forehead. The third eye was where all his power of cosmic destruction resided. If he opened that eye, there was no way China could survive. India's then–prime minister Jawaharlal Nehru, he claimed with utter certainty, had persuaded the Dalai Lama to invoke the devastating wrath that would instantly atomize the Chinese army. Such street-side phantasms let loose by the neighborhood fantasist merely reinforced my perception that the Dalai Lama was more apocryphal than real.

My first encounter with the real Dalai Lama came sometime in the early 1980s when he was visiting Bombay to attend a congress on synthesis between science and religion. I did not consciously look for his third eye, but it was reassuring that he did not have one. I vaguely remembered that my neighborhood storyteller had qualified his claim about the Dalai Lama's third eye by saying that it became apparent only during extraordinary times. The congress was clearly not one such extraordinary time. As a reporter assigned to cover the congress, I was expected to produce an offbeat story of the event, one that did not necessarily have any immediate news value. I remember asking the Dalai Lama, "Aren't we rapidly approaching a stage in human history where the dividing line between science and religion is fast vanishing?" The Dalai Lama laughed from the core of his being and said, "Religion is science with faith. Science is religion in search of faith." Even as he said that I realized that this story was not going to make that day's or any other day's paper. It is just as well that the remark had to hibernate for nearly two decades because it has now found a home in the more substantial context of a book.

The Dalai Lama has grown in my consciousness over the last fifteen years. Sporadic reading about him, Tibet, China, and Buddhism marked the run-up to my first substantial meeting with him in 1996. He was never in my professional focus till that year when I began working on a cover story for *India Abroad*, a New York–based Indian American weekly newspaper. The scope of the story was very general, covering the question of Tibet from many different angles. It was in this context that I first sought an interview with the Dalai Lama. It took place on the sidelines of Shoton, a Lhamo festival at the Tibetan Institute of Performing Arts (TIPA) in McLeod Ganj, the Dalai Lama's place of exile for four decades in India. Lhamo is a 580-year-old Tibetan tradition that began as a simple bridge-building project over the Kyichu River near Lhasa by the fourteenth-century scholar Thangtong Gyalpo. Legend has it that Gyalpo, hard-pressed as he was for money to build the bridge, turned to seven sisters in his workforce who excelled at dancing and singing. The scholar created an operatic style around the seven sisters' talent and traveled throughout Tibet staging performances to raise money for the bridge. The sisters' high-pitched martial singing and vigorous dancing earned them the sobriquet "the heavenly dancing goddesses," or Lhamo. The bridge was built and so was the Tibetan opera.

After the interview the Dalai Lama's aides invited my family, my wife, Kesumi, and my son, Jashn, for a ceremonial blessing. Kesumi is an Indonesian Muslim who was born in the Buddhist island nation of Sri Lanka. Having been used to Buddhist monks who do not hobnob with the laity, my wife approached the Dalai Lama with a great deal of circumspection, even trepidation. I am narrating this incident in some detail because I believe it influenced the Dalai Lama's decision to authorize me to write this book. The Dalai Lama sprang from his chair, went to the door, where my wife stood with our son, gave her an avuncular hug, massaged my son's head, and brought them in. Stunned by the gesture, my wife said spontaneously that she was a Muslim, I an agnostic, and that maybe our son would become a Buddhist. For a fraction of a second I could see that the Dalai Lama was touched by what was being said to him.

During one of my many subsequent visits to McLeod Ganj, a very senior monk, who bound me to the oath of never revealing his name, said, "Don't make the mistake of thinking that you were chosen for any worldly reasons." He left it at that with a cryptic clue hanging on my head forever. Be that as it may, I was chosen to write this ambitious book. It does not matter why.

The last four decades have seen one of the twentieth century's most intractable standoffs, essentially between a single individual and one of the world's mightiest nations. On the one hand there is a nation that has historically considered itself to be not only at the center of the world but a geopolitical entity that must keep open the option of extending its boundaries for all times to come. It is a powerful nation that has kept its over one billion people in a political, cultural, and economic straitjacket even while consolidating its position as one of the most decisive voices in world affairs.

On the other hand there is a simple yet profoundly learned and extraordinarily evolved monk whose very presence causes millions of his followers to be overcome with emotions. He speaks and practices tolerance of the most enlightened kind in the face of the systematic genocide of his own people by his gigantic adversary. Even if we set aside for a moment the fact that he is regarded by his followers as the reincarnation of one of human history's most revered and worshipped figures, the conflict pitting the Dalai Lama against China makes for a captivating struggle. The Dalai Lama's highly engaging personality adds to the standoff an incredibly dramatic edge.

As a journalist I have approached this book purely as a story whose characters are real and contemporary. Beyond that, during the course of my seven years of research I have discovered facets of the Dalai Lama that extremely few have had the privilege to explore. Many of my Tibetan friends tell me that they feel gratified for life if they manage to meet the Dalai Lama for a few seconds. "Look at your destiny that you have had the blessing to sit with His Holiness and talk not once, twice but a number of times. Never forget that something like this does not simply happen without a reason," Migmar, one of thousands of Tibetan refugees on the streets of McLeod Ganj, told me during a conversation.

For me the single biggest professional challenge has been to rescue from an ocean of often conflicting works a persona that is not only accurate but even original, and to present a profile that has never been written before. Given the kind of massive media profile that the Dalai Lama has enjoyed over the past fifteen years in the West in general and the United States in particular, it is difficult to find fresh material. Apart from books and newspaper articles there have been feature films and documentaries on the subject. Tibet and the Dalai Lama must be among the most extensively written about subjects in the world today. All this clearly made my task even more exacting.

By his own admission and according to many analysts of the subject, his long exile from Tibet has not only had a defining impact on the Dalai Lama personally but also has significantly influenced the evolution of the institution of the Dalai Lama in modern times. Some scholars even argue that the Dalai Lama's exile from the land of his birth and his separation from the trappings of his enormous power within Tibet has in fact salvaged the once sagging image of the Tibetan Buddhist clergy as a power-hungry elite that perpetuated itself in the morass of shocking ignorance and blind religious faith among its peasant and nomadic populace. The exile has also fundamentally shaped the dynamic of the Tibet-versus-China conflict.

It is from this standpoint that I recognize that a book that takes in its sweep all the elements of this conflict over the last four decades and presents it in a manner that is accessible to the uninitiated reader in any part of the world should have discernible merit. It is tempting to get sucked into the mystical vortex of the subject and produce yet another gawky account of something that has been so frivolously called exotic; a land with an average elevation of 13,000 feet and which forms an endless cold desert inhabited by people apparently frozen in a time warp, twirling strange-looking prayer wheels and chanting even stranger sounding mantras—these all are ingredients that naturally lend themselves to exotic interpretations. My challenge was to quickly go past those stereotypes and attempt to present something that goes beyond the obvious.

The conflict that the Dalai Lama finds himself right at the

center of is not merely about the geographical entity called Tibet. Geographical expansion is just one aspect of it. The conflict operates on a far more profound human level. It is a conflict that has all but destroyed a unique way of life and in the process taken, according to Tibetan estimates, close to a million lives quite remorselessly. It is a conflict that has ruthlessly dismantled a very valuable belief system, based not on unquestioning faith but on cogent intellect. While it is true that many elements of Tibet before the Chinese took over defied rational thinking, by and large it has been a society that has attempted to live by a system that rationally evolved over many centuries. It is also a conflict between a people who do not take up arms because they are convinced of the utter futility of violence and a nation-state that has no compunctions about expanding at any cost. Most important, it is a conflict between a single individual of enormous scholarship, enlightenment, and intellectual integrity and a nation that has routinely transgressed basic human values.

I set out to present a book through which a general reader can grasp some aspects of this great conflict and reach a conclusion that errs on the side of morality and humaneness. In one's effort to achieve that objective one always runs the risk of producing a hagiography that is rash in its judgment and naïve in its understanding of historical processes crystallizing for the past many centuries. I have no intentions of apportioning blame in the Tibet-versus-China debate. I merely want to understand through the life story of the Dalai Lama what it is that nation-states find so very unacceptable about independence of individual thought.

The conflict has already entered a phase wherein a battle of attrition is being waged by China to decimate the spirit of the Tibetans. Dr. Orville Schell, one of the foremost scholars of China and Tibet, author of fourteen highly regarded books, and dean of Berkeley School of Journalism, told me: "The trouble with the system that China now has is that it is very difficult to move in a deliberate and radically new way on anything. The whole path of reform has been tiny little piecemeal experiments which have become the de facto reality. In a certain sense the problem with Tibet is more symbolic than real, a little bit like Taiwan. So it is harder for China to move symbolically to clear major policy shifts and easier to move on piecemeal practical questions. I don't think this leadership feels capable of making such a shift. It is one of the great mysteries of China's political system how resistant it is to fundamental change and less resistant to superficial change[s] which in aggregate add up often into something major, but that's not Tibet's problem. So they are hoping that the Dalai Lama would simply die. What they fail to appreciate, however, is that he is their best hope to bring about some sort of reconciliation and to keep Tibet peacefully within the sovereign boundaries of China. They don't fully understand the negative consequence of what they are doing to themselves."

"It is possible that China is waiting for me to die in the hope that the cause will lose its center. But I think the Tibetan people have enough strength to keep up their struggle in my absence," the Dalai Lama told me in one of his many interviews.

A lot has been said about how the inherent pacifism of Buddhism, a philosophy that ordinary Tibetans consider pivotal to their lives, could in fact prove their greatest undoing. A race that was once martial and known for its conquests has steadily lost its edge because of centuries of pacifist conditioning. And in any case the sheer numbers do not favor the Tibetans. Even if every single Tibetan rises in armed rebellion, the prospects of their making any impact on China are bleak at best. "One billion Chinese, six million Tibetans—what can anyone do? Even if the Chinese say come cut my throat, who is going to do that? The Tibetans will get tired and the Chinese will still be there," is how the Dalai Lama's eighty-four-year-old brother, Thubten Jigme Norbu, puts it with a degree of resignation.

As long as the Dalai Lama is at the helm of Tibetan affairs there is no likelihood that the Tibet movement will turn itself into an armed struggle. The whole point of Tibet is that it must retain its moral and spiritual high ground because without that the conflict it faces could degenerate into any of the hundreds of armed insurgencies around the world.

I have attempted to tell a human story based on many fascinating anecdotes as well as the engaging mysticism surrounding the institution of the Dalai Lama as embodied by Tenzin Gyatso. The Dalai Lama's person combines three equal and at times competing elements of man, monk, and mystic. The very nature of the struggle he has had to wage since his childhood has forced him to let the man take primacy over the other two. The monk in him is, of course, an obvious reality but generally remains understated because of his increasingly mundane preoccupations. I have seen many occasions when the monk in him reigns supreme. There have been exceedingly few times when the mystic in the Dalai Lama has surfaced in recent years. He almost never talks about the mystique of his being. In fact, he tends to dismiss it completely. I have been witness to a couple of special teachings in McLeod Ganj where his mystique was in evidence. I was allowed to sit through a particularly advanced teaching for some six to eight people. At one particular point the Dalai Lama asked one of the people to choose a particular path of salvation. A symbol that emerged was indicative of wrath. At the precise moment that the Dalai Lama interpreted that symbol lightning struck somewhere quite close to the mountain where the ritual was being conducted. I don't know if anyone else noticed it but I was quite amazed at its timing, however fortuitously it may have coincided with the ritual. It may have been happenstance, but the Dalai Lama seems to have a knack for finding himself frequently amid such occurrences.

I have seen many spiritual masters in my career, but there are very few who switch so effortlessly between their ordinary mortal concerns, their renunciatory objectives, and their mystical calling as the Dalai Lama does. This book views the Dalai Lama from the three distinct standpoints of man, monk, and mystic and brings him within the grasp of general readers. The book is in no way driven by preconceived notions about who is right and who is wrong in the Tibet-China conflict. It would be simplistic, well-nigh foolish, to project one party as the villain and the other as the victim, especially since the Dalai Lama himself has steadfastly refrained from such knee-jerk characterizations. Insomuch as it means my taking a stand on the issue, I have written this book under definite promptings of my conscience in support of Tibet and the Tibetans. If I err, then I do so on the side of individual freedom against state supremacy.

I

CONTINENTAL
CATACLYSM

For tens of millions of years Nature has chiseled and sculpted Tibet unlike any other place in the world. It is as austere as it is awesome. Cataclysmic geological forces over the last seventy-five million years have pushed millions of square miles of Earth's crust northward over the ocean. The continental drift has moved what is now known as the Indian plate over 6,000 miles in 50 million years. The final phase of this tectonic crunch began about 25 million years ago when the Indian plate started literally ramming into the Eurasian (Laurasian) plate and began dredging the Tethys Sea with a force whose extent is still not fully understood. This powerful phenomenon carried with it a future history that defined many modern nation-states of Asia, their civilizations, their religions, their cultures, and their conflicts. Tibet has been at the center of this bewildering tectonic spectacle.

From an ordinary human perspective the time span may seem enormous and the pace of the drift impossibly slow, but in geological terms this is normal, considering the gigantic blocks of Earth's crust involved in this movement. A time-lapse cinematic perspective of the great crunch would reveal one of the most awe-inspiring occurrences in the planet's history. According to geologists, Tibet emerged as a hot and wet plane from under the sea between fourteen and eighteen million years ago, the era they call the late middle Miocene. Some fifteen million years before the present, the phase began wherein this tectonic union would elevate the land and turn it into the highest mountain range on Earth. With the formation of the Himalayas, which continues to this day, began the rise of the Tibetan plateau, arguably the world's largest, stretching over 1,550 miles (2,500 kilometers) from east to west with an average elevation of 13,000 feet. The Indian plate is still shifting northward at an incredible rate of 5 centimeters per year, which geologists describe with some levity as twice the rate at which human fingernails grow. Although there is clear evidence to suggest that the Tibetan plateau began rising before the rise of the Himalayas, it was during the last four million years that it acquired its fabled elevation.

Perhaps unlike any other region in the world, Tibet draws its fundamental character from its geography and geology; some say even more so than its history. Tibet without its rugged and stately mountains and vast plateau loses almost all its mystique, which has endured several centuries through medieval and modern times. If Tibet were a hot African nation with no mountains and monks as the predominant features of its landscape, chances are that it would not have inspired a million tales and captured the West's imagination. Not only is Tibet's geography at the center of its people's existence but it also determines the climate of a region inhabited by over two billion people. The Himalaya-Tibet region has been called the "water tower" of Asia. It supplies water to more than a third of the world's population and is the source of most great rivers in China and the Indian subcontinent. The Indus, the Ganges, the Sutlej, and the Brahmaputra—all rivers at the heart of the great Indian civilization—originate at the Kang Rimpoche in the northwestern corner of upper Tibet, more popularly known as Mount Kailash. This is also the putative home of Shiva, one of the great trinity of gods that Hindus worship along with Vishnu and Brahma. The east is formed by splendid gorges of the Salween, the Mekong, the Yangtze, and the Yellow rivers. These eight major rivers have shaped the two great civilizations of China and India.

As recently as a million years ago, or until the end of the Pliocene era, Tibet's climate was tropic or subtropic. But with the Himalayan range rising to 20,000-plus feet by the tail end of the Pliocene (about five to six million years ago), its climate started changing dramatically. The mountains blocked the movement of the monsoon winds rising over the Indian Ocean. Consequently, the Tibetan climate became a frigid alpine zone rather than subtropic, which would have been more in line with its latitude.

Tibet's reputation as an impregnable and aloof land, the roof of the world, owes everything to its geology and geography. Towering on its southwest are the greatest mountains on the planet—the Himalayas, the Karakoram, and the Pamir. Its northwest is the desert of Takla Makan, and the east has parallel gorges formed by the four rivers. The northeast is the only accessible area of Kokonor. Permafrost covers 2.15 million square kilometers of the Tibetan plateau throughout the year. Its 975,000 square miles (2.5 million square kilometers)—1,500 miles (2,500 kilometers) from the east to the west and 774 miles (1,200 kilometers) from the north to the south—form one-fourth of China, adding an enormous geopolitical weight to the country. The overriding appeal of Tibet to the outside world has been visual first and anything else later. The overwhelming yet majestic manifestations of nature have over the millennia created in the inhabitants of Tibet reverence for the elements. Mountains have traditionally enjoyed the exalted status of deities. Nature spirits have been invoked as a matter of routine. A whole set of prehistoric Tibetan belief systems that preceded the arrival of Buddhism was dominated by what to a novice and outsider seems completely outlandish. The prevailing belief system included nature and animistic worship, which incorporated rites and rituals that would seem rather bizarre to an outsider. For the Tibetans themselves it was just a way of surviving with humility in the midst of overarching Nature. These extremities of the Tibetan climate and geography are perceived as something of great value.

In my conversations with the Dalai Lama there was frequent reference to the fact that the climate in Tibet was free from "the heat, mosquitoes, snakes, insects, and dust of the Indian plains." This has also been a recurring theme in scores of interviews with ordinary Tibetan refugees even after they have spent decades in India.

Tsetsen Dolkar, a refugee who runs a small Tibetan curio shop in the narrow lanes of McLeod Ganj, summed up the feeling, saying: "I have been in India for nearly thirty years. But I still fear a rat might come out of my woodwork followed by a snake. My house near Lhasa was at such an altitude such creatures could not survive."

HISTORY OF TIBET

The known history of what is called Tibet today can be traced back to the seventh century, the era of the first hero-king, Songtsen Gampo. The time before that is buried in ancient myths including the one that says Tibetans were created by a monkey and a mountain ogress. Gampo's stature in early Tibetan history owes considerably to his success in getting Buddhist scriptures translated into Tibetan. For that reason he is credited with opening the doors so that Buddhism could enter this seemingly impenetrable land of awesome mountains and breathtaking valleys.

One of Gampo's queens was Bhrikuti Devi, a Nepalese princess who brought with her many Buddhist images, including one of Sakyamuni—the sage of the Sakya caste—namely, the Buddha. Before Buddhism came to Tibet the prevalent religion was Bon, a shamanistic worship of Nature spirits in which human and animal sacrifice, exorcism, magic, and sorcery were practiced. Bonism was soon merged into Buddhism, but many of its practices and beliefs were retained to varying degrees. In some ways Buddhism became a more refined face of the combination of the two. The fusion became known as Lamaism, from the word *lama*, meaning "master" or "teacher." Bonism exists to this day and is recognized by the Dalai Lama even as it continues to draw a large following among Tibetans.

It was the Tibetan monk Tsong-khapa (1358–1419) who carried forward the reform initiated in 1042 AD by Atisha Dipankara, an eminent teacher from India. Tsong-khapa founded the Geluk-pa (Virtuous Way) sect, or Yellow Hat sect, in the fourteenth century. The sect required celibacy among monks. After 1587 the Grand Lama of this school was called the Dalai Lama. Interestingly, the title of Dalai Lama was first conferred by the Mongol warrior-king Altan Khan, who proclaimed the head of the Geluk-pa sect as Dalai Lama Vajradhara (the All-Embracing Lama, Holder of the Thunderbolt). *Dalai* is a Mongolian word meaning "vast" or "oceanlike." *Lama* denotes "wisdom of a great teacher." Together the title means "a teacher whose wisdom is as vast as an ocean."

By 1641 the Dalai Lama had acquired temporal and spiritual authority over all of Tibet. Up until the current Dalai Lama, who is the fourteenth in the line of mystical succession, the Tibetans regarded the Fifth Dalai Lama, who reigned during the seventeenth century, as their greatest leader. This is because among other things it was during his time that the enormously large Potala Palace* was built as his residence.

The Chinese revolution of 1911 brought down the Quing Manchu dynasty and led to the loss of Chinese control over Tibet. In 1913 the Chinese authorities yielded to British pressure to hold a tripartite meeting (China, Tibet, and Britain) in Simla, India. A treaty was drafted by the British that divided Tibet into In-

---

*The Potala Palace, named after a hill in the southernmost tip of India commemorating Avlokiteswara, or the compassionate Buddha, known as Chenrezig to Tibetans, is far higher than St. Paul's Cathedral in London or Capitol Hill in Washington.

ner and Outer regions, the latter being autonomous. The outbreak of World War I in 1914 pushed Tibet out of the international spotlight. During the 1930s, when China became more unified, new efforts were begun to gain power over Tibet. After nearly two decades of uncertainty and the emergence of Communist China, the Chinese army captured the frontier fortress of Qamdo, 370 miles from the Tibetan capital of Lhasa. The Tibetan forces capitulated, with the current Dalai Lama sending a peace mission to Beijing.

On May 31, 1950, an agreement was signed granting nominal autonomy to Tibet but for all practical purposes bringing the area under Beijing's control. This, however, did not reduce tensions between the Chinese garrisons and the Khamba tribesmen of Tibet. In March 1959 the Dalai Lama rejected the Chinese request that he use his temporal power to rein in the tribesmen. The Dalai Lama was summoned to appear before the Chinese commander in Lhasa. The audacious summoning of someone whom the Tibetans regarded as the living Buddha sparked revulsion and large-scale antagonism toward the Chinese. On March 31, 1959, the Dalai Lama fled to India via Tezpur, the northeastern border town in the state of Assam, after a harrowing journey on foot and horseback. The Dalai Lama and his entourage were given political asylum in India.

Some 1,200 years after the Buddha lived his philosophy was introduced to Tibet, more out of royal matrimony than any conscious evangelical movement. Political expediency forced Songtsen Gampo to marry two foreign women, apart from the three Tibetan women he had already married. One of the two was Belsa, a Nepalese princess, and the other Gyasa, a Chinese princess. Both of them were devout Buddhists and brought with them strong

Buddhist influences. Historians believe that it was under their influence that Tibet began to gradually replace the indigenous animistic Bon religion with Buddhism. Both wives had brought with
them images of the Buddha which they had their king formally in-
stall in temples. While the door of Belsa's temple, known as the
Jokhang, faced west toward Nepal, that of Gyasa's temple, known
as Ramoche, faced east toward China. Although Buddhism was introduced with the blessings of the highest in the land, it did not
spread much for at least another 150 years. With spirit worship as
its core, Bon continued to influence Tibet's religious landscape as
well as political decision making. It would take the passage of
three successors for Buddhism to begin capturing the popular
imagination after Gampo in the reign of the thirty-seventh
Chogyal, Trisong Detsen. Detsen, overriding opposition from
pro-Bon ministers, invited Padmasambhava, or the lotus-born, the
foremost Indian Buddhist master of the day, to Tibet.

"Padmasambhava recognized early that the most effective way
of spreading Buddhism would be by interpreting its teachings in
the context of Tibet's prevailing mythology rather than dismissing
Bon altogether," the Dalai Lama explained. The Indian Buddhist
master traveled throughout Tibet and established the country's
first monastery, Samye, in AD 779. He initiated seven Tibetan
novice monks. These monks find a place of great reverence among
Tibetans even today. In 792 Detsen declared Buddhism as Tibet's
official religion.

History took yet another turn against Buddhism when four
decades after Detsen's death a coup by pro-Bon ministers installed
his grandson Lang Darma. His reign saw Buddhism come under
attack and monasteries overrun. Although there is no accurate
record, it is widely believed that Darma started the practice of

wearing hair in knots braided with red ribbons. The legend of the day that holds true to the present time was that he did so to hide his horns, signifying the fact that he was a wizard. Legend also has it that he had a black tongue. There are Tibetans who still stick their tongues out and scratch their heads while paying respects to high-ranking officials, the significance of the gesture being that they have neither black tongues nor horns.

For nearly four centuries after Darma's public slaying by the Buddhist monk Paljor Dorje using a bow and arrow, Tibet remained under virtual anarchy. From 842 when the Yarlung dynasty collapsed right up to 1247 when the Mongol warlords began overrunning Tibet, the country had practically no central governing structure. That made the area even more vulnerable to internal strife and external aggression. The Mongolian influence has been a crucial part of Tibet's history, especially since the middle of the sixteenth century. Altan Khan, leader of the eastern Mongols, and his grandnephew Secen Khungtaiji gave the Tibetans a clear choice—if they submitted, their religion would be accepted; if not they would be conquered and destroyed. The Tibetans chose submission in order to retain their religion.

It was in 1570 that Altan Khan invited Sonam Gyatso, the third incarnation of the Geluk-pa or Yellow Hat sect and abbot of the Drepung monastery, to his capital Hohhot (Khoto Khotan). During this meeting Sonam Gyatso recognized Altan Khan as an incarnation of Kublai Khan. This recognition was meant to help Altan Khan establish his lineage to the great Mongol warrior Genghis Khan. Whether Altan Khan was indeed a descendant of Genghis Khan by virtue of reincarnation is a moot question and could never be answered; but what the recognition of Altan Khan did was something of great value for the Tibetans in general and the Dalai Lama in particular. It helped the Tibetan monk secure Altan Khan's political patronage. More important, in return Sonam Gyatso was given the title of Dalai, which was the Mongolian translation of *Gyatso*. Thus was born the institution of the Dalai Lama. The two previous incarnations, Gedun Truppa (1391–1475) and Gedun Gyatso (1475–1542), were renamed as Dalai Lamas retroactively. After Sonam Gyatso's death his incarnation was discovered to be the great-grandson of Altan Khan. This coming together of the Mongol rulers and the Geluk-pa sect strengthened and expanded the influence of the latter over the whole of Tibet. The Mongol–Dalai Lama alliance was a mutually beneficial one, bringing both sides strengths in their respective domains.

Another significant Mongolian contribution to Tibetan history came in 1642 when Gushri Khan of Khoshot conferred spiritual and temporal authority upon the Fifth Dalai Lama, regarded as the greatest Dalai Lama with the exception of the current one, who is now described as the greatest of all time. This was a defining development in Tibetan history because over 350 years later the Dalai Lama's person continues to combine this supreme authority—some say now more so than ever before in the institution's over six-hundred-year-long history.

The Geluk-pa's choice of incarnation as an instrument of continuing spiritual and temporal authority represented a break from the practices of the other sects that mainly depended on hierarchical succession. The Geluk-pa, in fact, ended the overpowering influence of the Tibetan clans over the ruling elite since incarnation did not respect clannish affiliations.

The period under the Fifth Dalai Lama, Ngwang Lobsang

Gyatso (1617–1682), represents the equivalent of a Tibetan re-
naissance. Unlike Phagspa or the fifth Karmapa, heads of the often competing sects, the Fifth Dalai Lama did not shy away from
converting many monasteries of the other sects to the Yellow Hat
sect. After nearly eight centuries of anarchy, it was the Fifth Dalai
Lama who centralized authority in Lhasa.

For ordinary Tibetans, the most visible accomplishment of the
Fifth Dalai Lama still stands today in the heart of the now
Chinese-ruled Lhasa. It was he who began reconstructing the
seventh-century Dzong, the fort-residence of the Chogyal king,
which was destroyed by the Chinese. The Fifth Dalai Lama's
regent started building the great Potala Palace. While the construction of the 900-foot-long palace on a hill began during
the "Great Fifth's" reign, it continued well beyond his lifetime.
So overarching was the influence of the Dalai Lamas over Tibet
that the regent, Sangye Gyatso, had to conceal the Fifth Dalai
Lama's death for twelve years during the palace's construction. In
1694 when the Potala was completed, the regent announced the
death of the Fifth Dalai Lama. The objective behind this decep-
tion was to keep up the impression that the Dalai Lama was still
alive and, therefore, that the construction of the palace had his
blessings.

Unlike the previous four Dalai Lamas, the Fifth Dalai Lama
presided over a vast and fairly unified Tibet. The regent reasoned
that he could not risk waiting for the new incarnation to be found
and for him to grow to adulthood before taking over the reins. He
created an elaborate charade that the Fifth Dalai Lama had retired
from public life and gone into a secret retreat to pursue Buddhist
studies and meditation. It was a measure of the stratagem that

even meals were regularly taken to his quarters and drums beaten as part of the rituals. So much so that when very important visitors or officials sought an audience with the Dalai Lama the regent had a look-alike pose briefly as the Dalai Lama.

"The Fifth Dalai Lama is considered great because he unified Tibet, which had splintered over the previous eight or nine centuries. It was he who created a clear structure of governance," the Fourteenth Dalai Lama said.

The seven Dalai Lamas who followed the fifth were nowhere near as effective. A striking feature of their lives was that all of them died young, the youngest being nine (Luntok Gyatso, the Tenth Dalai Lama, 1806–1815) and the oldest forty-nine (Kesang Gyatso, the Seventh Dalai Lama, 1708–1757). Tibetan historians believe that none of them made a significant impact. In fact the Sixth Dalai Lama, Tsangyang Gyatso (1683–1706), pursued sensual pleasures and led a life of wine, women, and poetry. Despite his indulgences the Sixth Dalai Lama remains a hugely popular figure in Tibetan history. Tibetans judge his frailties differently and argue that his decadence was deliberate, aimed at testing their faith and sincerity.

"It seems he was not cut out for a monastic life but instead wanted to chase ordinary pleasures. The life of a Buddhist monk, particularly the Dalai Lama, is extremely demanding notwithstanding all the attendant devotion," said the Fourteenth Dalai Lama about the Sixth Dalai Lama.

By the time Thubten Gyatso, the Thirteenth Dalai Lama, was born in 1876, Tibet's tradition-bound society had been without a strong spiritual leader for nearly two centuries. Although all of the seven Dalai Lamas succeeding the "Great Fifth" were revered, they could not keep up the momentum that the Fifth Dalai Lama had generated. The Thirteenth Dalai Lama was crucial in the sense that he came at the threshold of Tibet's first brush with modernity.

The Thirteenth Dalai Lama went about overhauling affairs with a reformer's zeal. Centuries of primacy over the affairs of their land had bred complacency and corruption among monasteries and monks. The cliques around the preceding Dalai Lamas had become so used to their unfettered authority over the state that they had acquired what historians have called "profound arrogance." The Thirteenth Dalai Lama was quick to recognize the problems and understand how they could erode the credibility of the most revered institution of its kind.

Among many directives, the Thirteenth Dalai Lama discouraged the monks from getting too involved in secular affairs and increased the number of lay officials. He overhauled the legal system, abolished capital punishment, and reduced corporal punishment. He freed education from its elitist confines, restricted to the clergy, and made it accessible to the nobility and ordinary peasants. By all accounts the Thirteenth Dalai Lama had as modern a mind-set as could be expected within the limits of his tradition-bound life.

The Thirteenth Dalai Lama's nearly four-decade-long reign was both tumultuous and, by many accounts, replete with palace intrigues. Despite the heavy odds stacked against him, the Thirteenth Dalai Lama is considered as having been successful in breaking free from obscurantist traditions and introducing the Tibetan people to a more modern way of thinking.

"I believe the Thirteenth Dalai Lama did many things in his

lifetime that improved the quality of governance and life for the Tibetan people. After the Great Fifth, he was perhaps the most effective," the current Dalai Lama said.

TIBETAN ETHNICITY AND LANGUAGE

Two of the most important factors that modern Tibetans cite to strengthen their argument of their people's distinctiveness from the Chinese are their ethnicity and their language. While scholarly work on the two subjects remains sketchy at best, there is a fairly reasonable case to be made in their favor. It is nearly impossible to reach final conclusions on language or ethnic origins, which are always evolving, but there are significant pointers.

Warren W. Smith Jr., a highly regarded scholar who has done probably the most comprehensive work on Tibet in his seminal doctoral work *Tibetan Nation*, refrains from drawing any definite conclusions about the ethnic origins of the Tibetans or the source of their language. "One can never really say about the language or ethnic origins with any degree of certainty. I spent a whole year of research on that subject. What I have come up with does not entirely convince me one way or the other. I can only point in the general direction," he said to me in a brief conversation we had.

According to Smith's understanding, the very early Mongoloids who are regarded as one of the "primary races," are distinguished from the modern Chinese, who are secondary or differentiated Mongoloids. According to some theories, "Americanoid" or primary Mongoloids continued to exist in some isolated areas of Siberia and probably even Tibet, even as the Chinese developed by mixture and environmental adaptations "in divergence from primary Mongoloids." The argument seems to be that a common Neolithic culture existed in northern China, inner Asia, and Mongolia that eventually changed in response to varying ecological conditions.

Scholars of the archeology of ancient China have argued that the late Yang-shao culture of China reached as far to the west as the Tao Valley of Kansu and led to the subdivision known as the Kansu culture (3000–1850 BC). According to historian Kwang-chih Chang, the Kansu culture may have been culturally influenced from the northwest. The peoples of Kansu, known as the Chia-chia culture (approximately 2150–1780 BC), were likely of a different ethnic strain and probably of a distinct cultural tradition.

In all probability the modern Tibetans descended from the Chi'ang people whom the early Chinese knew from as early as the Shang dynasty (1700–1050 BC). The name *Chi'ang*, according to scholars, is formed by characters that mean "sheep" and "man," together meaning "shepherds." The Chi'ang and the Shang dynasties were constantly at war. It is quite possible that the Chi'ang were early Tibetans.

Author and scholar Owen Lattimore said: "The term *Chi'ang* or *Chiang*, written in a way that indicates the meaning 'shepherd,' is an old generic designation for non-Chinese tribes of the Kansu-Tibetan border. It appears probable that out of the early barbarians of this region, who were not yet true mounted nomads and probably had a mixed economy of herding, hunting, farming, and gathering of wild plants, some were incorporated and 'converted' into Chinese and some were crowded over to the north and northwest up to the Kansu-Tibetan border. The general term *Chi'ang* was applied to those who withdrew to the uplands of Tibet, where

some of them kept up at least a partial practice of agriculture in
the border valleys, while others took to a pastoral nomadism comparable to that of the steppe."

On the question of the distinctiveness of the Tibetan language
as well, the debate seems inconclusive. While some scholars say
that there are some similarities in the basic vocabulary of Chinese
and Tibetan, others such as Christopher Beckwith argue that
attempts to bracket Tibetan within a "Sino-Tibetan family" of
languages are mainly due to "contemporary political-racial considerations."

The Dalai Lama and many others along with him treat Tibetan as a distinctly different language. "I am not a great language
scholar, but from what I understand Tibetan and Chinese are totally different. And I am not saying that because it suits our campaign. This is irrespective of that."

The Tibetan legend that the Tibetan people descended from
the union of a monkey and an ogress furnishes an interesting link
between language and mythology. The word *mi* or *mu* means
"man" as well as "monkey" for both the Chi'ang and the Tibetan
people. Of course, the Dalai Lama does not support the idea that
the Tibetans descended from a monkey and an ogress. He merely
cites that as one of the many legends. "What is important is not
how the Tibetans came to be but the fact that they have always
been distinctly different from the Chinese."

Outside the realm of ethnographic and linguistic scholarship,
any number of examples can be cited to support either side of the
argument as to whether Tibet was always under the Chinese
suzerainty or existed as an independent entity. Among the more
compelling arguments, there is one that dates back to the seventeenth century during the reign of the Fifth Dalai Lama. The

Shun Chih emperor of the Manchu dynasty, who ruled China between 1644 and 1662, followed up on his father's plan to invite
the Fifth Dalai Lama to visit the Manchu court. Such visits are
fraught with protocol difficulties even during the best of times. In
the context of the difficult relations between Tibet and China they
acquire even more complicated nuances. The Fifth Dalai Lama
was invited in 1648 to the Manchu court in Beijing. On the face
of it such an invitation was of equal political importance to both
the Manchu empire and the Dalai Lama. The Manchu empire had
the Tibetan Geluk-pa sect's obvious influence with the powerful
Mongols in mind, while the Dalai Lama's interest was motivated
by the Tibetan wish to revive the Cho-Yon relations of the kind
that Tibet had enjoyed with the Mongol rulers starting from
Kublai Khan. *Cho* meant "religion" and *yon* meant "the secular pa-
tron." Both sides were motivated by a utilitarian purpose but neither was willing to concede that.

In the medieval world of diplomacy, where every action taken
by either player would be watched, analyzed, and interpreted by
political experts and historians, the Dalai Lama recognized that
his appearance in the court would be seen as the act of a suppli-
cant or unequal power. Soon after he began his journey in 1652
he sent a message to the Manchu emperor that perhaps it might
be a better idea for the two to meet at Khoto Khotan or Taika
Lake. The idea behind choosing a place outside the Great Wall was
very well thought out by the Dalai Lama. The region outside the
Great Wall was always considered by the Chinese as an expanse inhabited by "barbarians" who needed to be civilized. The Dalai
Lama knew that should the emperor leave his capital to meet the
Tibetan leader outside the Great Wall, the event would be of great
symbolic value for his stature as the king of Tibet. The Dalai

Lama's message divided the Manchu and Chinese ministers. While the former saw no harm in the emperor reaching out to meet the Dalai Lama, the latter argued against it, saying, albeit symbolically, that such a concession could make the Dalai Lama seem an equal of the emperor. On the other hand, were the Dalai Lama to appear in the Manchu court in Beijing it would mean that he was submitting to the emperor's supremacy in summoning lesser rulers. Behind this delicate protocol question was also the consciousness that any meeting between the Manchu ruler and the Dalai Lama outside the Great Wall would create a sense of equity between two inner Asian powers.

Ignoring the advice of his Chinese ministers, the Manchu emperor conveyed his intentions to meet the Dalai Lama at Taika Lake. This move was upstaged by the Chinese Grand Secretaries, who cited astronomical calculations that were unfavorable to the emperor's traveling at that time. Instead they recommended that the emperor send a high protocol official to receive the Dalai Lama. That way, they argued, the Dalai Lama would be accorded the respect due him. The emperor eventually yielded and sent Manchu princes to receive the Dalai Lama, with proper apologies for not having traveled personally for the fear of bandits and his preoccupation with the affairs of state. Interestingly, the Dalai Lama did not interpret this action as a slight to himself but instead reasoned that the rank of his interlocutors was, in fact, recognition that he was the legal king of Tibet.

The Dalai Lama reached the Manchu court in Beijing on January 15, 1653, where the emperor walked nearly thirty feet from his throne to receive him. The fact that the emperor condescended to actually walk thirty feet was quite a concession from his perspective, but not of such importance that history would record his gesture as signifying formally that he was treating the Dalai Lama as his equal. Covering the distance of thirty feet was unusual for the emperor, but the action was carefully choreographed in the larger interests of using the visitor's influence with the Mongols. The Dalai Lama was also exempted from the kowtow that all "barbarians" were required to perform before the emperor. The kowtow included three kneelings and nine head knockings. In yet another gesture of concession the emperor agreed to take his tea with the Dalai Lama. However, the royal munificence did not extend so far as to allow the Dalai Lama's throne to be as high as the emperor's.

The meeting between the emperor and the Dalai Lama is a classic example of the often ridiculous lengths to which the rulers in Beijing went to ensure that the Tibetans did not make the mistake of considering themselves as their equals in any way. More important, it underscores the conflicting interpretation of history in the China-Tibet context. While pro-China historians argue that the meeting was one of the many examples of how Tibet and its rulers, namely the Dalai Lamas, were never treated as true sovereigns, the more fair-minded scholars say that implicit in that very argument is proof of how much China has had to deny the obvious.

Most conflicts in human history have typically arisen over language, culture, ethnicity, religion, or territory. The question of Tibet is a typical one. Tibetans have consistently asserted their distinctiveness from the Chinese irrespective of whether there is any empirical evidence to prove their distinctiveness (and there is a fair of amount of that available too). The whole basis of the Tibetan struggle would be destroyed if they were to dilute that conviction by any degree.

The arrival of Buddhism in Tibet in the seventh century was in many ways the most defining development of its history over the last several centuries. It is the great convergence between Buddhism and Bon that accentuated Tibet's enchanting mystical and cultural traditions. This coming together of two traditions, one bewildering and beguiling in its magical sweep and the other stark, cogent, contemplative, and intellectually profound, remains the foundation of the way Tibet is perceived in modern times. Since Tibetan Buddhism drew on some elements of its predecessor Bon and also brought some of its own Tantric practices, it is a mystifying mix that has attracted Western attention.

From that convergence flows the institution of the Dalai Lama, which probably has no rival in its sheer combination of the metaphysical and the physical, the worldly and the otherworldly, the intellectual and the intuitive, the comprehensible and the esoteric.

The real story of Tibet begins in 1391 with the birth of Gedun Truppa, upon whom the title of the Dalai Lama was conferred well after his time. The story takes into its sweep legends, beliefs, mythologies, and history that appear so seamlessly connected it is often hard to tell one from the other. It is almost as if any attempt to distinguish one from the other is fraught with the risk of unraveling it all.

It is important to understand what happened centuries prior to the birth of Gedun Truppa, hundreds of miles south of Tibet in the foothills of the Himalayas. For it was there that the fountainhead of everything that the institution of the Dalai Lama is today erupted. It was there in the sixth century BC that a prince renounced his fabled kingdom and turned to the hard life of a wandering and wondering ascetic, raising profound questions and offering deceptively simple answers. It was there that from one man's lifelong quest emerged a philosophy whose full extent is still being studied 2,500 years later. It was there that Buddhism was born.

2

BUDDHISM
COMES TO
TIBET

Buddhism arose as a sort of spiritual revolt against the entrenched Brahminical order in India by those who were left out of the elite learned class. However, its spread in India was not dramatic. Indian scholars say that part of the reason for Buddhism's slow growth in the country was its lack of the elaborate and colorful rituals that could draw people by the hundreds of thousands. Buddhism, in contrast, emphasized the more cerebral aspects of life. It was more of a rumination or philosophical inquiry into issues that confronted human life. That a large number of Indians remained faithful to Hinduism in the face of the rise of Buddhism could be explained by the simple fact that Hinduism offered an elaborate distraction from the everyday life of struggle.

Although Buddhist scholars began traveling to China as early as AD 65, according to some sources, it was not before the fourth century that Buddhism began to make its presence felt on the margins of China's society, still dominated by the pre-Buddhist Bon religion, which was primarily an animistic religion that concentrated on spirit and nature worship.

According to John C. Powers of the Faculty of Asian Studies at the Australian National University, in AD 148 a monk named An Shih-kao from the Central Asian kingdom of Kusha began translating Indian Buddhist texts into Chinese in Lo-yang, which later became the capital of the Han dynasty. He along with others translated about thirty Buddhist texts during the next three decades. Given the strong indigenous culture and the derision with which the Chinese viewed foreign cultures, the monks took care that their translations were tailored to local sensitivities. In a sense their work was a loose Chinese interpretation of the Sanskrit texts.

According to Powers, during the reign of the Tibetan king Trisong Detsen (740–798), the Indian scholar Shantarakshita traveled to Tibet. Local resentments forced him to leave, but before leaving he urged the king to invite the great Padmasambhava.

Tibetan records show that Padmasambhava explained Shantarakshita's failure by saying he had encountered demons. The Indian master went on to defeat the demons and in the process impressed the king. In a sense this was a subtle reorientation of the essentially cerebral underpinnings of Buddhism to make it more amenable to Tibetan sensibilities.

Buddhism began some 2,500 years ago as one man's quest to confront the predicaments and dilemmas of life. That man was Siddhartha, who was born to riches, the heir apparent to an ancient kingdom of the Sakyas in what is now Nepal. His father, King Suddhodhana, and mother, Queen Maya, raised him sequestered from the stifling challenges of a common life. For the better part of his boyhood Siddhartha grew up thinking life had no rough edges, no challenges, and no suffering. He could well have grown to be a worthy successor to his father and lived happily ever after. That was not to be.

His life came rudely loose from its royal appurtenances when one day he was exposed to all human hardships, including poverty, sickness, old age, and death. During a rare brush with common life outside his palace he saw a funeral, as well as old and sick people on the street. That left a lasting impact. Already twenty-nine, married and the father of only one son, Rahula, Siddhartha decided to renounce worldly pleasures and set out in search of answers to life's troubling questions. He wandered along the sacred Ganges River holding spiritual dialogue with men of learning. Brahmins, then known as Bharat, dominated India; they were a class of people who monopolized scriptural knowledge and set the code for moral living. The young prince-turned-minstrel spent six years in rigorous search for answers. Sometime during those six years, when even the Brahmins failed to offer the answers Siddhartha was seeking, he began charting his own philosophical course.

His sojourn brought him to the Neranjara River near what is now Gaya in the northern Indian state of Bihar. Legend has it that one evening while sitting under a tree (now revered as the Bodhi tree or the Tree of Wisdom) on the riverside, Siddhartha found enlightenment at the age of thirty-five. It was then that Siddhartha, the prince who could have been king, instead became Buddha, the enlightened one.

He gave his first sermon at Isipatana (now known as Sarnath near Varanasi in the northern Indian state of Uttar Pradesh) to five ascetics in a deer sanctuary. For the next forty-five years the Buddha taught people of all backgrounds—traders, beggars, kings, monks, scholars, and ordinary seekers of truth. During those four and half decades of his life he founded a philosophy that transcends traditional religion and contains an intellectually rational and cogent way of comprehending life. If there is one thought that truly sums up what the Buddha taught, it is "One is one's own refuge, who else could be the refuge?" Implicit in this thinking is that humans are their own masters and there is no exalted entity or being that controls human affairs. In its purest form Buddhism ascribes the individual a position of total responsibility and thereby creates complete individual freedom. In his eighty years of life the Buddha never appropriated the role of savior as the founders of other great faiths or philosophies did. In fact, the very word *Buddha* in the Sanskrit language has an entirely intellectual connotation. It means the one who has comprehended answers to the questions, dilemmas, and situations of life. The Buddha is someone who has experienced a pure cerebral awakening. The Buddha argued throughout his life that this cerebral awakening is not reserved for only the chosen few but can be realized by anyone who cares to attain it.

Buddhist scholars have held that while the Buddha may have been conscious that there was a set of laws that governed everything in life, and that ordinary humans described as God the entity they thought embodied those laws, the Buddha recognized that in order for humans to live a normal, sensible, and generally calm life, divine intervention was irrelevant. It was in order to eliminate people's dependence on an exalted entity called God that the Buddha developed a set of four simple truths. These four truths formed the first-ever sermon that he delivered to the five ascetics.

Before dwelling on the Buddha's Four Noble Truths, it is important to understand that the Buddha encouraged people to doubt. He believed that doubt was a great obstruction in the path of Nirvana (the ultimate truth or reality), but he also saw it as the first important step to learning. Unless that step was taken and that obstruction was overcome, Nirvana could not be achieved. In keeping with his vision, the Buddha never laid down any articles of faith. Doubt and ignorance were not condemned as sins but were seen as shortcomings that could be addressed through knowledge and understanding.

While developing the concept of the Four Noble Truths, the Buddha was quite clearly drawing on his experiences beginning with his first brush with the realities of life as he saw it after he emerged from the sequestered existence of his palace.

The Buddha identified the Four Noble Truths as Dukkha, Samudaya, Nirodha, and Magga. Many students of Buddhism make the mistake of translating *Dukkha* rather loosely as "grief." They then take an enormously irrational leap to conclude that Buddhism is at its heart pessimistic. Nothing could be further from the truth. Buddhism is neither pessimistic nor optimistic; it is simply realistic. A Sanskrit term describes Buddhism as *yatha bhutam*, or "the way it is." There is a matter-of-factness about Buddhism that can be unsettling for those pursuing it out of an ill-founded expectation that it might offer something exotic and "oh, so oriental." I was witness to this disconnect during one of the Dalai Lama's public audiences on a misty November morning when fogs had just begun to envelop the pine trees around his bungalow. One of those in a long queue of people waiting to be blessed by the Dalai Lama was a wheelchair-bound Tibetan man. As the Dalai Lama emerged with one end of his robe draped over his right forearm, the Tibetans in the line fell to the ground as if hit by some mysterious force. The Tibetan man in the wheelchair appeared to be a familiar figure for the Dalai Lama's minders. The Dalai Lama laughed and told the man, "I have not seen you for some time. I am told you are not keeping well."

The man started to weep and in between the sobs he managed to say in Tibetan, "I may die soon. I am not well at all."

The Dalai Lama became serious and handed the old man a bottle of Tibetan medicine. "Try this one. It might work. If it does not, we know we all have to die. Do so peacefully."

I was struck by the matter-of-fact acceptance of death as just another development in life. I managed to ask a quick question, much to the discomfort of the Dalai Lama's minders. "Death does not seem to trouble you much," I ventured.

"Something that happens to every sentient being should not be considered extraordinary. Besides, that knowledge should liberate rather than scare us," he said. A couple of Americans behind the old man broke into spontaneous applause at the Dalai Lama's pithy answer.

While the term *Dukkha* ordinarily denotes pain, suffering, anguish, or sorrow—and the Buddha did mean all of those—it also addresses more profound concepts. Impermanence, insubstantiality, and emptiness are all incorporated in the term *Dukkha*.

Samudaya, the second noble truth, arises out of the first one. At its core it means "thirst, desire, greed, or craving that leads to Dukkha." The thirst or desire or greed or craving could be for sense-related pleasures, wealth, ideas, ideology, dogmas, views, opinions, and beliefs. The Buddha reasoned that all the conflicts in the world are essentially born out of selfish desire or thirst. Beyond this, he argued that such selfish desires lead to re-existence or re-becoming, the theory of karma and its consequence of being reborn.

The third truth, Nirodha, relates to liberation from this cycle of being reborn, or the cessation of Dukkha and the attainment of Nirvana. Nirvana is really elimination of desire or thirst, which in turn stops one from being reborn. Admittedly, this is probably the shortest and the most inadequate explanation of a concept that scholars can spend years trying to fathom. However, in an introduction to Buddhism and its truths, Nirvana ought to be explained as freedom from the cycle of rebirth caused by an incessant desire or thirst.

The fourth noble truth is Magga, or the path to the cessation of Dukkha. It is the middle path and the path that the Buddha chose. This path eschews both extremes—the path of decadent sensuous pleasures on the one hand and the path of asceticism that demands self-mortification on the other. The Buddha spent over four decades teaching about the middle path.

On the face of it these seem to be simple or even simplistic truths, but as they unravel themselves through the Buddha's interpretation they acquire a truly profound dimension.

The version of Buddhism that reached Tibet was Mahayana Buddhism. *Maha* means "great" or "big" in Sanskrit and *yana* means "vehicle" or "system." Mahayana Buddhism is a version of the philosophy which is less doctrinaire and more open, unlike the competing Hinayana, or "smaller vehicle," Buddhism. In retrospect, Hinayana Buddhism could not have flourished in Tibet, because of that country's long tradition of animism and shamanism, both of which were incorporated in Tibetan Buddhism. Incidentally, Tibetan Buddhism also has a strong dose of Tantra, which was a set of mysterious practices that offered a quicker way to Nirvana.

Padmasambhava, who founded a monastery near Lhasa around AD 750, retained many elements of Tantra even as he went about adapting Buddhism to local conditions. As Buddhism took root in Tibet, it created abbots and ordained religious mendicants, novices, and neophytes (children on probation). It also gave birth to the Red Hat sect of Tibetan Buddhism, which was quick to consolidate its position. While on the surface it seemed that Buddhism had managed to transplant itself firmly in Tibet's religious landscape, trouble was lurking below the surface. Bon shamans, feeling pushed out of their position of supremacy, began recapturing lost ground. They were so aggressive in their campaign that they managed to force Buddhism out of the national discourse for over a century. It did not reemerge until 1042 when the great Indian Buddhist master and reformer Atisha Dipankara (982–1054) visited Tibet. He spent the remaining twelve years of his life resurrecting Buddhism in all its doctrinal glory. He sought to eliminate the influences of Bon and brought Buddhism back into the reckoning as the religion of choice.

Tibetan Buddhism was divided into four sects: the red sect, the yellow sect, the white sect, and the variegated sect. Some Tibetans include the black sect as the fifth one, headed by the Karmapa. Both the red and white sects spend considerable time studying

Tantras rather than the more spiritual aspects of Buddhism. The Yellow Hat sect, to which the Dalai Lama belongs, was founded by Lopsang Drakpa, better known as Tsong-khapa, in the fourteenth century. The Yellow Hat sect is the mainstream of Tibetan Tantric Buddhism, which emphasizes discipline and learning. Lamas of this sect are expected to spend twenty years on scholastic study before studying Tantras.

The Karmapa is considered by many Tibetans to be the first incarnate lama. The debate over who commands unassailable supremacy over Tibet's religious and political affairs often runs into problems because of the complex hierarchical definitions among the various sects. The most widely accepted belief is that the Dalai Lama is at the helm of Tibetan life in theory, even though in practice the heads of various sects conduct their own affairs without having to seek the Dalai Lama's blessing. Most Tibetans believe that the Dalai Lama recognizes the Karmapa and even the Panchen Lama, but the Chinese government disagrees. Those who disagree say that the Dalai Lama's authority has never historically gone beyond the Geluk-pa school.

The Chinese say that even in terms of historical chronology the first Karmapa, Dusum Khyenpo, lived in the twelfth century, over three hundred years before the Geluk-pa school was founded and before the First Dalai Lama was recognized. Many scholars say that the Gyalwa Karmapa line holds the distinction of manifesting as the first appearance of reincarnated lamas in Tibetan Buddhism. Those who support this argument also point out that five Karmapas reincarnated before the First Dalai Lama appeared, hence the Dalai Lama could not possibly have been the one to decide on matters related to the Karmapa incarnation or succession. However, supporters of the Dalai Lama say that since 1638 the

Dalai Lama has been at the helm of Tibetan life and by virtue of that he remains the predominant influence. The Tibetan government-in-exile has maintained that it has the powers to recognize the reincarnations of all four schools.

It was in response to internecine rivalries among various religious sects that Tsong-khapa advocated a return to the traditional Buddhist way of life. The reform also required that witchcraft, sorcery, and magic be eschewed and that celibacy, abstinence, and vegetarianism be laid down as conditions for a disciplined monastic life.

Historically, starting in the early thirteenth century spiritual and temporal powers have been fused in Tibet. According to Tibetan chronicles, in 1239 the Mongol general Godan sent troops to mount an attack on Tibet. The Mongolian troops managed to reach all the way to Lhasa. Unsettled by the aggression, the Tibetan leadership decided to nominate Sa-pan, the abbot of the Sa-skya monastery, as their interlocutor to negotiate with the Mongols.

Sa-pan and Godan met at the latter's camp in 1247. What created the first favorable impression was that the abbot cured Godan of his ailments. But more important, according to Tibetan sources, what also played a part in drawing the Mongol warrior closer to Buddhism were the elaborate rituals that the abbot performed. Apparently fear of the unknown and the mysterious changed the quality of discourse between the two. The two reached an arrangement under which, while Tibet would submit to the Mongolian authority, Sa-pan was appointed as a Mongol official with the rank of vice-regent. Kenneth Chen, in his book *Philosophy East and West*, wrote, "The Mongol general undoubtedly realized that, although he could subdue the Tibetans by force, he could not hope to occupy the country by force for any length of time, for he knew that he could not cope with the magic and sorcery of the Tibetan priests—it would be much safer to exercise his rule through a Tibetan."

The Godan–Sa-pan arrangement was, according to Chen, the beginning of "the marriage of spiritual and temporal powers in the hands of the Sa-skya abbot, arranged for by an external power, the Mongols." However, the Sa-skya abbot failed to impose his authority on other monasteries, causing widespread resentment among other sects.

The rise of the Yellow Hat sect came about through a reform movement that sought to address some of the venality that characterized the earlier rule. The yellow sect both combined the features of Bonism as well as cast itself as a direct descendant of Atisha Dipankara's philosophy. One of the main attractions of Buddhism in general and the Yellow Hat sect in particular for Tibetans was the belief in reincarnation. Even though the Buddhist belief in reincarnation was driven mainly by the logic of the karmic cycle, for the Tibetans it held the promise of something more magical, accustomed as they were to Bon.

Since the proclamation of the Dalai Lamas in 1587, the reincarnation of the Dalai Lama has been central to Tibetan life. By the sheer virtue of his being born into an era in which communication technologies had already made their mark in the world, the Fourteenth Dalai Lama's birth has been the best recorded among all Dalai Lamas so far. His birth in obscure northeastern Tibet and his subsequent rise to world prominence has been extensively chronicled.

3

CLUCKING LIKE A
HEN AND BREAKING
UP FIGHTS

Thick and dark clouds swirled around Mount Kyeri towering over a large valley before dawn came
upon Tengster village in northeastern Tibet. The
recurring thunder and lightning added to the austere
magnetism of the Kyeri, which was worshiped by the
four-hundred-some people of Tengster as the abode of
their protecting deity Kye.

It was too early in the day to wake up, but some
miles away, inside a mud-brick house, a woman in her

early twenties was awakened by the impending thunderstorm. She lay on her stone bed next to her husband, Choekyang Tsering, for a while. She gently massaged her pregnant belly and smiled to herself. Something told her a momentous birth was imminent but she did not quite know what this meant. She had gotten up and begun morning chores when she felt cramps in her stomach. She knew it was time but continued to work. Babies were nothing new in her life. The one about to be born was her ninth child, and, in all, she would have sixteen children. Only seven of them would live.

She went to the cow barn to tend her stock of six *dzomos*, a cross between a yak and a cow, some eighty sheep and goats, several chickens, and three horses. On the way she cleaned the gutter made from branches of juniper wood in preparation for the rains. Women in Tengster, or for that matter anywhere in Tibet, did not let their pregnancies interfere with their daily life. Many of them delivered their babies by themselves. Prenatal care and midwives were unheard of. Allopathic doctors did not exist at all.

Tengster, which in Tibetan means "roaring tiger," is set amid rolling hills in the province of Amdo. The climate there had three fairly defined seasons. Summers were strong. Rains were relatively plentiful considering Tibet's otherwise dry climate. Winters were particularly severe and brought inches of snow. Tengster was atop a small hill that overlooked the valley, where the pastures were generally not farmed. Nomads brought their herds there for grazing.

The month of July 1935 saw intermittent rains and some glorious rainbows. While children of Tengster chased those elusive arches of seven colors, Sonam Tsomo clutched her stomach, once again massaged it, and sat down near a haystack. The dzomos chewed their cud and shook their heads, while chickens scampered near her as she prepared to deliver the baby. Half an hour later an eight-pound boy was born.

Two important details, which would be used much later to illustrate the boy's high birth, were not readily noted because of Sonam's labor pains. The infant did not cry, and he came out with his eyes wide open. "My mother once told me after I was chosen as the Dalai Lama that she did not see any extraordinary signs that are supposed to attend the birth of a special child. I did not feel anything special either," the Dalai Lama said. "I remember though that I was born with my eyes open and I did not cry. It could be because I was already into my fourteenth incarnation and had developed clarity about life."

Other signs that some momentous birth may have happened were reported, but the Dalai Lama tends to be rather dismissive about them. His father Choekyang Tsering's sudden recovery after weeks of illness was considered one such sign. He had been shunning work till the morning of July 6, when he awoke feeling fine and made offerings of butter lamps before a Buddha statue at the family altar. His wife bantered: "Were you ill or just lazy all these weeks?" Choekyang said in all earnestness that he had indeed been ill but that this morning he had felt "spontaneously cured." A while later a neighbor from one of the thirty-odd houses surrounding the family's six-room cottage came running to the couple and informed them that a rainbow was touching the roof of their house.

The boy was named Lhamo Thondup, which meant "wish-fulfilling goddess." "Gender was not very important while naming babies in Tibet. I was a man and yet they called me a she-god." Some of the Dalai Lama's earliest memories do not foreshadow the life ahead, and, if anything, they charmingly underline his keen sense of humor.

"There were no toilets in Tibet in those days. Nature's calls were answered out in nature. I remember one day when I was two years old; I was sitting outside to do the big job, as the Westerners call it. In the midst of it all I suddenly spotted a camel for the first time in my life. I was so scared that I ran home without finishing whatever it was that I was doing . . . It took my mother some time to clean me up. Some days later I was equally scared when a worm came out of me. Obviously, they did not deworm their children in those days."

Lhamo's father, Choekyang, was a man of medium height who was easily angered. He had a a small farm and grew barley, buckwheat, and potatoes. He was nowhere near being called nobility, but he was not bonded to a master. The family led a fairly comfortable life.

Choekyang's only regret about the boy who would be the Dalai Lama Vajradhara (the All Embracing Lama, Holder of the Thunderbolt) was that he did not share his father's passion for horses. "My father could have spent his life talking about horses. He understood horses instinctively. I, on the other hand, was scared of them. He tried to introduce me to the joys of understanding this graceful animal but he could not."

Choekyang treated Lhamo like any other ordinary child and occasionally spanked him. "Once I pulled his mustache while he was sleeping. He promptly slapped me."

The Dalai Lama describes his mother, Sonam, as "one of the kindest people I ever knew." He remembers a tragic story about a severe famine that hit China in the late 1930s.

"The famine had forced many Chinese families to leave their villages and look for livelihood elsewhere. I was told of a Chinese couple showing up near our house with a dead child in their arms. They were begging for food, which my mother gave them. She then asked them if they needed help to bury their dead child. They said no, adding that they would eat it. My mother was horrified to hear that. She called them inside and gave them our entire stock of grains and whatever else we had.

"I was very attached to my mother. I saw in her a woman of great strength and compassion who never complained no matter how hard her life became."

By the time Lhamo was born his parents were already accustomed to one of their own being declared a reincarnate. The Dalai Lama's eldest brother, Thubten Jigme Norbu, and his immediate elder brother, Lobsang Samten, had already joined a Buddhist order. Thubten was declared the reincarnation of Tengster Rinpoche, a high lama, and was installed at Kumbum, one of the most famous monasteries. Lobsang was sent to the same monastery to be a monk, although he was not chosen as a reincarnate.

Until he turned three, Lhamo accompanied his mother everywhere. Once in a while she would pass on some of the minor chores to her son, who was ever eager to help. Once she sent him to the chicken coop to pick up eggs. He did not return for hours, making the family anxious. They finally found him sitting near a nest "pretending to be a hen." "The only problem was I could not lay eggs myself."

With two of his brothers already in the monastery, neither Lhamo nor anyone else in the family had anticipated the great future that lay ahead of him. In Tibetan Buddhist tradition it is considered practically impossible that one family would have more than one *tulku,* or reincarnate. "It had to be a great surprise if one more child was declared a tulku in the same family. From the many conversations that I had with my parents, especially with my mother, in later years, it is clear that we had not anticipated anything more. I too would have gone to the village school like another elder brother, Gyalo Thondup."

Lhamo's parents were religious, but not such that they could be called devout. They followed the main Tibetan Buddhist practices such as making an offering of butter lamps and water at the family altar. As in all Tengster homes, they too had a flagpole from which they raised a white banner inscribed with prayers. Lhamo would occasionally point at the banner and ask what was written on it. "Of course, I was too young to understand when they explained what was written on it. The most commonly used words were 'Om Mani Padme Hum' [Hail the Jewel in the Lotus]. I later learned that each syllable of this line symbolized six divisions of the mandala [the Tibetan wheel of life]. But as a boy my only worry was that too much wind might rip the banner apart from the pole."

Two of Lhamo's favorite pastimes were turning into a clucking hen and breaking up fights and defending the underdog "whether between humans or animals.

"I have memories of running after those I perceived to be the tormentor in any fight. I just could not take the sight of the weak being harassed. A lot of my well-wishers used to point out with great delight how these qualities presaged my life ahead. I personally thought of them as ordinary qualities which all good people ought to have."

Since he barely had three years of ordinary childhood, Lhamo's early life was hardly considered of any consequence. In many ways he was a typical Tibetan child who loved eating *tsampa*, a staple meal made from ground barley, mixed either with tea or milk and rolled into balls. "I find most non-Tibetans do not like tsampa. The Chinese, of course, can't stand it."

Lhamo may not have stood out as a child, but there were tell-tale signs that something was very different about him. He would frequently pack bags and say he was going to Lhasa. When the family sat down for a meal, he invariably took the position equivalent to the head of the table.

"As a child, I was told, I never had problems relating to anyone. It was as if there were no strangers in the world. All these were described as signs of high birth. But I still remain unconvinced."

While Lhamo was growing up free from any worry about the world outside his village, about a thousand miles away in the Tibetan capital of Lhasa anxiety and concern had begun to unsettle the government. Some eighteen months after the death of the Thirteenth Dalai Lama Reting Rinpoche, the regent of Tibet was sandwiched between continuing skirmishes with the Chinese on the eastern frontier on the one hand and the uncovering of a plot to overthrow the government by a lay official named Lungshar on the other. The twin trouble seriously threatened the stability of Tibet, which was so used to the commanding presence of the Thirteenth Dalai Lama.

The regent was also troubled by the fact that there were no reports of the reincarnation of the Thirteenth Dalai Lama. He knew that only the discovery and enthronement of a new Dalai

Lama, however young, could prevent the affairs of state from spinning out of control.

So Reting Rinpoche, along with monks and lay officials at the thousand-room Potala Palace in Lhasa, began planning a search for the fourteenth successor. The Thirteenth Dalai Lama had left only a few clues of where he might be found.

4

FROM A PRANKSTER TO THE DALAI LAMA REINCARNATE

On the last day of the tenth month of the Tibetan Year of the Waterbird, which fell on a Saturday in the middle of December 1933, Choskyi Gyaltsen, the Thirteenth Dalai Lama, knew something was amiss. A man given to working long hours, he did not quite feel up to working. His personal physician, Champa La, advised him to rest since he knew the Dalai Lama was quite ill.

Between 1 and 2 a.m. on Sunday morning, the Nechung oracle, a medium with powers to invoke spirits, administered some medicine to the Dalai Lama. It is not entirely clear what the oracle administered but Champa La was recorded as having told him in a strongly disapproving tone, *"Men di norra nangzha."* (You have made a mistake in the medicine.) Whether this was deliberate or a genuine mistake remains generally unexplained. A few hours later the Thirteenth Dalai Lama breathed his last.

Tibetans believe that if someone dies on a Sunday or a Tuesday it could lead to sickness or other serious problems for the family of the deceased. Since the Dalai Lama had no family, his death on a Sunday was believed to signal troubled times ahead for Tibet as a whole.

The lifeless Thirteenth Dalai Lama looked contemplative as he sat cross-legged in the lotus posture. He seemed to be gazing southward as thousands of ordinary Tibetans filed past chanting mantras and twirling prayer wheels without really looking at him. After the day of tributes the hall was empty except for the forlorn figure of the fifty-eight-year-old Dalai Lama and a few monks going about their chores. Quite mysteriously, the Dalai Lama's head tilted eastward. One of the monks noticed it and gently turned it southward again. The next morning the head had again turned eastward.

Official records of the day show that a seasoned wooden pillar of a nearby temple inexplicably developed a star-shaped fungus at its base and a dragon flower popped up seemingly out of nowhere near a stairway of the main courtyard of the palace. "The buildup of clouds in the northeastern sky resembled thousands of charging elephants," one account said. All these were considered portentous signs.

Tibet was plunged into palpable sadness as people wept openly at the passing of the Thirteenth Dalai Lama. Yeshi Dorjee, a *thangka* painter who lived not too far from the Potala Palace, recalled, "It was as if everything and everybody had frozen. It was very cold and bleak. When I heard His Holiness had passed I was painting. I put my brush aside, went out, looked in the direction of the Potala, and prayed. Something told me times were changing for the worse for Tibet."

Inside the palace the regent and his subordinates as well as other monks began preparing for a life without the Dalai Lama. "I heard about His Holiness's head facing the east being seen as a signal that perhaps his reincarnation would be found in that direction," Dorjee said.

Generally, there is a gap of between nine months and two years between the passing of the Dalai Lama and his reincarnation. Since 1475, when the First Dalai Lama died at age eighty-four, reincarnates have been born within a maximum of two years. In many instances the gap was less than a year.

Worried about the absence of any reports of the Thirteenth Dalai Lama's reincarnation, Reting Rinpoche decided to seek clues about the next Dalai Lama in the Lhamoi Latso, a mysterious lake about ninety miles from Lhasa. Although that is not far in modern terms, in the Tibet of the 1930s, with the mountainous terrain lacking any roads, even that short journey was anything but easy. It took ten days to reach Lhamoi Latso.

The lake, set in the midst of snow-laden peaks reaching 18,000 to 20,000 feet, has mystical powers that were first discovered by Gedun Gyatso, the Second Dalai Lama, in the sixteenth century.

Reting Rinpoche and his team reached Lhamoi Latso in the

summer of the Tibetan Year of the Wood Hog. Intermittent rains and fierce winds made the blazing sun feel less intense as the regent and his team spread across the lakefront. The regent went into deep contemplation and after a while opened his eyes. He peered into the lake waters with a great deal of anticipation. His body quivered as he saw three Tibetan letters—*A*, *Ka*, and *Ma*—appear and disappear all at once. He then had a vision of a three-story templelike structure with a golden roof and walls with greenish blue tiles. He also saw a narrow pathway curving into a small hill and ending near a single-story house with a gutter.

With a mixture of excitement and disbelief the regent embarked on a return journey to Lhasa, all the while thinking about the significance of the revelations. They pointed to the coming of a new Dalai Lama, but he and his colleagues were perplexed since there were no reports of the birth of the Fourteenth Dalai Lama.

The abbots of the Drepung, Sera, and Ganden, Tibet's three most important monasteries, went into conference, as did high-ranking lay officials led by the regent. All of them remembered that the Thirteenth Dalai Lama's head had rolled toward the east after his death. Piecing the clues together, they had to look in eastern Tibet for a blue single-story house by a hill close to a temple with a golden roof and green blue tiles.

After considerable debate, the spiritual and temporal authorities decided to turn to the state oracle at the Nechung monastery. The Nechung oracle is a monk or a nun who acts as a medium through whom deities known as *dharampal*, or protectors of religion, communicate. The oracle is called upon to invoke spirits every time a decision of great significance is to be made. The invocation is an elaborate and haunting ritual in which the oracle, clad in brocaded flaming-yellow robes with a mirror on his chest, goes into a convulsive trance to the tune of large Tibetan drums and oboes. He dances uncontrollably and rolls his eyes as a deity enters his body.

The oracle gave instructions to send three search teams, one each to Dakpo in the southeast, Kham in the east, and Amdo in the northeast. By the time the search teams were ready to leave, the winter had begun to descend on Lhasa. It was sometime in September of 1938 when the expedition began. On the eve of his departure, Kyitsang Rinpoche, a Buddhist scholar in his sixties from the Sera monastery, was concerned about a heavy snowfall. What lay ahead of him was an arduous journey stretching at least two months on horseback and on foot in what would turn out to be his life's most important mission. Although the day of the journey was determined after astrological calculations, the snowfall was a discouraging factor.

The next morning as Kyitsang Rinpoche gathered his group, the sun broke through and began melting the snow. On any other occasion this would have been considered a normal weather occurrence, but on that day they saw something more in it.

By the time the team reached Kham two months later, traversing inhospitable steppe land and huge mountains where the temperatures often plunged to subzero, they received word that the Panchen Lama, who is second only to the Dalai Lama, had identified three possible child claimants as the reincarnation. But one of them had died before the team reached him. The second likely reincarnation was a boy who had grabbed the Panchen Lama's rosary and refused to let go of it some months before during an initiation ceremony known as Kalchakra.

But that boy turned out to be a disappointment, as he failed to recognize the Thirteenth Dalai Lama's rosary. He was also unusually shy and ran out of the house crying. That left only one possible reincarnate. It is not quite clear how the Panchen Lama went about identifying possible reincarnates. Tibetan reference materials and experts say the process works based on a combination of intuition and word of mouth in a small society where there are hardly any secrets.

The abbot and sixty nomadic horsemen welcomed Kyitsang Rinpoche and Tsedrun Lobsang at the Kumbum monastery. After a rest the cavalcade left the precincts of the monastery. The two men from Lhasa were almost thrown off their horses when they saw a three-storied temple with greenish blue tiles. They also saw a pathway curving around a hill and ending near a blue single-story house with a gutter. Another fortuitous detail that was later discovered but probably not known then was that while returning from a visit from China and passing through the province of Amdo, the Thirteenth Dalai Lama had stopped near a place not too far from where his reincarnation was born. Signs so far pointed toward success.

An elaborate ruse was designed to make the would-be reincarnation's job difficult. Accordingly, the abbot wore an ordinary robe while Lobsang was dressed up more ornately to make him look like the head of the party. As the convoy entered Tengster village, children ran after it and the entire farming community turned out despite the bitter cold. Sonam Tsomo carried Lhamo on her waist and stood in the doorway. She did not know the search team was heading for her house. The abbot and the others entered her house much to her consternation. Lhamo seemed amused by the presence of so many people.

"My memory of that day is quite clear. I remember that so

many people came to our house. I recognized many of them although I had never met them. I don't want to make it sound dramatic but it was as if I had never left the scene for a long long time," the Dalai Lama remembered.

As the abbot sat down, Lhamo jumped onto his lap and grabbed his rosary saying, "I want this rosary." Sensing an opportunity to test the boy, Kyitsang Rinpoche said he could have it only if he recognized the abbot. "I told him promptly that he was a lama from the Sera monastery. The abbot asked me to recognize Tsedrun Lobsang and I did."

Sixty-odd years after the event the Dalai Lama spoke about it as if it were yesterday. "I knew that they were trying to test me, but being a boy I did not understand it fully. I distinctly remember how their faces lit up when I recognized the abbot and Tsedrun Lobsang."

The Dalai Lama said it is hard to describe how he could recognize all of them. "Remembering the past is a process that is not easy to explain. Something stirs up your subconscious memories and pours them out without any seeming effort. As I said, I felt as if I had never left the scene."

The search team was struggling to suppress its joy first and its reverence next. A coded message was sent to Lhasa about the possible discovery. A reply was received four weeks later instructing the search team to test the boy further by asking him to recognize some personal belongings of the Thirteenth Dalai Lama. Care was taken to present the boy with sets of two items that looked alike in order to confuse him. Throughout the period of scrutiny no one was told whose reincarnation Lhamo could well be.

On the day when the search team returned to Lhamo's house

his father was not at home. Possessions such as two black rosaries, two yellow rosaries, two sticks with iron and bronze handles, respectively, and ivory drums were laid out before Lhamo. The boy was also shown two ivory drums, one ornate and the other simple. He chose the latter and correctly so. The boy's ease at setting the real apart from the fake without any apparent effort clinched the issue. "I was later told that I even said that my dentures were kept in a particular chamber and in a particular chest. They found them there.

"This may seem mysterious and even magical for most people, but when I saw those objects what I felt was nothing extraordinary. It was as if I was looking at things I was accustomed to. In my private moments I do try to analyze some of these so-called powers. But I am afraid I am not able to do it," the Dalai Lama said.

After Lhamo's effortlessness in clearing the tests, the search team realized that the letters A, Ka, and Ma denoted Amdo, Kumbum, and the hermitage of Karma Shar-ston, respectively. Once all the tests confirmed his reincarnation, it was revealed to his family that he was the reincarnation of an important lama. "My memory of their reaction is almost nonexistent. But I remember a lot of faces full of tears and devotion toward me. Of course, I did not understand what all the fuss was about, but from that day I stepped up my demand to go to Lhasa."

The news of the Fourteenth Dalai Lama having been born in their midst made the simple inhabitants of Tengster exultant. There were frequent celebrations and parades through the village's narrow lanes. A mischievous three-year-old prankster, whose cheeks they used to pinch with so much relish, had suddenly become a living Buddha, completely beyond their league, beyond bounds and perhaps beyond their comprehension.

"Once in a while I do try to remember how people's reactions changed. I remember the sudden distance people kept from me. I also remember other children wanting to play with me but not being allowed. Nothing had changed for me but everything had changed for everyone around me. Funny but true."

5

#

FAREWELL
TO THE
WORLDLY WORLD

L hamo Thondup's farewell to the worldly world was
not without serious obstacles. The biggest of them
all was General Ma Pu-feng, a corrupt Muslim
warlord in charge of administering Amdo, then part of
the Chinese province of Chinghai. The discovery of the
Fourteenth Dalai Lama in a village under his jurisdiction presented the general an irresistible opportunity to
make some money. General Ma told Kyitsang Rinpoche
he would let the boy incarnate leave for Lhasa in ex-

change for 300,000 silver dollars. The ransom money had to be arranged by Kyitsang Rinpoche from Lhasa.

But the payment of that ransom was not enough. Sensing yet another great opportunity, General Ma also dictated that the boy be formally declared the reincarnation of the Thirteenth Dalai Lama at the Kumbum monastery. This demand was made with an eye on raising the monastery's standing as a place where the new Dalai Lama was first sheltered. Such a move was motivated by the obvious pecuniary gains to be had from generous contributions that the faithful would make to a monastery that had had the honor of heralding a new Dalai Lama.

Kyitsang Rinpoche quickly understood the motive behind the general's demand. There was no way he could agree to this. The eminently pliable general told the dignitary from Lhasa he was willing to give up his demand for 300,000 silver dollars. Instead he demanded the entire set of the Thirteenth Dalai Lama's robes, throne ornaments, and complete editions of the sacred Buddhist texts of Kangyur and Tengyur inscribed in gold letters. Lhasa had no choice but to comply. The ransom was arranged through a group of Muslim merchants who were on their way to Mecca for the hadj.

Unaware of the petty behind-the-scenes machinations of a corrupt general, Lhamo Thondup led as normal a life as a living Buddha is allowed to. Utter reverence replaced the village inhabitants' affections for him. His parents began to maintain a studied distance from him. Whenever he made demands typical of his age they were granted without demur, unlike before, when he would often be reprimanded.

Then sometime in the summer of the Year of the Earth Hare, or 1939, Lhamo Thondup was woken up well before dawn and

dressed up. "I remember waking up cranky and bleary-eyed wondering what was going on. My mother told me we had to go to the
Kumbum monastery. I did not understand why a child should be
woken up in the middle of the night, dressed up, and taken somewhere." The Kumbum Jampa-ling monastery was founded in 1583
by the Third Dalai Lama, Sonam Gyatso (1543–1588), near Lake
Kokonor. It was at that site that Tsong-khapa (1357–1419), the
founder of the Geluk-pa tradition, was born.

That dawn changed four-year-old Lhamo's life forever. It
ended his ever so short affair with the laity and elevated him to a
status that only a handful of human beings have held. On July 10,
1939, barely a week after his fourth birthday, Lhamo Thondup
and his family began his life's first defining journey. Some 350
horses, yaks, camels, and mules were lined up for a convoy of fifty
people. A special *dreljam*, or palanquin, was mounted on two mules
to carry the boy who would be the Fourteenth Dalai Lama and
Lobsang Samten, a brother who was three years older. For a boy
whose definition of the world extended a little beyond the threshold of his door, what was to unfold over the next six decades was
going to be the human equivalent of the geological cataclysm that
had created his homeland.

The convoy's route from Amdo to Lhasa passed through the
Sandal Valley with dozens of lakes. "Although I was still a child I
recall a sense of total wonder during the journey. One could see
the lakes shining in the bright sun. Every time I saw herds of *drong*
[wild yaks] or *kyang* [wild asses] or groups of *gowa* and *nava* [small
deer] I felt I was discovering something extraordinary."

The travelers had to journey for nearly three months, traveling
every day from dawn to noon and then pitching yak-hair tents, before they would reach the outskirts of Lhasa. "Even for a Dalai

Lama this was a very long time not to get bored," the Dalai Lama said with his trademark guffaw. "Just to fight boredom I would rag and nag my brother Lobsang, provoke him into an argument, and then invariably win. Once in a while Kyitsang Rinpoche would regale us with some humorous stories to break the monotony of such a long journey. We often came to blows and I must say it was my brother who was always at the receiving end. He often cried at the end of the fight. In retrospect it seems he was being indulgent toward his kid brother."

It was toward the autumn of 1939 when the convoy reached the banks of the Thuptopchu River. The Tibetan government sent two aristocrats and ten officials along with a yellow tent belonging to the Thirteenth Dalai Lama and four yak-hide coracles.

Since secrecy about whose reincarnation the boy really was had to be maintained, even his parents were not let in on what their son was about to be anointed. After their halt on the banks of the Thuptopchu River, the convoy crossed the Tonghor pass and reached Bumchen village. Lhasa was still a couple of weeks away. The yellow tent was erected in the midst of a carpet of yellow flowers in full bloom. Inside the tent was the ornate throne on which the boy Dalai Lama would sit. Mandalas were offered to him. By this time Kyitsang Rinpoche had decided it was now fine to let it be known to people who the boy really was.

"Although my parents knew that I had to be someone important, they were not told till then whose reincarnation I really was. I remember that it was near Bumchen that they knew for sure what all the fuss was really about. From whatever little I remember I think they were overcome with joy and gratitude. In retrospect, they, particularly my mother, realized what it meant to have a son who would be the Dalai Lama. She understood that I would go away from her world for all practical purposes. I don't know if I felt sad or a sense of loss. There was so much going on I don't quite recollect how I felt," the Dalai Lama said.

Meanwhile in Lhasa, the Kashag, or the Cabinet, decided that it could no longer keep the discovery a secret. Apart from everything else, according to Tibetan astrological calculations the boy Dalai Lama had to enter Lhasa before the end of the eighth month of the Tibetan calendar since the period after that was considered inauspicious.

As the convoy moved closer to Lhasa, Tibetans turned out in the hundreds, carrying incense and prostrating before him. Most wept openly without looking up so that they would not commit the sacrilege of looking him directly in the eye. His path to the Shapten monastery, his first stop after reaching Lhasa, was full of people waiting for a glimpse. Such overwhelming devotion could have spoiled even the sanest of human beings, but for the four-year-old Dalai Lama it seemed like any other day.

THE METAMORPHOSIS

There is no detailed perspective available on what went on in the mind of a child on the threshold of virtual divinity. Going by the Dalai Lama's own feeling on the subject and by piecing together the many accounts of the months leading to his ascension, it appears that essentially the four-year-old boy just went along with the flow. It is difficult to argue that the Dalai Lama remained so composed in the face of the ever growing devotion because as a child he did not quite understand what was going on. Several hours of close observation of the Dalai Lama in different situations and many personal conversations with him clearly revealed that he knew perfectly well what lay ahead of him. The strange sense of familiarity that he demonstrated every step of the way to his eventual enthronement also strengthened the view that the Dalai Lama was in complete control. Several incidents illustrate this point.

One took place on the twenty-fifth day of the eighth month of the Tibetan Year of the Earth Hare 2066 (1939). As the Dalai Lama began the last phase of his journey to Lhasa on the path marked with white and yellow chalked lines along which large incense burned, the Nechung oracle, looking fearsome and locked in a mysterious trance, peeped into the palanquin carrying the Dalai Lama. The Nechung oracle looked so disturbing that even some of the horses in the convoy were frightened by the sight. But the boy Dalai Lama responded without any outward sign of fear or shock or even surprise. For a four-year-old uprooted from the simple life of his village and thrown into such overpowering tumult to remain unaffected in the face of such sights and sounds is hard to explain. When the Nechung oracle, with his face contorted, peeped in, the Dalai Lama's instinctive reaction was to put a *Kata*, a white ceremonial silk scarf with eight auspicious symbols woven into its design, around him. Such instances abounded during the run-up to the Dalai Lama's installation.

The Dalai Lama does not normally speak of what lies behind the obvious. He tends to be dismissive about questions aimed at finding out what the metamorphosis meant to him as a child. It is in keeping with his self-effacement that he hardly, if ever, comes out with a response that gives a glimpse into some of the most private recesses of his being. But during one interview with me he offered a rare disclosure: "What might seem like a fundamental change to you was merely a continuation for me. Although a lot of the details were new, by and large I did not react to the goings-on around me because I felt so very familiar with the surroundings. It is hard for me to describe what I felt or if I felt anything at all. For instance, the Nechung oracle incident. I know the normal reaction for a child would have been to be frightened by what I saw, but then to me it did not appear anything out of the ordinary. It was a sight I had seen very often and for a long time."

Sir Basil Gould, the political officer of Sikkim who represented the colonial British government in India at the enthronement of the Fourteenth Dalai Lama, wrote that he was struck by the "extraordinary steadiness of his gaze," which clearly demonstrated that the boy recognized many of the close associates of his predecessor. "The next thing they noticed was the devotion and love, almost passing the love of women, of the Abbots who attend him. Next perhaps, the beauty of his hands. And meanwhile all had become aware they were in the presence of a Presence," Gould wrote. It is interesting that Gould should have mentioned the Dalai Lama's hands, because even now they strike most people who meet him as "captivating."

Sometime in December of 1997, during a general audience, when the Dalai Lama blesses people, a Sikh man patiently awaited his turn in the backyard of the Dalai Lama's official residence in McLeod Ganj atop a mountain some 6,000 feet high. Sikhs typically come from the Punjab region of north India and follow Sikhism, an Indian religious philosophy that is barely five hundred years old. The Sikh man kept telling others in the line: "Look at His Holiness's hands. It seems they were made specially to bless the world." A Swiss tourist ahead of the Sikh man agreed in his broken English and said: "Hands of a baby ... very innocent and still divinity ... I mean divine."

The Dalai Lama, of course, tends to laugh off such attentions as "not only embarrassing but ... what do you call it ... foolish you see."

Tempa Tsering, the Dalai Lama's brother-in-law and former secretary for international affairs of the Tibetan government-in-exile, explains: "His Holiness does not like people making such a big deal out of what he is. It is his genuine conviction that he is an ordinary monk. Of course, Tibetans and millions of other Buddhists do not for a second believe that description, but he sincerely believes that he should be treated as an ordinary monk. He cannot comprehend why people should talk about things like hands with any fascination."

For someone who for almost all of his seventy-one years of life has been regarded as a divinity, the Dalai Lama comes across as exceptionally humble. "Not much has been written about his metamorphosis from being a simple village child to the Dalai Lama. One reason is that His Holiness does not like to encourage anything that seems like reverence or devotion. The other more compelling reason could be that not too many people have that kind of access to discuss such details," Tempa Tsering said.

During the course of several interviews and interactions, I directly and indirectly tried to find out what the Dalai Lama himself thinks of such curiosity. Laughter was the most common response. When he did choose to respond he would say things like: "You see, I do not analyze such things," or "Let me remain a simple monk," or "I am like you, only a little luckier." The most telling response was "We can all be Buddhas. What it takes is awakening."

6

LHASA IN TURMOIL

Thankga painter Yeshi Dorjee's fingers quivered as he picked up his brush that October morning in 1939. He was only twenty-four and had not known any ailment. Often commissioned by the Tibetan government to liven up monasteries, painting was Dorjee's passion, and he believed his was "one of the steadiest hands" in Lhasa. The tumult in the air seemed to unsettle him. He knew the new Dalai Lama was on the outskirts of the "abode of the gods." He kept mixing wrong colors. It was as if he had never painted in his life.

"That morning I decided that till His Holiness arrived I would not paint. I was just too excited. Perhaps his arrival would inspire me to recover the lost time," said Dorjee, practically blind and deaf at eighty-two years when I met him in McLeod Ganj in 1997. He remembered Lhasa acquiring an "extraordinary brightness" in the run-up to the Dalai Lama's arrival. "October is a cold month there, but in 1939 when His Holiness arrived everything seemed just right. It was very bright, unusually so. As a painter I would have loved to work more with light like that. But something in the air prevented me from working. It was as if I was being commanded to pay attention to the one who was about to arrive," Dorjee said almost mystically. Dorjee said people in Lhasa knew that the Dalai Lama was at Rigya monastery, about two miles east of the capital, which was agog with the boy's fabled supernatural powers. "Many in Lhasa thought the new Dalai Lama was blessed with supernatural powers. I knew that could not be true because the Dalai Lamas do not indulge in magic and sorcery. They are more philosophical beings than magical ones," Dorjee said. In the late 1930s Lhasa was a city of about 15,000 people, nearly half of whom were monks. It had been without the presence of a Dalai Lama for nearly six years and was in a mood to stretch the limits of credulity. In those days the city extended barely one mile and there were people everywhere. "If someone had said the Dalai Lama came flying on his own wings from Tengster, many would have believed it because they were desperate for the Dalai Lama to return to Lhasa," Dorjee said laughing.

Being a painter, who conceives life visually, Dorjee remembered quite vividly the colors that attended the welcoming ceremonies. "The Dalai Lama's tent was bright yellow because that is the signature color of the Dalai Lama's tent. Inside there were designs in blue, red, and yellow. I remember the pole on the roof of the tent had a figure of a peacock. That is why they call the tent the Peacock Tent," Dorjee said. What lent drama to the Dalai Lama's already very considerable presence in their midst was the presence of thousands of people waiting, with prayer wheels, incense sticks, white silk scarves, or simply folded hands, along the route from Rigya to Lhasa. "There was a group of Chinese soldiers that led the procession, followed by mounted bodyguards with their Mongolian hats. The regent was there closest to the palanquin carrying His Holiness. I also saw the Dalai Lama's father and mother and his two brothers," Dorjee said.

"I caught my first glimpse of the boy who had come to save us. He looked in complete control of himself. I was told he was only four years old but he seemed to know everything. It was as if he was coming back home after a short break," Dorjee said.

The journey from Rigya to Lhasa took the Dalai Lama's cavalcade two days because of all the rituals and the reception on the way. First he and his entourage were on their way to the Jokhang Temple, the holiest of Tibetan shrines, first built in the seventh century by King Songtsen Gampo and then reconstructed in the seventeenth century. The temple, at whose smaller replica near Dharamshala the author spent considerable time, has a powerful impact on visitors. The main entrance to the Jokhang is topped with a golden, eight-spoked Dharma wheel, with two golden deer on either side. The eight spokes of the wheel signify the Eightfold Path to enlightenment. The deer remind the visitors that the Buddha gave his first sermon in a deer park. Even the replica of the

Jokhang Temple near Dharamshala leaves visitors awestruck. The
visitor's gait changes perceptibly as he or she enters the complex.
The original Jokhang houses the Jowo Buddha, a Buddhist sculpture that Gampo's Chinese queen Gyasa brought as part of her
dowry. Legend has it that after Gampo's death, Gyasa hid the
sculpture in the temple. The historic Buddhist sculpture is said to
survive to this day. Like the mysterious stories that surround
everything in Lhasa, there are many surrounding how the Jokhang
was built on a lake. The most readily believed legend says that
Gampo tossed a ring from his finger and decided to build a temple wherever it fell. It fell in a lake where a white stupa appeared
magically, compelling him to build the temple there. Quite like the
original walls of the first courtyard, those of the replica in India
are also lined with hundreds of votive lamps. The flickering lamps
lift the already striking ambience of the temple to a new high.

Once he was inside the temple the Dalai Lama's head was
shorn of all his hair by Reting Rinpoche, the regent, as part of his
initiation as a monk. His name, Lhamo Thondup, had to be for-
feited to acquire his religious name, Jamphel Ngwang Lobsang
Yeshe Tenzin Gyatso, which means "Holy One, Tender Glory,
Mighty in Speech, Compassionate One, Learned Defender of the
Faith, Ocean of Wisdom." As always the Dalai Lama has a humorous take on it all. "I had a great lock of hair. All gone in one shot.
I could no longer comb my hair. My hair vanished but I acquired
a much bigger name. There was so much in that name that I had
to try very hard to live up to some of the attributes people
thought I had," the Dalai Lama said even as he found it hard to
control his laughter.

I asked him which one of his given attributes he really thought he had. "I am supposed to say all in case people feel disappointed. I think I am mighty in speech, that is for sure. I talk so much. The rest I don't know," he said with tongue firmly in his cheek.

After the ritual tonsuring and renaming, the Dalai Lama was taken to the Norbulingka Palace. Although the Norbulingka, which means "jeweled garden," is the summer residence of the Dalai Lamas, Tenzin Gyatso was taken there despite its being early winter. "Even in the winter I was quite struck by the palace's beauty," the Dalai Lama said. Built by the Seventh Dalai Lama in the eighteenth century, the Norbulingka was until that time a work in progress. Successive rulers kept improving upon it, adding more buildings and structures, till it turned into a cluster of palaces and pavilions with 350 rooms, surrounded by a lush green park full of musk deer, peacocks, pheasants, fish, and other animals. "The Norbulingka's soil was very fertile. There were all sorts of trees such as poplars, juniper, as well as flower trees. Many of the tree seeds were imported from India," the Dalai Lama said he later found out.

Life in the Norbulingka, by his own admission, was unending fun and joy. At four he was considered too young to begin formal studies of Buddhist scriptures. Being the chosen one, he could pretty much do what he chose. He spent most of his time playing with his brothers Gyalo Thondup, twelve, and Lobsang Samten, eight. The Dalai Lama's parents and brothers were lodged in a farmhouse, about a fifteen-minute walk from the palace. He had enough time and "deviousness" to visit them regularly with an attendant, although he was not supposed to. "One of the main attractions for me was the food at my house. One could eat eggs, fish, and pork. As a Buddhist monk I was not supposed to eat nonvegetarian food. But I could not resist then. I was even caught eating an egg by a senior official. I had to ask him to leave and he did," the Dalai Lama said.

Just as some people inside the palace began to wonder about the boy lama's high birth, he sprung a surprise. The Thirteenth Dalai Lama had told his mother that he had left his teeth behind in a particular closet inside a particular quarter of the palace. The boy was taken to the spot where he pointed at a wooden box. When it was opened, an aide found a set of dentures that had belonged to his predecessor. "I just knew it. I don't know how but I did. Of course, I could not wear them then. I don't wear them now either," he said yet again making light of his curious past memories.

From the end of October 1939 to the beginning of February 1940, the Dalai Lama lived in the Norbulingka. He did not know he had a far bigger initiation and enthronement ceremony ahead of him, the one that would forever establish him as the temporal and religious leader of Tibet. He said he never quite paid attention to what was to come because at his age, and notwithstanding that he was supposed to be into his fourteenth reincarnation, he did not quite understand all the fuss being made over him. It was true that every time he was thrown into a situation, as when the Nechung oracle unexpectedly thrust his head in his palanquin, the Dalai Lama reacted with uncanny familiarity. A sense of having been here before is something he was born with. If he was prescient about what life held for him, he never chose to reveal what he knew. "I would say I felt more familiar than prescient," the Dalai Lama explained, without caring to elaborate, although many of his aides strongly believe he is a man of strong prescience.

The people of Lhasa seemed to think that six years under the regent and the first six days in the presence of the Dalai Lama

could not be more different. The people of Tibet in general and
Lhasa in particular have always enjoyed a strong bond with the
Dalai Lamas. Since the Fourteenth was coming after an interreg-
num of nearly six years, they were expecting a change. "Under the
regent it was a normal life without any great highs. But the moment the Dalai Lama came onto the scene, it seemed we were all
lifted to a level or two higher. I became more prolific in my work
and perhaps even better than before. We were secure under the regent, but we were happy in the presence of the Dalai Lama," Dorjee said.

By early February, the regent, the Kashag, and all the high officials were busy feverishly finalizing plans for the upcoming enthronement. While the world's mind was focused on the rise of
Adolf Hitler and the mighty military machine in Europe, at
12,000 feet, in the bosom of the Himalayas, the people of Lhasa
were preparing to enthrone the new god-king. "I am not sure if
anyone in Lhasa really knew that Europe was about to be devastated by a big war. They did not even know Europe existed. They
were pleased that the new Dalai Lama was about to take over their
destinies," Dorjee said.

The lay Tibetan authorities chose the auspicious time of
Losar, the new year, the Year of the Iron Dragon, to anoint Lhamo
Thondup as the Fourteenth Dalai Lama. February 22, 1940, was
chosen to be the day of the enthronement. "I was quite unaware
of what was being planned. I had some idea that something important was about to happen but I did not really know what," the
Dalai Lama said.

But the people of Lhasa, Dorjee included, knew precisely what
was about to happen. "The Potala was without its chief resident
for a long time and Tibetans without their chief inspiration," Dor-

jee said. "That was about to change. I remember having done a special thangka to mark the upcoming ceremony. I am not sure where I left the painting. It is gone forever."

The Dalai Lama's elder brother Thubten Jigme Norbu, who was not part of the enthronement ceremony because he was still at his Kumbum monastery, said, "I knew the enthronement was around the corner. I was longing to attend but I could not. I had my own responsibilities at the Kumbum. By the time of the enthronement the word had got around in Tengster who my younger brother really was. With that my importance too went up."

7

·

TIBET'S NEW RULER
IS NOT ALL
OF FIVE YEARS OLD

February 21, 1940, was a glorious day in Lhasa.
The temperature that morning was about 50 degrees. In Lhasa, at 12,000 feet with no clouds, the
sun felt stronger than 50 degrees. Lhasa looked deliri-
ously festive. "I don't remember Lhasa looking so glorious before and since February 21, 1940," painter
Yeshi Dorjee said. "I did not see a single face without
a smile on it."

Inside the Potala Palace, in his residential quarters,

Lhamo Thondup prepared to assume a role he did not choose but one that he accepted with an effortlessness well beyond his age. Not all of five years old yet, he displayed an intuitive familiarity with what he was about to become. He was told he was born to be the king of all that he surveyed in Tibet and was about to be formally anointed. He woke up early as always. "I think it was around three a.m. It was very cold still and I wanted to sleep more. They told me that day was going to be important," he remembered.

Outside the Potala, along the route leading from the Norbulingka, a smell of burning incense wafted through the air. All along the route sat thousands of men, women, and children in their finest silk robes, hats, and jewelry. Blue and red dominated the colors. There was spontaneous singing among women and applause among men. All classes, the landed and the landless, the gentry and the common, the trader and the peasant, were all out in force. Fathers carried sons on their shoulders and mothers their daughters. "I remember not a single person in Lhasa was indoors that day. Whatever possessions people had, their best clothes, jewelry, and shoes, they came out wearing them. It was as if they all had a family wedding. The smell of incense is still fresh in my nose after nearly six decades," Dorjee said.

The procession carrying the Dalai Lama was a lesson in elaborate protocol. Sir Charles Bell, the British officer in Lhasa, wrote in his eyewitness account details that brought the scene alive:

> *First came servants, on ponies and foot, dressed in green tunics, blue breeches and broad, red-tasseled hats, carrying the Dalai Lama's food, kitchenware, garments and bed-clothes; grooms to be ready for their master at the Potala; attendants carrying tall banners to ward off evil spirits; some members of the Chinese delegation, high lamas followed by the State*

Oracle and the Chief Secretaries; the lead ponies of the Dalai Lama in gorgeous silk trappings; the head monks of the Potala monastery in claret robes fringed with gold and silver embroidery; junior lay officials in their long mantles of many colors, black shirts and white boat-shaped hats set sideways on the head and tied down under the ears; lay officers in ascending order of rank, all stiff in heavy brocade. And then through the clouds of incense which were drifting across the route, and between lines of standard-bearers, came two long double lines of men in loose green uniforms and red hats with white plumes, holding draw ropes—which would be needed for the climb up to the Potala—and men in red with yellow hats, bearing, as they moved with short shuffling steps, the yokes which supported the poles of the Dalai Lama's great golden palanquin.

From inside that ornate palanquin the world looked stunning to Lhamo Thondup. "I don't remember all the details but I do remember rows and rows of people in blue and red robes. I remember the fragrance of the incense. I remember peering through the golden curtains and finding my guards walking in measured steps. I also remember part of the peacock umbrella. I have some memory of the regent in his yellow hat," the Dalai Lama said. This was the ceremony marking his arrival in the Potala Palace on February 21. The next day was going to be even bigger. The Dalai Lama's residential quarters were predominantly red. By the red lacquered pillars was his seat atop a red wooden sofa. The hall had a full-length window in front that let the sunlight in all day. The Dalai Lama said the combination of the red carpet, red pillars, and orange wall paintings made for a "stunning effect" in the sunlight. "I remember that very well till today," he said.

Soon after the break of dawn the next day, guests began coming into the massive audience hall at one end of which lay the Lion

Throne, the ceremonial seat for the Dalai Lamas. The hall was packed to capacity with laity as well as high officials. Gifts laid out near the throne included two horses sent by the maharaja of Sikkim, as well as a large number of gifts from the British government carried by Sir Charles. They included a brick of gold, freshly minted by the Calcutta Mint, ten bags of silver, three rifles, six rolls of broadcloth of different colors, a gold watch and chain, a music box, two pairs of budgerigars, and a garden hammock. The British officer personally presented a gold clock with a singing nightingale, a pedal motor car, and a tricycle. There were other gifts such as golden Buddha statues, bags of gold dust, an elephant tusk, and silver ingots.

"I remember the cuckoo clock very well. I also remember the pedal motor car. My first instinct was to open up the clock but I did not," the Dalai Lama said.

The Dalai Lama entered the hall preceded by the blowing of Tibetan horns and trumpets. He managed to climb the first few steps of the throne but then had to be carried. Once he settled down on the Lion Throne, the view seemed enchanting. "There were so many people bending in reverence in front of me. Many came to prostrate in front of me. I found that funny. I smiled once in a while," he said.

The degree of self-assurance that the child at that age showed in the face of such overpowering ceremony did not escape Sir Charles's attention: "the extraordinary interest of the child in the proceedings, his presence, and his infallible skill in doing the right thing to the right person at the right time."

When I reminded the Dalai Lama of Bell's description, he seemed amused by it. "I never thought of it that way. As I said I had a strong sense of familiarity about what was happening in front of me. I did not have to put in any extra effort. It was as if I had done that before," he said.

Bell's claim that of all the gifts that the boy received he liked the British ones the best had some veracity. "I was fascinated by what Sir Charles brought, especially the budgerigars, which I kept asking for till they were brought to me. I am not sure if that meant I liked the British better than the rest," he laughed.

Once the installation ceremony was over after a daylong series of events, the Dalai Lama was chaperoned back to his living quarters. His brother Lobsang Samten too was allowed to stay in the palace, close to his room. Lobsang did not particularly like living in the palace because during the day it was lonely and at night it was scary because of the long shadows that its inmates cast on the walls as they walked in front of lamps. "My brother was scared of the long shadows cast by the staff moving about against the lamps. I on the other hand did not react to all that. Besides, there was a guard outside my room," he said.

The view of the Kyi Chu River from the palace was gorgeous but every time the Dalai Lama looked outside he realized he could not go there when he wanted. There was a telescope mounted on the terrace of his quarters, from which he would explore the sights of Lhasa town in the foothills. "The sight of other children playing freely used to make me wonder occasionally why I could not do it. I soon began to play with the palace servants," he said. The Dalai Lama's carefree childhood lasted another year. By the time he turned six, he was enrolled in a course of Buddhist studies that would last the next eighteen years. It mainly centered on metaphysical inquiry and meditation. "Early on I realized I was very interested in many profound questions. I was equally interested in what any child would be interested in as well. By the time I turned ten, I know I was well and truly into Buddhist studies," he said.

The winters from December to April were spent in the Potala, which the Dalai Lama thought was "not a very nice place to live," and the summers were spent in the Norbulingka, "which was a great place because I could go out into the open and commune with nature." As he grappled with concepts such as nothingness and impermanence, the two basic core principles of Buddhism, the Dalai Lama also involved himself with more mundane preoccupations such as repairing broken clocks, "or breaking the good ones and then fixing them." He also liked to tinker with automobiles. "I surreptitiously drove one in my teens and almost broke it. They could not scold me much for that," he said.

Life inside the Potala was quite structured and regimented for both the Dalai Lama and Lobsang. Both had to wake up well before dawn and bathe. The only concession that the chosen one was afforded was that he got heated water, unlike his brother who had to make do with cold water. The bath was followed by an hour of meditation. Seven a.m. was breakfast time. Breakfast was butter tea and tsampa. At 9 a.m. the officials and monks of the palace would get together for soup, rice, and yogurt. This hour also coincided with a daily audience. This was followed by two hours of school, which neither the Dalai Lama nor Lobsang really looked forward to. What kept them under control were two whips on the wall, which were used occasionally on the elder brother, at times to compensate for his brother's mischief. "Lobsang endured some tough punishment for me because they really could not punish the Dalai Lama," the Dalai Lama said.

Dorjee, who returned to his life as a thangka painter after the festivities subsided, said that by the late 1940s "the air in Tibet began to change again." With the rise of the Communist movement, Dorjee said he felt things were beginning to spin out of control. "One could hear in conversations on streets that the Chinese were planning something big in Tibet. With the Chinese one had to be worried because they always did things with great deliberation," he said.

The political upheaval in China was fraught with serious consequences for Tibet. In 1949, when the Dalai Lama turned fourteen, Tibet's relations with China had plummeted and were on a shaky foundation. "The Communists did not like the very basis of Tibet. They did not like Buddhism. They did not like religion. Although I found many aspects of Communism commendable and agreed with them, I began to see that at its heart it did not want people to seek spiritual awareness. I could see that what we stood for was in direct conflict with what they stood for," the Dalai Lama said.

When the People's Liberation Army invaded Tibet in 1949, the Dalai Lama knew, as did someone like Dorjee, that the Chinese were not acting on a short-term plan but a long-term strategy. "When they invaded in 1949, my heart sank. It was clear that they were not going to stop at that," Dorjee said.

A year later, the Dalai Lama was requested by the regent, the Cabinet, and the National Assembly to assume full political authority at fifteen, three years short of traditional majority. "The situation in Tibet was such that it had to rally around a symbol. I was seen as that symbol," the Dalai Lama said. As a teenager he had to balance the hard questions his Buddhist scriptural studies posed along with the ever-growing demands that his position as the supreme political authority made on him. From 1949 onward the Dalai Lama was forced into playing dual roles as the leader of the Tibetan Buddhist church as well as the de facto head of state at whose door stood one of the world's fiercest armies.

"What a change from when the Dalai Lama reached Rigya in October 1939 to November 1950 when he was compelled to take over the reins of Tibet because the Chinese did not like us! In February 1940 Lhasa was in great spirits celebrating the arrival of the new Dalai Lama. In February 1950 we were not sure if we would survive as a country," Dorjee said, sitting inside his two-room house in McLeod Ganj. "I can no longer see but I can still see in front of my eyes when the Chinese soldiers stormed into Lhasa. They all looked so young and yet so cold. They seemed to be brainwashed by Mao into thinking that we were barbarians and we needed to be civilized and freed from the 'oppression' by the Dalai Lama. Such lies, blatant lies," Dorjee said, and requested that I not talk to him about history anymore. "I am very old and I can't bear to face the fact that I will never see Tibet again," he said.

Unlike Dorjee, who could express his optimism and pessimism without any inhibition, in the Potala Palace the Dalai Lama had not only to weigh every word that he spoke but also to measure every step he took. "It was just five years since the end of the Second World War. The world did not have time for Tibet and what China was doing to us. I had to make every effort to see if we could coexist peacefully," the Dalai Lama said. Quite evidently those efforts did not yield much, as events in the following months were to so shockingly underscore.

8

■

INDIA, CHINA, AND TIBET

The India factor in the destiny of Tibet has not been explored with any degree of seriousness. The two nations have been brought together not just by their shared spiritual traditions but also by something more elemental in geological terms. They are as geologically connected as they are spiritually joined. The Dalai Lama describes India as Tibet's "Arya Bhoomi," or land of inspiration. India's role in the past, present, and future of Tibet has appeared marginal partly because the country's successive leaderships, beginning with its very first government in 1947, have chosen not to thrust themselves onto the center stage. The success of the Dalai Lama's campaign to keep the question of Tibet alive internationally can be substantially attributed to the unfettered existence he has enjoyed in India. "We are forever grateful to India and its people for doing so much for Tibet and Tibetans. If you look at it in terms of the number of years of my life spent here, India is my home," the Dalai Lama said.

If Buddhism is the pivot around which Tibet has revolved for at least a millennium, then it could be argued that for at least that long India has been integral to its existence. For centuries Indian Buddhist masters visited Tibet, laying the foundations of its spiritual life. In modern times it is hard to imagine Tibet without Buddhism. It is anybody's guess whether Buddhism has been good for Tibet or has set it on a course where its people became so docile and unsuspecting that they eventually lost control of their own land and destinies. These are questions that have no final answers. Great historians see history in cold, unemotional terms, without bringing their personal biases, prejudices, preferences, and wishes to bear upon the processes they are chronicling and interpreting. Such an assessment of Tibet would invariably create a picture wherein India's influence on the land has been as much as, if not more than, China's.

Ten months after India became a republic on January 26, 1950, emerging from nearly two hundred years of subjugation by the English colonialists, China annexed Tibet, the only buffer state between the two Asian giants. Historians are not clear if the timing of Tibet's annexation was deliberate or fortuitous, preoccupied as India was with repairing two centuries of plunder and impoverishment. Less than three years earlier the subcontinent had been overwhelmed by one of human history's most brutal and tragic upheavals when Pakistan was carved out as a separate country. The partition of India along religious lines by the retiring British colonial power led to sectarian bloodletting of the worst kind. Hundreds of thousands of Hindus and Muslims were butchered, as neighbors turned foes overnight. Millions were driven out of their homes with nothing more than the clothes they wore on their backs, subject to the fallout of an arbitrarily drawn border.

When the People's Liberation Army (PLA) walked into Tibet practically unaccosted, India, Tibet's most important neighbor to the southwest, could no more than look askance. It was in no position to challenge its aggressive neighbor. Its own nationhood was nascent, its exchequer was practically empty, its 300 million people were largely poor, and its military laughably ill-equipped. Most important, a dazed new republic was still trying to comprehend the partition of India and its bloody aftermath. India's first prime minister, Jawaharlal Nehru, summed up the country's predicament accurately in a letter to the country's home (interior) minister, Sardar Patel: "We cannot save Tibet, as we should have liked to do, and our very attempt to save it might well bring greater trouble to it. It would be unfair to Tibet for us to bring this trouble upon her without having the capacity to help her effectively. It may be possible, however, that we might be able to help Tibet to retain a large measure of her autonomy.

"It must be remembered that neither the UK nor the USA, nor indeed any other power is particularly interested in Tibet or in the future of that country. What they are interested in is embarrassing China," Nehru said.

Patel, a man of austere expressions unlike the more literary

Nehru, responded with characteristic brevity, saying, "[E]ven though we regard ourselves as friends of China, the Chinese do not regard us as friends." Nehru's critics—and there are legions of them in India—argue that the aristocratic prime minister, generally an astute judge of geopolitics, had a blind spot when it came to China. Even at the height of India's campaign for independence from the British, his views about China were highly complimentary. During an address to the Sino-Indian Cultural Society at Santiniketan, near Calcutta, on December 23, 1945, Nehru said, "[The Second World War] has certainly brought us nearer and closer to China than ever before, both physically and psychologically. The war has made China look to the west of her rather than to the east of her. The centre of activities in China came nearer to India with the development of communications by road and air. Today it is possible to be in the heart of China after a brief day's journey. All these factors, which might have taken place in course of time, but which have been expedited by the war, have led to the closest associations and approximations between China and India." In the same address Nehru also clearly indicated how he expected India and China to work together:

> *India and China, which have played a different part in world affairs, are passing through some kind of turmoil today. In China it has taken the obvious course of a civil war and in India the trouble is deep-seated. These differences among our own people result in a certain weakening of our ability to influence the world which is extremely unfortunate. Now that hostilities have ceased in the Pacific Theatre, India and China should have had the privilege of directing the future course of events. A strong and united China and a strong and united India must come close to each other. Their amity and friendship will not only lead to their mutual*

*benefit but will also benefit the world at large. There are in China and
India certain elements and traditions, which the West does not have,
elements which are essential for world equilibrium.*

*However that may be, one thing seems to be dead certain and that is
this: There is going to be no equilibrium in this world unless there is
equilibrium in India, China and South East Asia. There is not going to
be harmony or peace even for a short time, and much less for a long time,
unless the problems of Asia are settled satisfactorily, unless aggression and
interference by western countries in Asian affairs cease once for all.*

With such sanguine views of his future adversary, Nehru had evidently misread China's real intentions as the world was emerging from the ferment of World War II. What did not help matters, according to some critics, was that two of Nehru's closest advisors were Krishna Menon, former Indian ambassador to the United Nations and defense minister, and K. M. Pannikar, India's ambassador to China, both avowedly socialistic in their political leanings and close to China. Instead of focusing on the more immediate and eventually territorially consequential annexation of Tibet, Nehru chose to concern himself with the Korean War (1950–1953).

The Chinese invasion of Tibet came only five years after the curtain came down on World War II, with Europe, America, and Japan experiencing deep war fatigue and struggling with devastated economies. Post–World War II estrangement and tensions in Europe had divided the world into western and eastern blocs. The U.S.-led western bloc was locked in a simmering war of nerves with the Soviet Union–led eastern bloc. Notwithstanding the world community's dwindling appetite for wars, North Korea, assisted by the Soviet Union and China, invaded

South Korea, prompting the United States to jump in along with a UN coalition.

In Nehru's judgment, partly backed by the analysis provided by Menon and Pannikar, the Korean War could weaken the case for the People's Republic of China's (PRC) entry into the United Nations, which in turn could undermine his vision of creating a new axis of nonaligned powers in Asia, including India and China.

The Republic of China (ROC) came into existence in 1912, at the end of the Qing dynasty, bringing to a conclusion over two thousand years of imperial rule. Over the course of its existence the ROC was troubled by warlordism, Japanese invasion, and civil war before it was overthrown by the Communists in 1949. Although the ROC had been a founding member of the United Nations since 1945, the rise of the Communist Party and its seizure of power in mainland China did not automatically mean that the PRC would be the natural successor to the ROC's UN seat. Until 1971 the ROC was recognized as the sole legitimate government of China, even though it was based in Taiwan. But a resolution passed by the UN General Assembly in 1971 withdrew that recognition and instead recognized the PRC as the legitimate representative. Nehru's hope that China would be an active and influential member of the nonaligned movement, a grouping of countries claiming to be independent of either the western bloc or the eastern bloc, was belied by Beijing.

Nehru's logic of keeping China on India's side may have made sense at the time. But in retrospect it appears to have been counterproductive. Despite India's having been reduced to a shadow of its former self by frequent foreign invasions prior to 1950, there were those who thought that India could make a difference in Tibet. *The Economist*, not known for its particularly complimentary view of India in those days, wrote in an editorial, "Having maintained complete independence of China since 1912, Tibet has a strong claim to be regarded as an independent state. But it is for India to take a lead in this matter. If India decides to support independence of Tibet as a buffer state between itself and China, Britain and the U.S.A. will do well to extend formal diplomatic recognition to it."

The annexation of Tibet took Nehru by surprise. He complained that he had been "led to believe by the Chinese Foreign Office that the Chinese would settle the future of Tibet in a peaceful manner by direct negotiation with the representatives of Tibet." Given the history of the Chinese Communists it is hard to imagine why Nehru would take the Chinese Foreign Office's promises at face value.

In April 1951 Beijing had managed to coerce Lhasa into entering into the Seventeen-Point Agreement that was entitled "Agreement of the Central People's Government and the Local Government of Tibet on Measures for the Peaceful Liberation of Tibet." The nomenclature was carefully chosen in describing Tibet's government as a local government and China's as the central government. The language of the agreement was openly weighed against Tibet. "The Tibetan nationality is one of the nationalities with a long history within the boundaries of China, and like many other nationalities, it has performed its glorious duty in the course of the creation and development of our great Motherland," it said.

The Tibetan delegation sent to discuss the agreement was presented a draft that did not address most of their misgivings. Already weakened by the 1950 aggression, the delegation felt obliged to enter into some sort of an agreement to prevent any further military hostilities by Beijing. Describing the circumstances that eventually led to the Tibetan delegation being coerced into signing the agreement, the Dalai Lama said, "Our delegation told the Chinese forcefully that Tibet was an independent state. They produced strong evidence to support it but the Chinese did not agree. They drafted a revised agreement that contained seventeen articles and it was presented to the delegation as an ultimatum. Our delegation was prevented from making any alterations. Not only that, they were abused and threatened with personal violence as well as further military action against the people of Tibet. They were not allowed to refer the articles to my government or I."

The Tibetan delegation signed the agreement without using the official seal. They used personal seals. "I know for a fact that they did not use our official seal. In that sense the Seventeen-Point Agreement was no agreement in effect yet. But the Chinese conveniently concluded it was a done deal. I repudiated it then and I do so now," the Dalai Lama said.

Three years after the Seventeen-Point Agreement was enacted, during his second visit to China in May 1954, the first being in 1939, Nehru seemed to hit it off with Chinese prime minister Chou En-lai. Nehru was impressed with the "terrifying strength" that the Chinese displayed in their nation building. The visit was to be fateful as India and China signed the famous five-point agreement, known as the Panchsheel Agreement, that spoke of "mutual non-aggression," "mutual noninterference in each other's internal affairs," and "peaceful coexistence." The agreement was viewed with a great deal of suspicion by Nehru's political opponents, many of whom believed it had effectively doomed Tibet's future.

Jyotindra Nath Dixit was an aspiring career diplomat at the time and would later become India's foreign secretary and national security advisor and distinguish himself as one of the most bril-

liant foreign policy strategists. He put Nehru's position in a larger
perspective. In interviews in 1997, Dixit, who died in January
2005, said, "It is easy to dismiss Nehru's China policy as seriously
flawed and naïve. But if you look at the geopolitical circumstances
within which it evolved, it makes perfect sense. It is true that the
great prime minister did take China at its face value but his basic
premise that India and China had to work together, an idea which
is being executed by both in the twenty-first century, was not inherently wrong.

"Their sheer size and reality of their geographical proximity
dictated that the two had to find a way of being on the same side
while approaching many international issues. Nehru's vision of
keeping China on India's side in his quest to create a nonaligned
axis could not be faulted. However, what could be questioned was
his administration's inability to see the reality of China's individual interests and ambitions."

Dixit said that what critics describe as Nehru's failure was really
a consequence of hindsight. "In the circumstances that Nehru was
in it would have been unwise of India to assume an openly antago-
nistic position to China simply because we did not like their politics. I would say this though. India's China policy under Nehru
certainly needed a heavy dose of skepticism and doubt," he said.

That skepticism and doubt were conspicuously missing from
India's China policy was explicitly clear in the 1954 Panchsheel
Agreement between the two, four years after Beijing took over
Lhasa. Around the time of Nehru's visit to Beijing in May of that
year, the Chinese government was tightening its control over Tibet
by deploying over 200,000 troops. It was no surprise to anyone
that China was willing to sign an agreement that spoke of mutual
noninterference. If Tibet mattered to India because of their

centuries-old trade and cultural and religious ties, the 1954 visit did not appear to underscore any commitment to a relationship with Tibet. In fact, if anything, it seemed to undermine some of those ties with serious formalization of Sino-Indian relations. Nehru's incredulity in 1950 over the Chinese invasion of Tibet was hardly expressed in his exchanges with the Chinese leadership during his first official visit.

"Although we were deeply troubled by the Chinese invasion and India's relatively muted response, I was optimistic about Prime Minister Nehru's visit," the Dalai Lama said. "We had always seen India as the land of our inspiration and a civilization that would always stand by us. When the Panchsheel Agreement was announced, I was quite doubtful about Beijing's real intentions. Mutual noninterference meant telling India don't talk about Tibet."

By the time Nehru visited China, Beijing's stranglehold on Lhasa was firm and increasing. It was clear to most Tibetans that short of an extraordinary twist in geopolitics they had lost their land forever. If the Dalai Lama then had a sense of foreboding, he did not reveal it to anyone. "It was becoming obvious to me that Tibet was being lost to China," he recalled. "But that the situation would be so hopeless as to drive me out eventually was not."

Nehru's Beijing visit turned out to be an exercise in great Asian bonhomie between him and Chou En-lai, inspiring the Indian leader to eventually coin an enduring but much reviled expression "Hindi-Chini Bhai Bhai" (Sino-Indian brotherhood). Despite his admission that he was unpleasantly surprised by the Chinese action in Tibet four years before his visit, Nehru appeared all too willing to put Sino-Indian relations beyond concerns over the developments in Lhasa. Notwithstanding Nehru's candid response that since India was not in a position to help Tibet to an extent where it could resolve the issue it should not do anything at all, Tibetans in general and the Dalai Lama in particular had expected New Delhi to use its influence much more than it eventually did. "I understood Prime Minister Nehru's compulsions and logic. But I also thought he underestimated India's and his own standing in world affairs," the Dalai Lama reasoned.

Two years after Nehru's visit an opportunity presented itself for the Dalai Lama to meet Nehru personally during the 2,500th anniversary of the birth of the Buddha in India. The Dalai Lama was invited by the Maharaj Kumar of Sikkim to attend the celebrations, much to the concern of the Chinese that he might not return. In fact, the Chinese assessment was not off the mark since the Maharaj Kumar was actively plotting to convince the Indian government to grant the Dalai Lama asylum and to enlist U.S. support for the plan. The Dalai Lama arrived in New Delhi on November 26, 1956, along with the Panchen Lama.

The meeting between the sixty-seven-year-old Nehru and the twenty-one-year-old Dalai Lama was very cordial, but the two, separated by more than forty-five years, found it hard to form an immediate bond. One was a world statesman, patrician in his background and expansive in his political philosophy and yet astute in the art of realpolitik, having been at the core of one of the world's greatest political movements against imperial subjugation. The other, although highly intuitive, was untested in world affairs, naturally self-effacing, and driven by his faith in the inherent goodness of all human beings. Nehru and the Dalai Lama were as far apart as any two men could ever be. What united them, however, was their deep understanding of the ethos of Indian civilization as it is manifested in Buddhism. "Nehru was a remarkable man, a great leader and intellectual," the Dalai Lama explained. "I understood that he had to look after India's interests but I did not think India's interests were separate from Tibet's. That is where we disagreed.

"I could see that while his heart was with us Tibetans his head was preoccupied with the difficult issue of balancing India's old ties with Tibet and the necessity to work with China. But I still think that Nehru had more power as India's leader than he gave himself credit for," the Dalai Lama said.

"We met many times during my stay in New Delhi. I explained to the prime minister our situation. He reiterated his position that India could not do much for Tibet and suggested that I work out all outstanding issues with Chou En-lai who was scheduled to visit India in January. Nehru also said no one in the world recognized Tibet's independence, so it would be best for us to work within the Seventeen-Point Agreement. Of course, I had expected more from Nehru but he had his own compulsions," the Dalai Lama rationalized. Nehru's position on the Chinese invasion of Tibet was less than critical, governed as it was by his wish that the two Asian giants should work in tandem on major international issues.

During that visit the Dalai Lama indicated to Nehru his wish to seek asylum in India. "Nehru was not in favor at that point," the Dalai Lama recalled. "My impression of Nehru was that he was genuinely concerned about the Tibetans but he was equally concerned about India's future."

The 1956 visit to India gave the Dalai Lama a glimpse of the possibilities should he choose to leave Tibet. His meeting with Chou En-lai turned out better than he had expected. When he complained that reforms were being imposed on the Tibetans by the Chinese, Chou En-lai seemed genuinely surprised. "He seemed very friendly and willing to hear me out on our issues. He even promised us that he would convey to Mao our feelings," the Dalai Lama said.

Chou En-lai also met the Thubten Jigme Norbu, the elder brother of the Dalai Lama and the first incarnate lama in the family who went on to become the abbot of the powerful Kumbum monastery. "My impression of Chou En-lai is he was inclined to resolve our issues but didn't quite have the authority to do so. After all everything flowed from Chairman Mao those days. I told His Holiness my feelings. I said things did not look good despite what Chou was saying," Norbu said.

Chou En-lai returned to India from his European tour and met the Dalai Lama again. "He told me that the situation in Tibet had worsened with revolt against the Chinese presence becoming more intense. I got the sense that he still did not comprehend why the Tibetans would want to revolt. He then told me that the PLA would act to put down any revolt," the Dalai Lama said.

By the time the Dalai Lama returned to Lhasa in March 1957, he and most others in the capital knew that his life there was becoming untenable. But Tenzin Gyatso still believed that he could turn the tide. "I believed then that I could reason with the Chinese and convince them of the futility of their action in Tibet. But when I look back now on those days it seems China never did anything to retract. The Chinese thinking has always been that they are the center of the world, which is of course so wrong. The Chinese would never hesitate to do something once they have set their mind on it even if it was wrong," the Dalai Lama said.

The Dalai Lama's last two years in Lhasa, following his visit to New Delhi, were portentous and foreshadowed the impending doom.

9

SUGGESTIONS
OF FRATRICIDE

Sometime in late 1950 as the People's Liberation Army prepared to overrun Tibet, a handful of its officers met Thubten Jigme Norbu. Their mission was to win Norbu over to their side and play him against his more illustrious sibling.

The deal being offered to Norbu by the Chinese interlocutors was breathtakingly cynical. "Overthrow your brother and we will make you the governor general of Tibet," is what he was told by the officials. As if this was not startling enough, the officials suggested something even more cynical—fratricide as a possible option, should the Dalai Lama refuse to cooperate.

"They said they would destroy everything Tibetan, its religion, its culture, its customs and so on [in case we did not cooperate]." Norbu, eighty-four, who runs a Tibetan cultural center in Indianapolis, Indiana, remembered vividly. "They said if His Holiness does not cooperate with the Communists then I should kill him. I had to exercise a great deal of self-control in the face of such an abominable suggestion. They said those who committed such acts for the cause of Communism would be rewarded with high office. I don't know why but I always hated Communism.

"It was clear that the Chinese did not like anything about us Tibetans. They would come to me every day and tell me all sorts of things. They would criticize everything, from our habits to our clothes. They would comment on our monks' robes saying we wasted so much cloth. They would say just wear a jacket and pants. They would then criticize religion in general and Buddhism in particular," Norbu said.

Tibet came into Beijing's crosshairs immediately after the rise of the Communist Party in China in 1949. Soon after the Communists took power, China's political elite began plotting ways to "liberate" Tibet from "imperialist forces and the reactionary feudal regime in Lhasa." Tibetan chronicles before Tibet was invaded have references to "supernatural" indications of the trouble ahead. One report said that during meditation in the Ganden monastery the Dalai Lama saw the statue of Yamantaka, the deity of terror and destruction, move its head and look to the east with a fierce expression. There was a series of natural disasters, including a powerful earthquake and droughts. There were also reports of freak births to both humans and animals. Temple edifices were reported to have crumbled for no apparent reason.

Among the prominent reasons used to justify their impending action against Tibetans—their habits of dress not being the least of them—the Communist Party spoke of the practice of slavery or serfdom in Tibet. They also accused Tibetans of human sacrifice. While slavery or serfdom did exist in Tibet, where poor families often sold their children to bidders paying them *shoring*, or the "price of mother's milk," it was equally prevalent in China as well. According to many estimates, there were up to four million children in servitude in China in the 1930s.

There is some evidence that the ghastly ritual of human sacrifice existed in Tibet, but it predated the arrival of Buddhism. In any case it did not enjoy any official sanction from the Tibetan government or the Buddhist clergy. What kept the stories about human sacrifice alive was a burial practice that some Tibetans followed. When young boys died their bodies were buried in a standing position under important buildings. In some cases, instead of actual bodies, images were buried. But this was not a cruel religious tradition; it was merely a form of burial.

Determined as it was to bring Tibet under its control, the Communist regime did not take much time to act. By October 1950, the PLA had entered Chamdo, the capital of Kham province and headquarters of the Tibetan Army's Eastern Command. Kham was practically overrun by the PLA, which took the province's Governor Ngawang Jigme Ngabo prisoner. Simultaneously, the Chinese army was also quietly infiltrating Tibet's northeastern border province of Amdo, ever careful that its action not attract international attention.

The mounting Chinese military presence forced the fifteen-year-old Dalai Lama and a band of his high government officials to evacuate the capital and set up a provisional administration near the Indian border at Yatung. The Chinese understood that the Dalai Lama's action could send a wrong signal within and outside Tibet. In July 1951 the Dalai Lama and his select government officials were persuaded by Chinese officials to return to Lhasa.

"Even at that early age my recollection is that of a determined Chinese army bent upon taking control of Tibet. We were persuaded to return with the idea that we could still ward off any further inroads by the Chinese," the Dalai Lama recalled some forty-five years after the fact. Less than two months after the Dalai Lama and his officials invested their faith in the Chinese promises, 3,000 Chinese "liberation forces" took over Lhasa in September 1951. During the next three years Beijing moved rapidly to consolidate its hold over Tibet, stationing 220,000 PLA troops there by 1954.

In April 1956, the Chinese set up the Preparatory Committee for the Autonomous Region of Tibet in Lhasa, headed by the Dalai Lama. "Quite craftily the purpose of the committee was described to be to modernize the country. It was not lost on the discerning members of the Tibetan government, including the Dalai Lama, that the committee was in effect expected to toe the Chinese lines on any imminent claims that they would make," Tempa Tsering, a brother-in-law of the Dalai Lama and an influential functionary of the Tibetan government-in-exile, said.

In the late fifties, Lhasa became increasingly politicized and a nonviolent resistance grew with the rise of Mimang Tsongdu, a popular and spontaneous citizens' group. Posters denouncing the occupation went up across town. Stones and dried yak dung were hurled at Chinese street parades. During that period, when the directive from Beijing was still to woo Tibetans rather than oppress them, only the more extreme Mimang Tsongdu leaders and orators faced arrest.

By February 1957, many areas in eastern Tibet were in ferment as local Kham and Amdo guerrillas inflicted heavy casualties on the Chinese army. The attacks forced the army authorities to relocate 100,000 forces from western to eastern Tibet. Attempts at disarming the fierce Khampa tribesmen escalated the resistance to the level where the PLA was compelled to begin bombing the area. Monasteries were pillaged and nobles, monks, and guerrilla leaders were arrested. Many of them were publicly tortured and executed to send a wave of terror down on others who might have contemplated joining the resistance.

The fighting in distant Kham and Amdo forced thousands of Tibetan refugees to flee to Lhasa, already inundated with 30,000-strong PLA troops who were watching nervously as the capital's population grew dramatically. Hundreds of temporary shelters and camps sprung up on the outskirts of the capital. In the next few months revolt began brewing across Lhasa. Tens of thousands of guerrillas and ordinary Tibetans in and around Lhasa began locking themselves into combat with the Chinese troops as winter came in 1958. By end of 1958 a full-scale revolt was staring the Chinese military command in the eye. Finally, they had to pull out their trump card—threaten to bomb the Dalai Lama's palace if the revolt was not contained.

"I remember as 1959 began I was so preoccupied with the finals of Geshe Lharampa [the doctorate in Buddhist philosophy with emphasis on metaphysics]. Metaphysics is a very tough subject and requires a lot of concentration. Even the Dalai Lama has to study seriously. He cannot cheat and pass," the Dalai Lama said, laughing. "But I also had the events outside the Jokhang [temple] on my mind. Lhasa was not happy those days. People were angry at the presence of the PLA."

On March 1, 1959, two junior Chinese army officers paid a visit to the Dalai Lama at the Jokhang, the spiritual hub of Tibetan Buddhism. Built in 647 during the rule of Songtsen Gampo, the temple was also a place of learning for the Dalai Lamas. The ostensible reason for the visit by the two soldiers was to invite him for a performance and tea at the Chinese army headquarters. They wanted him to commit to a date right then. "I said I could do so only once the ceremonies surrounding my final exams were completed," the Dalai Lama said.

Tempa Tsering put the invitation in perspective. "This visit was extraordinary for many reasons but I can tell you the two most important ones. For one, invitations of such nature are always conveyed through the Kashag [the Tibetan Cabinet]. For another, such parties were normally held at the palace and not at the military headquarters. Something was not right about that invitation," he said.

"In those days of 1959 there was something odd in Lhasa's air. You could sense that we were in serious trouble and that had nothing to do with just the presence of a large number Chinese troops. They were merely symptoms of the time," Norbu said.

Five days after the two junior army officers met the Dalai Lama at the Jokhang, General Tan Kuan-sen, one of the three military bosses of Lhasa, called the chief official abbot to inquire when the Dalai Lama would attend the performance at the army camp. After some back and forth March 10 was fixed. March 8 was Women's Day, on which the Chinese general Tan Kuan-sen used to hector the people of Lhasa and threaten to bomb monasteries unless the Khampas relented in their attacks.

On the morning of March 9 two Chinese officers visited the commander of the Dalai Lama's bodyguards, requesting that the commander meet Brigadier Fu at the military headquarters. What Fu had to tell the commander was portentous. Fu said the Dalai Lama's visit to the army headquarters from the Norbulingka Palace would have to be without any ceremony. No bodyguards would be allowed to accompany the Dalai Lama and no Tibetan soldiers would be allowed inside the headquarters.

"That seemed like a clear signal since His Holiness was always accompanied by a retinue of twenty-five armed guards on such visits. People of Lhasa would invariably line the route of his journey. What the Chinese were asking us to do sounded very suspicious," Tsering said.

"I was told by my aides that the Chinese were up to no good. I did not want to make an issue out of it since I wanted to gauge the Chinese mind," the Dalai Lama said. However, Lhasa's citizenry thought otherwise. On the day of the scheduled visit some 300,000 Tibetans surrounded the palace in order to prevent the Dalai Lama from visiting the Chinese headquarters.

"I remember the huge crowd outside the palace. I remember people were quite anxious. I remember that they did not want me to leave the palace because they feared for my safety. They thought I might be forcibly taken to Beijing to attend the Chinese National Assembly. Looking at their emotions I had no choice but to decide against the visit to the army headquarters," the Dalai Lama said.

That decision turned out to be fateful. From that point onward life started spiraling out of control in Lhasa. Two days later thousands of women took to the streets carrying banners reading TIBET FOR TIBETANS. A delegation of women presented an appeal for help to the Indian Consulate. An Indian diplomatic source who was present at the time, said, "Although the people in Lhasa seemed feisty and determined to take on the Chinese, it was obvious to anyone who bothered to go beyond the obvious that the Tibetans had already lost their land to the PLA. I knew we were seeing the last days of an autonomous Tibet."

With the Dalai Lama turning down the invitation, the battle lines were drawn in Lhasa between the Tibetans and the Chinese. Mimang Tsongdu members went around barricading narrow streets even as the Chinese troops were fortifying their positions. The Dalai Lama and his aides began to plan a move that was to change his life and the history of Tibet forever. They decided to escape.

"I knew my stay in Lhasa was no longer tenable. In my private moments I felt sad that I had no option but to leave," the Dalai Lama recalled nearly forty years later, sitting on an ochre-colored sofa in his private study in McLeod Ganj one afternoon. He looked reflective, nostalgic, and somewhat emotional. "You see, too much was going on for me to stay. My aides thought I had to leave in order to stay alive."

According to Tibetan records, on March 15, 3,000 of the Dalai Lama's bodyguards left Lhasa to take up their positions along his likely escape route. The Khampa tribesmen, whom the Chinese wanted the Dalai Lama to rein in, deployed some of their most trusted men at strategic points. Nearly 50,000 heavily armed Chinese troops were breathing down on Lhasa and outnumbering the Tibetan forces several times over.

On March 17, Lhasa woke up with knots in its stomach. Something seemed amiss. By the afternoon, the Chinese gave up all pretense of a "peaceful accession" of Tibet. The army fired two mortar shells at the summer palace of Norbulingka. Their rounds fell short of the palace walls but landed close enough for the Dalai Lama to make up his mind.

"Everybody in the palace said I ought to leave immediately. I was not sure since I wanted to stay back for the people of my country. I was told if I stayed alive I could still make a difference," the Dalai Lama said.

The penultimate hour came at 10 p.m. that night. In an action fraught with irony the Dalai Lama was forced to discard his ochre robes and instead wear a soldier's uniform and carry a gun. He set out on the long journey to India. Two days later fierce fighting broke out, with poorly armed civilian Tibetans engaging the Chinese troops in hand-to-hand combat. Hundreds of shells were fired at the Norbulingka. Tibetan sources say thousands were killed in the next few days. Two hundred members of the Dalai Lama's bodyguard were executed publicly by a firing squad. Three of Lhasa's most important monasteries, Ganden, Sera, and Drepung, were bombed and severely damaged. According to one estimate, over 86,000 Tibetans were killed in the span of a few days in the aftermath of the Dalai Lama's escape.

After two weeks of treacherous mountainous journey on horseback, the Dalai Lama and the officials accompanying him reached the Indian border at Khenzimane Pass on March 31, 1959. Two days later they reached Tawang, which was the headquarters of the North East Frontier Agency (NEFA). The region is now known as Arunachal Pradesh, one of the India's twenty-seven states.

"We were all very tired. I remember I had an attack of dysentery, a problem I found was quite common to India. I was in India, the land of our spiritual inspiration. I was both happy and sad, sad that we were forced to leave our home but happy that we were in India where Buddhism began," the Dalai Lama said.

On April 3, India's first prime minister, Jawaharlal Nehru, told parliament that New Delhi had granted asylum to the Dalai Lama, his family, and others who had accompanied him. On April 18, the Dalai Lama along with his mother, sister, brother, three ministers, and some eighty others left for Tezpur, Assam. He was received by Indian officials and nearly two hundred journalists who had gathered there to cover what they called "the story of the century."

"I remember journalists were curious about everything, about who I was, how I proposed to deal with the occupation of Tibet, when I planned to go back. These days when I think about that time I tell myself that the questions have not changed. I am still in India and the Chinese are still in Tibet," the Dalai Lama said in a rare wistful moment.

Among the pronouncements that the Dalai Lama made at Tezpur was a strong repudiation of the Seventeen-Point Agreement (see pages 111–114) of May 1951, which he said China made him sign "under duress" in Beijing.

The Dalai Lama and his entourage did not quite know what the future held for them in India. They did not know where they would be resettled. They did not know how long they would live in the country. The only thing they knew was that they were refugees, very important but refugees nevertheless. "It struck me immediately that I had lost my home. At that point I did not know how long my exile would be but I sensed it was not going to be a short one," the Dalai Lama said. The entourage was told by the government of India that the Dalai Lama would be offered an exile home in Mussoorie, a scenic Himalayan hill town in north India. It was known that that would at best be a temporary arrangement. The Dalai Lama's staff was told that Nehru had decided that eventually they would be shifted to a quaint Himalayan hamlet called McLeod Ganj in the state of Himachal Pradesh. "It did not really matter where as long as the place was not very hot," the Dalai Lama said.

THE SEVENTEEN-POINT AGREEMENT, MAY 1951

Agreement on Measures for the Peaceful Liberation of Tibet. Signed and sealed in Beijing on 23 May 1951.

[The preamble to the agreement stressed that Tibet had a "long history within the boundaries of China," outlined the aggressive imperialist forces in Tibet that needed to be "successfully eliminated" and claimed that both parties (Tibetans and Chinese People's Government—CPG) had, as a result of talks, agreed to "establish the agreement and ensure that it be carried into effect."]

1. *The Tibetan people shall unite and drive out imperialist aggressive forces from Tibet; the Tibetan people shall return to the big family of the Motherland—the People's Republic of China.*
2. *The local government of Tibet shall actively assist the PLA to enter Tibet and consolidate the national defenses.*
3. *In accordance with the policy toward nationalities laid down in the Common Program of the Chinese People's Political Consultative*

Conference (CPPCC), the Tibetan people have the right of exercising national regional autonomy under the unified leadership of the CPG.

4. The central authorities will not alter the existing political system in Tibet. The central authorities also will not alter the established status, functions and powers of the Dalai Lama. Officials of various ranks shall hold office as usual.

5. The established status, functions and powers of the Panchen Ngoerhtehni shall be maintained.

6. By the established status, functions and powers of the Dalai Lama and of the Panchen Ngoerhtehni are meant the status, functions and powers of the Thirteenth Dalai Lama and the ninth Panchen Ngoerhtehni when they had friendly and amicable relations with each other.

7. The policy of freedom of religious belief laid down in the common program of the CPPCC shall be carried out. The religious beliefs, customs and habits of the Tibetan people shall be respected and lama monasteries shall be protected. The central authorities will not effect a change in the income of the monasteries.

8. Tibetan troops shall be reorganized step by step into the PLA and become a part of the defense force of the CPR.

9. The spoken and written language and school education of the Tibetan nationality shall be developed step by step in accordance with the actual conditions in Tibet.

10. Tibetan agriculture, livestock raising, industry and commerce shall be developed step by step and the people's livelihood shall be improved step by step in accordance with the actual conditions in Tibet.

11. In matters relating to various reforms in Tibet, there will be no compulsion on the part of the central authorities. The local

government of Tibet shall carry out reforms of its own accord, and, when the people raise demands for reform, they shall be settled by means of consultation with the leading personnel of Tibet.

12. In so far as former pro-imperialists and pro-Kuomintang [Guomindang] officials resolutely sever relations with imperialism and the Kuomintang and do not engage in sabotage or resistance, they may continue to hold office irrespective of their past.

13. The PLA entering Tibet shall abide by all the above-mentioned policies and shall also be fair in all buying and selling and shall not arbitrarily take a needle or thread from the people.

14. The CPG shall have centralized handling of all external affairs of the area of Tibet; and there will be peaceful coexistence with neighboring countries and establishment and development of fair commercial and trading relations with them on the basis of equality, mutual benefit and mutual respect for territory and sovereignty.

15. In order to ensure the implementation of this agreement, the CPG shall set up a Military and Administrative Committee and a Military Area HQ in Tibet and—apart from the personnel sent there by the CPG—shall absorb as many local Tibetan personnel as possible to take part in the work. Local Tibetan personnel taking part in the Military and Administrative Committee may include patriotic elements from the local government of Tibet, various districts and various principal monasteries; the name list shall be set forth after consultation between the representatives designated by the CPG and various quarters concerned and shall be submitted to the CPG for appointment.

16. Funds needed by the Military and Administrative Committee, the Military Area HQ and the PLA entering Tibet shall be provided by the CPG. The local government of Tibet should assist the PLA in the purchase and transport of food, fodder and other daily necessities.

17. This agreement shall come into force immediately after signature and seals are affixed to it.

Signed and sealed by the delegates of the CPG with full powers by Chief Delegate Li Weihan [Chairman of the Commission of Nationalities Affairs] and three delegates [and by] delegates with full powers of the local government of Tibet by Chief Delegate Kaloon Ngabou Ngawang Jigme [Ngabo Shape] and four delegates.

10

NEW GODS IN TIBET

Tibet without the Dalai Lama was like Tibet without its mountains. The place felt incomplete. For Tibetans, his absence, although considered temporary, meant having to reinvent life as they had known it till then. The country had lost its most important reference point. "I was told later that the people of Lhasa felt a sense of bereavement after we left. They were depressed, anxious, and angry. I felt as much for them," the Dalai Lama said.

The dramatic exit of someone they considered divinely ordained and someone whom they believed was endowed with un-
fathomable powers had a devastating psychological impact on the
Tibetan people. Scholars have not adequately studied what happens to a people when the one in whom they have reposed their
most sacred trust is suddenly removed from their midst. The Dalai
Lama's flight created a vacuum that people filled with varying
emotions. One typical response was summed up by painter Yeshi
Dorjee who said, "The people of Lhasa believed that the Dalai
Lama's escape from Tibet was part of a larger divine plan. They
believed, and some still do after these many decades, that he would
return to Lhasa more triumphant and powerful than ever before.
They just had to continue believing it would happen one day." Another typical response was to go into complete denial and pretend
that nothing had changed, a reaction that was widespread among
the older generations of Tibetans. The third response, which was
nowhere as pervasive as the first two, was to believe that there had
been a change in divine leadership and the Chinese were the new
gods in Tibet.

The remarkably easy defeat of the Tibetan army at the hands
of the PLA and the subsequent escape of the Dalai Lama from
Lhasa were seen by a minority within the Tibetan people as a clear
signal that Mao Tse-tung was the new presiding deity of Tibet.
This minority felt disillusioned that the god in whom they had invested so much faith and trust was after all not invincible but had
frailties they had never suspected. Quite like the neighborhood
children of my early years did, this minority had ascribed to the
Dalai Lama powers which he never claimed to possess.

"I remember some of my neighbors here in McLeod Ganj
wondering if the Dalai Lama was really the kind of powerful

monk they had come to believe in or was he really just a myth," Dorjee said. "My explanation to them was the Dalai Lamas never presented themselves as anyone other than learned, enlightened Buddhist scholars. They have the same human weaknesses that we all have. How can one monk take on the might of the PLA? Some Tibetans feel disillusioned because they wrongly believed the Dalai Lama to be invincible. It is their fault and not the Dalai Lama's."

Wang Lixiong, a Chinese writer, wrote in the April 2002 issue of the British journal *New Left Review*:

> *As to who had more actual power between the Dalai Lama and Mao Tsetung, there could scarcely be any doubt. At the Battle of Chamdo in 1950 the crack troops of the Tibetan Army were totally overwhelmed by the PLA; the Dalai Lama had to take refuge in Yatung. In 1959, with tens of thousands of rebels demonstrating in the streets of Lhasa, it took the PLA only 20 hours or so to prevail, and the Dalai fled into exile. The Tibetans were inevitably disturbed by the disparity. The divinity before whom they had prostrated themselves turned out to be less invincible than they thought.*

Lixiong argued that Beijing was unlikely to have understood the developments in Tibet in terms of religion. In other words he was suggesting that the people of Tibet needed something, anything, to believe in. The author rephrased Karl Marx's maxim that religion is the opiate of the masses:

> *The period of 1960 to 1966—from the final suppression of the Rebellion to the start of the Cultural Revolution—saw a movement from "awakening" to overall mobilization in the region. The predominant image*

of the time was of Mao waving his red-starred military cap from a
distant, temple-like building; Tibetans were only too familiar with the
strong religious flavor of such a sight, which had always evoked in them a
powerful emotional response. They plunged into the frenzy of the
Cultural Revolution fired up both by fideistic fervor and material
interest. Yet even as they shouted "atheist" slogans against the monasteries,
the underlying pulse was still there; it was simply that Mao had replaced
the Dalai Lama as the god in their minds.

Lixiong erroneously interpreted this turn of events as the Tibetans' forsaking the Dalai Lama as "the eternally damned" and accepting Mao as the more "powerful ruler" who would "endure forever." He drew interesting parallels between Dalai Lama worship and Mao worship and how the first effortlessly morphed into the other. In Lixiong's judgment the Tibetans did not have much problem with "switching sides," accustomed as they were to following a certain kind of omnipotent figure, be it Tenzin Gyatso or Mao. "If the actual ceremonies of Mao worship were slightly different, their spiritual essence was close enough to lamaism to make it an easy switch," Lixiong wrote. "To hang Mao's picture in a cottage and bow to it daily, to recite his 'highest instructions' while clasping the Little Red Book, was not so far removed from the accustomed daily prayers and prostrations before the household image of the Dalai Lama."

Lixiong argued that what the Tibetans needed was a set of placatory rituals that Buddhism offered. In modern information technology parlance, if the Dalai Lama was Windows 2000, Mao was Windows XP. Making the transition was only a question of a few adjustments in their beliefs. While Lixiong's analogy is intellectually apt, it misses a fundamental point about the Tibetan people's psychology. It is entirely possible that some of them indeed felt and behaved the way the author contends. But by and large it was not as if since ordinary Tibetans had a desperate need to believe in anything or anyone, and had no qualms reorganizing their pantheon and installing some Han gods in it. The notion that they swiftly turned to Mao instead of Tenzin Gyatso and to the Little Red Book instead of Om Mani Padme Hum* and enlisted themselves in a new religion called the Cultural Revolution is not just cynical, it is simplistic. Lixiong's contention also betrays a lack of understanding about why people feel compelled to believe in something far more mystifying and unattainable than just mundane ideological options. People believe in religion because they consider it a loftier objective than their daily humdrum preoccupations. They worship figures such as the Dalai Lama because rightly or wrongly they see in them qualities and attributes they believe they themselves cannot possess but are worth aspiring to. Whether the person at the receiving end of their worship, devotion, or reverence is deserving of such attention is an altogether different debate. It is possible that many Tibetans replaced the Dalai Lama with Mao in their hearts, but the extent of that change of deities was nowhere near as widespread as the Communists would have liked it to be. It is surprising that over four and a half decades after he left the Dalai Lama still retains his hold over the Tibetans in Tibet, while Mao has all but faded.

*The literal translation of the mantra is "Behold! The jewel in the lotus!" But the Dalai Lama offers a more elaborate meaning. "The six syllables, Om Mani Padme Hum, mean that in dependence on the practice which is in indivisible union of method and wisdom, you can transform your impure body, speech, and mind into the pure body, speech, and mind of a Buddha."

Many of the Dalai Lama's advisors, while aware that in the immediate aftermath some Tibetans did turn to Mao and Communism instead of the Dalai Lama and Buddhism, had a different explanation. One very senior official said, "The issue is not one of the Dalai Lama versus Mao and Buddhism versus Communism. The people of Tibet do not believe in the Dalai Lama and Buddhism because they have been coerced into doing so or because they want to believe in something. Unlike Communism, which is dogmatic and regimental, Buddhism is open to individual interpretation. Their belief comes from a sense of conviction about what the institution of the Dalai Lama represents and what Buddhism stands for. To argue that in one fell swoop Mao and Communism replaced the Dalai Lama and Buddhism is to demonstrate how utterly ill-informed one is about the Tibetan people and their psychology."

One recurring theme that supporters of the "liberation" of Tibet harp on is that the Tibetan peasantry and others at the lower rungs of the societal pecking order accepted their own oppression and exploitation as a matter of destiny. Those who support this school of thought also say that fatalism, a uniquely Indian philosophy of accepting one's station in life without any challenge, came to Tibet with Buddhism, bringing with it the same sense of resignation that was pervasive among India's common masses. Nowhere does Buddhism, or for that matter Hinduism, hold the view that suffering in this life will bring a reward of a fabulous life in the hereafter and hence there is no point for people to challenge any oppressive or exploitative regime that is run by the divinely ordained. The idea that the Buddhist clergy created this elaborate charade in order to perpetuate their exploitative rule over the dispossessed masses is so fantastic that it takes the discourse to a wholly irresolvable level. Like all organized religions, Tibetan Buddhism has also been vulnerable to misuse by the clergy. The Tibetans and the Dalai Lama do recognize serious shortcomings. "I have heard this argument many times before. I no longer find it necessary to refute it," the Dalai Lama said. "A lot of Chinese scholars have argued that the Dalai Lamas were essentially feudal lords who kept up the façade of spirituality in order to hide oppression and exploitation of their own people. This is completely wrong. Buddhism never demands unquestioning devotion or faith. Buddhism is more cerebral than any other philosophy that I know of. However, I do recognize that in many of the monasteries religion was misused as an instrument of control and over the centuries, the Dalai Lamas have done everything in their power to ensure that the monks do not abuse their authority."

The Dalai Lama's departure from Lhasa threw the city into "unspeakable frenzy," according to Tempa Tsering. "Contrary to what the Chinese argue, the Tibetans resolutely rejected the change of guard in Lhasa," he said. "They rose in rebellion that became impossible for the PLA to control for months. Death and destruction were the order of the day. Again the Chinese argue that ordinary Tibetans themselves turned against the monasteries and anything that reminded them of the Dalai Lama. This is laughable. How do they explain that over four decades after His Holiness was forced to leave he still remains the most revered figure in the whole of Tibet?"

Tsering's point of view finds vindication from a most unlikely source. Lixiong cited annual economic growth of 10 percent in Tibet between 1991 and 1999, which was higher than in China proper. He said that per capita income for farmers and herders grew by 9.3 percent per year and for urban residents by 19.6 percent. He conceded that while Tibet was "more prosperous now than ever before in its history" that progress had not won PRC the allegiance of the Tibetans. In fact, he noted that an increasing number of them were still drawn to the Dalai Lama, who he noted with some telling humor, "has never given them a penny." Notwithstanding their progress, thousands of Tibetans still try to cross over the Himalayas to enter either India or Nepal.

Lixiong's assertion was independently echoed by a new lot of refugees whom the author interviewed in 1997 in McLeod Ganj. The refugees said that many retired Han Chinese officials frequented monasteries to find out more about Buddhism and many of them eventually embraced it. One young monk said, "I met a retired policeman who said he felt so disillusioned with his life that he decided to seek some answers through Buddhism. In fact, he even said he was very sorry he did things against the Tibetans under orders from his superiors he now recognized to be wrong."

Coming from a Chinese writer of obvious intellectual clarity, the conclusion that more Tibetans have become attached to the Dalai Lama, notwithstanding the economic growth and resultant prosperity that Chinese rule has brought to Tibet, is quite stunning. "Although Mao did not like religion, I feel he understood that Buddhism was unlike religion. He knew that Buddhism was about rational discourse. At some level early in my life I also admired some of the concepts of Communism. So you see one cannot be dogmatic about anything," the Dalai Lama said.

To this day the Dalai Lama believes that the Chinese and Tibetans together could have created something valuable without one surrendering independence of thought and freedom of religious practice to the other. When he escaped Tibet, the Dalai Lama did not have a specific idea what life ahead held for him and how long he would stay outside his homeland. What he knew for sure was that he had to make the best of whatever came his way.

11

McLEOD GANJ,
DHARAMSHALA, INDIA

McLeod Ganj barely manages to hold on to the mountain that lies on a spur of the Dhauladhar (white ridge) range in the Pir Panjal region of the Outer Himalayas. Even in 2005 it would be an exaggeration to describe McLeod Ganj as a town. In 1960, when the Dalai Lama first came here, calling it a town would have been a downright falsehood. Then it was merely a cluster of a handful of cottages, one church, and one graveyard built by the British in the early part of the twentieth century. At best it was a hamlet that had sprouted amid a forest of pine, Himalayan oak, rhododendron, and deodar trees. Reputedly one of the wettest places in India, McLeod Ganj is often lost in the clouds. In this one-street town, where everyone knows everyone else, mists provide the only sanctuary. At 6,000 feet (1,800 meters), the town's altitude is a relative low point when contrasted to the Dhauladhar range, which rises rapidly to over 17,000 feet (5,200 meters) from the unremittingly beautiful Kangra Valley. Till the 1940s, along with Dharamshala, a town some 328 yards (300 meters) downhill, McLeod Ganj was an occasional hill resort for the imperial British rulers who came here to escape the debilitating heat of the Indian plains. The town draws its name from David McLeod, who was the lieutenant-governor of the neighboring Punjab state.

"The difference between Lhasa and McLeod Ganj was so much. Lhasa had no vegetation, hardly any rain, and obviously no forest. But McLeod Ganj struck me as so very beautiful and full of forests. I think I saw more rainfall in my first few weeks here than I had in my entire life in Lhasa," the Dalai Lama said. The Nehru government's decision to resettle the Dalai Lama and his entourage in McLeod Ganj was motivated by his compulsion to keep as much distance as he could between India's political heartland of New Delhi and the Dalai Lama without appearing to be an impolite host. In equal measure, Nehru, as a generous host, also had climatic considerations in mind since his guest was not used to the heat and dust of India's plains.

Quite fortuitously, the Kangra Valley turns out to be of some historical significance, since Buddhism can trace its earliest roots there. Some thirteen centuries before the Dalai Lama arrived, the Chinese monk-pilgrim Hsuan Tsang wrote that there were about fifty monasteries in the region with around two thousand monks in AD 635. Although it was not on the route of a series of invasions of India from its north by Central Asian warriors, Dharamshala and McLeod Ganj were affected by the changing ethnographic landscape. The British posted a regiment at Dharamshala in 1849. Six years later Dharamshala became a small but thriving administrative headquarters of the Kangra District. Lord Elgin, viceroy of British India and a former governor-general of Canada, grew so fond of Dharamshala that he recorded his wish to be buried here. After his death in 1863 he was buried in the graveyard of St. John's Church in the Wilderness. Historians say that had Lord Elgin lived longer, Dharamshala might have become the summer capital of British India instead of Simla, another hill station in Himachal Pradesh.

Coming to McLeod Ganj was not just a geographical dislocation for the Dalai Lama and his entourage; it was a profoundly transforming experience in that they had to socially, emotionally, culturally, and even financially reorient themselves to life as refugees. Moving from the one-thousand-chamber Potala Palace to a modest British bungalow was the least of their problems. But the Dalai Lama personally played down the challenges. "As a Buddhist monk I had taken the vow of poverty. I could possess nothing. I could not have personal wealth or property. Personally it made no difference to me whether I lived in the Potala Palace or this charming bungalow," the Dalai Lama said, sitting in the verandah overlooking a small courtyard, beyond which stretched miles of wilderness. "Initially I missed Lhasa and my people terribly. But soon I became used to the life in exile. India was like a second home to me. Over forty years later it has practically become my first home."

For a mountainside bungalow the Dalai Lama's official residence is a fairly large one, perhaps in excess of 10,000 square feet. Painted light yellow, it has several rooms, but his living quarters are quite modest, consisting of a single bed and no trimmings whatsoever. His personal audiences are mainly conducted in a large living room with ochre sofas in the middle. Unlike in Lhasa, where the Potala Palace was large enough for anyone to lose one's way, the McLeod Ganj bungalow seemed even smaller than an outhouse. The challenge of balancing his revered status among Tibetans as a god-king and leading his life as an ordinary political refugee was more difficult for the Dalai Lama's minders than for the monk himself. His life in the Potala was one of meticulously orchestrated seclusion from the laity. Occasions when he left the palace were rare, and when they came they were surrounded by a mix of monastic, royal, and ritualistic appurtenances. For one, he never walked. A palanquin draped in yellow silk carried by twenty guards dressed in green cloaks and red hats was the preferred means of transport. Typically, the Dalai Lama's cavalcade consisted of hundreds of minders, monks, musicians, and monastic police with whips. By his own admission, the whips were not merely decorative; they were used every once in a while to keep importunate devotees at a distance. Most lay Tibetans never had the gumption to look the Dalai Lama in the eye. Many would cringe in servility in his presence, but for those few who were so overcome by his presence that they would want to get close, whips were put to some use. "I strongly disapproved of such show of authority and pomp. I would put myself in their position and wonder how I would feel if my leader traveled with so much show. I would not like it," the Dalai Lama said.

The show of authority and pomp was the first casualty of life in exile for the Dalai Lama. While his secretariat did its best to cushion him from the onslaught of the commonplace that a refugee must battle, the change in circumstances also had unexpectedly positive consequences. "My brother was always a democrat at heart. He might have enjoyed being deferred to and revered for a short while, but His Holiness was never really comfortable being treated with so much attention," Thubten Jigme Norbu said. "In many ways life in exile has been good for His Holiness because he was exposed to a life which he could never have explored had he remained in Lhasa, in the Potala cut off from the rest of the world. He soon began to find out what real life was.

"My brother is a very inquisitive man. He does not like to be confined. He likes to reach out and mix with people, engage in a dialogue. Sometime his status as the Dalai Lama gets in his way. In Lhasa it would have been impossible for him to do many of the things that he does in exile," Norbu said.

Being tenacious people, the Tibetans who came with the Dalai Lama quickly began to rebuild their lives in McLeod Ganj. If they believed that their stay in India was going to be a temporary one, they did not quite show it. Many of them knew in their heart that they had been permanently displaced and any hope of returning home must remain in a distant realm with no bearing on their daily survival. They had no choice but to get on with their lives. The first few months in McLeod Ganj were spent mainly putting down roots, creating a semblance of administrative infrastructure around the Dalai Lama, and evolving a plan to ensure that Tibet was not forgotten by the rest of the world. "During my early days I would sometimes speculate in my mind what lay beyond the Dhauladhar range. I could sense in the air that we were in the

vicinity of Tibet but were still so far. Could I jump over the mountain and land in Tibet, I would ask myself," the Dalai Lama said,
giving a rare glimpse into his state of mind in 1960. But he knew
that he did not have the luxury of brooding over what could have
been, but must instead prepare for what was ahead of him. What
lay ahead did not seem encouraging.

The sense of statelessness was overpowering for the Dalai
Lama's entourage in the early days. And for someone who embodied the state itself, the challenge was even greater. "In my private
moments, I used to wonder what life held for Tibet. Being a Buddhist, impermanence is the core part of my philosophy. I knew being stateless would not be a permanent situation. State was a state
of mind, after all," the Dalai Lama said.

Life in exile makes anyone, especially the Dalai Lama on
whom rests such enormous responsibility, become inventive and
innovative. It is conceivable that centuries of tradition of Tibetans'
having given special treatment to the person of the Dalai Lama
would have given him very little incentive to press ahead with his
agenda of democratizing institutions. Silk palanquins, whip-
wielding monastic police, grand palaces, high thrones, obsequious
aides, delirious devotees, and relentless attention to even the smallest gesture would have all made for a powerful argument—even
for someone as enlightened as the Dalai Lama—not to disrupt
traditions by introducing democracy. But the Dalai Lama had already made up his mind while in Lhasa to dismantle the unassailable supremacy of his order.

"The Thirteenth Dalai Lama introduced many democratic
measures in the governing structure. He was a progressive at heart
and knew that eventually the Dalai Lamas must not control the

state of affairs. We began developing a democratic constitution soon after settling down in McLeod Ganj. By 1963 I decided to formally announce a democratic constitution based on Buddhist principles. I knew then, and I believe today as well, that institutions are more important than the person of the Dalai Lama," he said.

Life in exile offered the Dalai Lama and his staff no time to rue their fate. The year that he arrived in India the Dalai Lama appealed to the United Nations to focus on the issue of Tibet. That appeal led to the first UN resolution asking China to respect the human rights of Tibetans and their desire for self-determination. Two more resolutions were adopted in 1961 and 1965. Apart from the questions of democratizing Tibetan institutions and internationalizing the Tibetan cause, the Dalai Lama had a third, far more long-term plan to take care of. "To my mind the most important challenge was how to preserve Tibetan culture, heritage, language, and traditions. While we had to ensure that the Tibetan refugees in India had decent means of economic survival, we had to also ensure that their culture and heritage not only remained intact but even flourished," he said. One of his first acts in exile was setting up the Tibetan Institute of Performing Arts in 1959, as well as the Central Institute of Higher Tibetan Studies, a university for Tibetans in India. "We also had to preserve centuries of our spiritual knowledge and Tibetan Buddhist teachings. I knew then that the Chinese were bent upon erasing our culture and heritage forever. I had to find a way to preserve it in India," he said.

Although the Dalai Lama was formally called upon to assume full political power as a head of state and government in November 1950, in Lhasa, it was only after coming to India that he began to get the full measure of the workings of a government. In Lhasa, despite his official title and the tradition requiring the government to consult him on all matters, the Dalai Lama never really got involved with affairs of state on a daily basis.

In McLeod Ganj, the situation was fundamentally different. He had to become hands-on and drive the decision making. "The loss of one's home was a serious one but I had to continue with our struggle for the liberation of Tibet. That meant acting on several fronts," the Dalai Lama said.

When the Dalai Lama announced the promulgation of a democratic constitution on March 10, 1963, to coincide with the anniversary of the 1959 revolt, China saw red. China accused India of a "serious provocation" in not preventing the Dalai Lama from issuing the statement from its soil. Beijing also said that New Delhi had not "reconciled" itself to China's sovereignty over Tibet. A year later on the same day, the Dalai Lama issued another statement, yet again to the annoyance of China, which reiterated its protest to India. In a clear signal to Beijing that New Delhi did not share China's view of the Dalai Lama's activities in India, the Nehru government allowed the Tibetan leader to embark on his first foreign tour to Buddhist countries in Asia. The government also allowed him to send his representatives to other countries such as Switzerland. By March 1964 Nehru was seventy-four and a very sick man. It is likely that given the humiliation of India in the 1962 Indo-China War (in which China brazenly took over Indian border territory), and the possibility that he believed time was not on his side, Nehru decided to dramatically alter his policy toward China.

"I got the sense that Nehru was realizing he should have been less trusting of China. That could be one reason why in the last two to three years of his life, he did an about-face while dealing with the question of Tibet and China. He no longer seemed to want to soft-pedal the issue with Beijing," Jyotindra Nath Dixit said. "Nehru was completely disillusioned with China, and had he lived longer I would not have been surprised to see a radically new aggressive approach by India toward China."

12

MAO, BUDDHISM, AND TANTRA

By the time the Dalai Lama was born, Mao was already a seasoned political thinker and revolutionary at forty-two. Born in 1893, Mao was a contemporary of the Thirteenth Dalai Lama. When Mao and the Dalai Lama met for the first time, China's "maximum" leader was past sixty, while his Tibetan counterpart was barely in his twenties. From all available accounts, including comments by the Dalai Lama himself, the two got along well. In many ways the rela-

tionship between Mao and the Dalai Lama was akin to that between the Dalai Lama and Nehru. Both Nehru and Mao were absolute masters of their ideological crafts and the Dalai Lama saw
great merit in both although he did not agree with their policies.

The Dalai Lama remembered quite vividly and with sneaking
admiration the first time he shook Mao's hand in Beijing. "Mao
had a firm handshake. He had the handshake of a man who was
very sure of himself," he said. Author Mary Craig has quoted the
Dalai Lama as saying he felt "in the presence of a strong magnetic
force" when he met Mao. In fact, it has also been suggested that
the Dalai Lama wanted to become a member of the Communist
Party. "Sure, Mao had a great presence but I was not fooled by
what his intentions were vis-à-vis Tibet. I did see merit in the
Communist ideology insomuch as it claimed to stand for the ordinary people's rights, but to say that I wanted to become a Communist was, you see, exaggeration. I was born to be a Buddhist,
and Buddhism recognized well before any other comparable philosophy what the Communists came to understand over 2,500
years later in terms of human welfare," the Dalai Lama said.

At a purely personal level Mao understood the position of un-
critical reverence that the Dalai Lama enjoyed within Tibetan society. Mao too had reached that exalted status within his own
universe, where—and quite paradoxically so—young Communists
saw him as an alternate god. It is hard to back the theory that part
of Mao's motivation in taking control of Tibet was to eliminate a
rival god in the person of the Dalai Lama. There are those who
believe that, notwithstanding his public protestations, in his heart
Mao was quite fascinated by Buddhism, especially some of its
darker practices such as Tantra. Senior Tibetan sources say they
know for a fact that Mao was not opposed to Buddhism per se but

only insomuch as it represented a philosophy that could rival Communism. They say the "Great Helmsman" quite enjoyed and even encouraged others to worship him even though it stood in stark contrast to what his Communist ideology stood for.

Mao was on record having said this about the Dalai Lama. According to the January 1995 *Tibetan Review*, Mao said, "The Dalai Lama is a god, not a man. In any case he is seen that way by the majority of the Tibetan population." For a man who considered religion the "opiate of the masses," Mao saw no contradiction in the fact that Communism had emerged as a new religion and he himself as its new god. "We did not discuss religion in great detail but I could see that he was not comfortable with it. He was certainly aware of Buddhism. He was also aware of Tantra," the Dalai Lama said.

There are stories that Mao was a practitioner of Tantra, which his personal physician Li Zhisui claimed helped him retain an insatiable sexual appetite until a very late age. Zhisui also wrote about the deification of Mao. "The Mao cult spread in schools, factories, and communes—the Party Chairman became a god," he wrote.

It will always remain in the realm of speculation what it was that drove Mao to launch such an onslaught against Tibet and its people. One obvious but not necessarily complete explanation was that it was about territorial control. Another explanation was that the People's Republic of China sought to expand the Cultural Revolution to a land and a people China considered barbaric. There is a widespread belief that Mao himself was quite unaware of the devastating effects of the Cultural Revolution on Tibet's culture. Although Mao triggered it, the Cultural Revolution was hijacked by the youth of the country, who turned it into a revolt against the status quo in every walk of life. It is a matter of record that a considerable number of young Tibetans enlisted themselves in the movement and some of them did turn against the Buddhist establishment. Critics of the Dalai Lama have frequently argued that he and his government-in-exile have chosen to sweep under the carpet the fact that many young Tibetans took part in the Cultural Revolution and in fact joined their Han Chinese counterparts in destroying many symbols of the Lamaist supremacy. "It is quite possible that some young Tibetans did join the Cultural Revolution. Many of them were carried away by the force of the moment. But to argue that the Cultural Revolution co-opted young Tibetans in a large measure is to falsify history. It is simply not true. The notion that the Dalai Lama represented a structure similar to what Han Chinese Communists were rebelling against in their own country is absurd," Tempa Tsering, the Dalai Lama's brother-in-law, said.

Mao survived seventeen years after the Dalai Lama left Tibet. It was long enough for the Dalai Lama to observe the effects of the Cultural Revolution. The brutality that Mao's Red Guard unleashed in Tibet was followed in McLeod Ganj with a great deal of sadness and a sense of helplessness. All that was going on in Tibet seemed to confirm what the Dalai Lama was reported to have seen during a meditation session before the Chinese invasion. The expression he saw on the face of Yamantaka, the deity of terror and destruction, was so fierce that it could only have meant a catastrophe of great proportions. The Dalai Lama did not choose to talk about what, if anything at all, he saw during that meditation in the Ganden monastery.

The Dalai Lama observed that Mao did not appear to be in full control of all that his own Red Guard was doing. "I am not quite sure if Mao knew or approved of the level of brutality and violence in Tibet. I am not absolving him of the responsibility, but the man that I met did not seem the kind who would preside over all this," the Dalai Lama said. Yet it was that very man who presided over the doom of Tibet.

The dawn of 1976 was significant for both the Tibetans and the Chinese. There were reports that the Nechung oracle had made some dramatic predictions that sent the Dalai Lama into what was claimed to be his longest retreat in India. During retreats the Dalai Lama typically goes into complete seclusion for several weeks and engages in rarely talked about practices and rituals. Retreats offer the Dalai Lama an opportunity to regenerate spiritually. Some believe the Dalai Lama may use such retreats to create special and sometimes dramatically destructive circumstances against an order of things he disapproves of. The 1976 retreat, according to the Dalai Lama, was "an extremely strict practice which required complete seclusion over several weeks. It was linked to a very special teaching of the Fifth Dalai Lama." However, according to author Claude B. Levenson, the result of that particular retreat was quite dramatic, including "a major earthquake in China with thousands of victims. [The earthquake occurred in Tangshan in July 1976.] Then Mao made his final bow upon the mortal stage. This prompted an Indian who was close to the Tibetans to state, 'That's enough, stop your praying, otherwise the sky will fall on the heads of the Chinese.' " The earthquake affected Mao personally since, according to his physician, the bed he was sleeping on shook and the house where he was rattled.

There are claims that during the retreat the Dalai Lama performed a secret ritual to "liberate" Mao. Around the time Mao died on September 9, 1976, the Dalai Lama was in Ladakh, a part of Jammu and Kashmir state that borders Tibet, to conduct a Kalchakra initiation. According to the Dalai Lama's autobiography, the day after Mao died, "it rained all morning. But, in the afternoon, there appeared one of the most beautiful rainbows I have ever seen. I was certain that it must be a good omen."

"Retreats are deeply spiritual in nature and no aspect of any retreat is meant to harm anyone or anything. People make all sorts of claims about what the Dalai Lama does during a retreat. I can tell you on complete authority that none of what is claimed is even remotely true," one senior Tibetan monk said.

Mao's death removed the Dalai Lama's most important historic reference point in China. Mao was the last link in China between the Dalai Lama and Tibet. Although he was the man who set the stage for and carried out the invasion, occupation, and takeover of Tibet, Mao still represented a time when Tibet was free. At least for a brief period the Dalai Lama and Mao had managed to establish a semblance of a working relationship. Mao saw in the Tibetan leader a means to understand Tibet's feudal and religious order. In turn the Dalai Lama saw in Mao a person who had at least the capacity to understand the importance of an amiable relationship between the two lands, if not the will to actually forge such a relationship. Mao's successor, Deng Xiaoping, was a completely unknown entity for the Tibetans in exile. Quite to the surprise of the Tibetan government-in-exile, Deng was quick to concede the mistakes made in Tibet in the name of the Cultural Revolution. He gradually removed many of the restrictions imposed on Tibet during the days of the revolution. In 1978 Deng gave the Dalai Lama an opportunity to return to Tibet, and the PRC leader also offered to discuss everything except complete independence. The Dalai Lama did not oblige. Many historians say this was a grave error of judgment by the Dalai Lama, but the Tibetan leaders and his advisors argue otherwise. In 1977 the Dalai Lama had not considered options other than independence, even though he recognized the limitations of his government's ability to actually make it happen.

In retrospect, it seems that the 1978 offer was worth exploring, if only to expose whether Deng was sincere or was merely grandstanding. But it was clear then, as it is even more so now nearly thirty years later, that once the Chinese occupied Tibet, they had absolutely no intention of vacating it. Tibetans say Mao did nothing for a short-term gain. When he took over Tibet it was forever, at least as "forever" could be defined within the modern geopolitical context. Mao and his party cadres sincerely believed that Tibet had to be liberated from the stranglehold of the Buddhist clergy, and Tibetans from their centuries-old serfdom. They were not concerned with the annoying little detail that the Tibetans themselves did not mind the religious and political order that had survived for centuries. Deng's dramatic reversal of many of Mao's policies did raise some hopes in the Tibetan exile community, but that was short-lived, as the next ten years proved.

13

■

TO TALK OR
NOT TO TALK

During the last two decades of the twentieth century the complex nature of Sino-Tibetan relations was on full display. Even a nation like China, known to be unyielding and driven by a sense of finality in matters of territorial control, had to make repeated attempts to engage the Dalai Lama directly and indirectly to evolve some sort of practicable solution. The early Chinese position that with the 1950 takeover Tibet had fully and finally been returned to its natural geopolitical forebear has never really been accepted by the Chinese leadership itself, if several attempts at reconciliation with the Dalai Lama made over the decades were any indication. There was the realization within the leadership that Tibet was an unnatural addition to China's territory. There was also the realization that as long as the Dalai Lama remained outside his land, his potential to create secessionist troubles would only grow.

The Dalai Lama himself joked about this once. "Had the Chinese leadership been fair and decent and reasonable to Tibetan brothers and sisters, it is possible that my name would not have grown so much internationally, since I would have stayed on in Tibet," he said. He also said he would have much preferred to be less known internationally and would have settled for an autonomous Tibet instead rather than become famous internationally but remain without a state.

In March 1979 there was the first high-level contact between the Chinese leadership under Deng Xiaoping and the Tibetan leadership represented by Gyalo Thondup, the Dalai Lama's elder brother who was then fifty-one years old. Thondup, according to Thubten Jigme Norbu, the Dalai Lama's eldest brother (he was fifty-seven then), remembered the Deng-Thondup meeting well. During a series of interviews in Bloomington, Indiana, where he runs a Tibetan center, the eighty-three-year-old Norbu said, "It certainly appeared that Deng was inclined to make some headway in establishing serious contact with His Holiness. However, I was not sure if Deng could change the monolithic thinking of his own party leadership. He was embarked on an ambitious agenda of rolling back his compatriot Mao's policies and it seemed that was a daunting task."

Norbu said his brother came back from the meeting with the

impression that Deng was personally keen to resolve the issue but that Deng was also conscious that he had to manage a diversity of often conflicting opinions within the Communist Party. "That was clearly a factor weighing down anything pathbreaking that Deng may have had in his mind. For some reason I have never been optimistic about such talks because China is not interested in the return of the Dalai Lama to his homeland," Norbu said.

Writing for Phayul, a Tibetan news Web site, on July 11, 2005, two Tibetan experts, Tashi Rabgey and Tseten Wangchuk Sharlho, said,

> *Deng indicated a serious interest in opening talks with the exiled Tibetan leader by agreeing to allow fact-finding missions from Dharamshala to investigate the conditions in Tibet firsthand. In these first heady days of Deng's leadership, it seemed that the discussion of anything short of Tibet's political status might be possible. Given the remarkable political resolve signaled by Deng's initiative, why then did the talks of the early 1980s fail to lead to substantive dialogue between Beijing and the Dalai Lama?*
>
> *No doubt Deng's initial offer of engagement demonstrated an unambiguous interest in normalizing relations with the Dalai Lama. But however promising this initiative might have appeared on the surface, it soon became apparent that there was in fact little basis for substantive talks at this early stage. The gap in expectations between the two parties was too wide to contemplate serious dialogue. For Beijing's part, the boldness of the new Tibet policy had been founded on a miscalculation of China's stakes in engagement with the exiled Tibetan leadership. The Chinese leadership was concerned in part to bring to an end to the Dalai Lama's rogue existence in exile and to enhance the legitimacy of Chinese rule in Tibet. But the decision to court the exiled Tibetan leadership was also prompted by strategic considerations.*

It certainly seemed then that the Deng initiative was too conciliatory for its own good. It was also weakened by the fact that it
sought to revive the 1950s era when it seemed possible that the
Dalai Lama would return to accept positions of qualified authority that the Chinese were willing to grant then. The inherent flaw
in Deng's offer was that it failed to recognize that the Tibetans
themselves, especially those in exile led by the Dalai Lama, had
long rejected the 1950s consensus. In particular, they had repudiated the Seventeen-Point Agreement, which they said they signed
under duress.

Looking back on those days in the 1980s when for a brief
while it seemed that the prospects of his return to the land he
loved were not as bleak as they had been, the Dalai Lama's perspective is a mixture of hope and apprehension. "By the time the
Deng initiative came I had already spent nearly twenty years outside Tibet. I was exposed to a world that most Tibetans had never
even thought about. Being outside of Tibet I could understand the
issue in a broader geopolitical context. Despite being an optimist
I knew that Deng's initiative, while laudable, lacked the conviction
of his own party machinery," he said.

In a particularly expansive mood, which Tibetan analysts said
was not based on facts, Deng offered Thondup that Beijing would
allow four fact-finding missions made up of exiled Tibetans to
learn firsthand the conditions of the land they had left. China
even went to the extraordinary length of acceding to the exiled Tibetans' demand that the Tibetan delegates would not travel on
Chinese passports. Behind this extraordinary offer was unfounded
confidence that Beijing's performance in modernizing Tibet and
freeing it from the shackles of Lamaist supremacy was so stellar
that when the fact-finding missions visited they would be told that

the Dalai Lama no longer mattered to them. According to Rabgey and Sharlho,

> *As a signal of their flexibility at this early point, the Chinese*
> *accommodated not only demands regarding the itinerary and composition*
> *of the delegation, but also the unwillingness of Tibetan exiles to travel on*
> *overseas Chinese passports. Confident in their success in transforming the*
> *region, Chinese officials were more concerned about the possibility of open*
> *displays of hostility against the Dalai Lama's representatives during the*
> *course of the visits. Local Tibetans were thus instructed to restrain*
> *themselves from physically attacking the visiting exiles. Beijing was*
> *consequently caught off-guard when the first of the exiled delegates arrived*
> *in the summer of 1979 only to be greeted by ecstatic crowds numbering*
> *in the thousands expressing their devotion to the Dalai Lama. To their*
> *alarm, there were even calls being openly made for Tibetan independence.*

Author and Tibetan scholar Warren W. Smith's account of the overwhelming response of the Tibetan people to the first delegation, led by the Dalai Lama's younger brother Lobsang Samten, is even more telling. In his book *Tibetan Nation*, Smith said that in Amdo, where the delegation first went in August of 1979, Samten and others were "mobbed" by Tibetans "desperate" for any contact with the representatives of the Dalai Lama. The Communist cadres were red-faced at this spontaneous show of solidarity with the visitors because they had sold Beijing a contrary picture. They then argued that there was no way the delegation would receive a similar response in Lhasa, where Tibetans had openly accepted the Chinese ideology and supremacy. What happened in Lhasa was even further off from what the cadres had led Beijing to expect. Despite having been instructed not to react with any emotions and

LEFT: The Dalai Lama at age two. *(Courtesy Demton Khang Photographic Archive)*

BELOW: Proud parents of the Fourteenth Dalai Lama pose in Tibet on February 21, 1940, with two other sons. The infant peasant boy was installed spiritual and temporal leader of Tibet on February 22. *(AP photo)*

ABOVE: The Dalai Lama at his formal enthronement in Lhasa. *(Courtesy Demton Khang Photographic Archive)*

RIGHT: Tibet Buddhism's Fourteenth Dalai Lama, born Lhamo Thondup on July 6, 1935, is shown wearing royal robes in a golden palanquin at his enthronement as the spiritual and temporal ruler of the theocracy in Lhasa, Tibet, February 22, 1940. The Dalai Lama Tenzin Gyatso assumed full political power on November 17, 1950. *(AP photo)*

BELOW: The Dalai Lama, third from right, with his family: from left, mother Dekyi Tsering, sister Tsering Dolma, Takster Rinpoche, Gyalo Thondup, Lobsang Samten, and Jetsun Pema. *(Courtesy Demton Khang Photographic Archive)*

Thousands of Tibetan women silently surround the Potala Palace, the main residence of the Dalai Lama, their spiritual and temporal leader, to protest against Communist Chinese occupation and repression, on March 17, 1959, in Lhasa, Tibet. Only hours later fighting broke out and the Dalai Lama was forced to flee to safety in India. *(AP photo)*

Communist Chinese leader Mao Tse-Tung, seen in uniform in the center, is flanked by the two religious leaders of Tibet, who came to Peiping for the National Congress meeting, on September 11, 1954. The Panchen Lama, considered to be the spiritual leader of Tibetan Buddhists, is seen on Mao's right; the Dalai Lama, the temporal leader considered more powerful, but reportedly less pro-Communist, is on Mao's left. *(AP photo)*

ABOVE: The twenty-four-year-old Dalai Lama, left, with his younger brother Tenzin Choegyal, right, while escaping to India in 1959. *(Courtesy Demton Khang Photographic Archive)*

RIGHT: The Dalai Lama with his entourage during his escape to India in 1959. *(Courtesy Demton Khang Photographic Archive)*

BELOW: The Lhamo Latso lake, which has the reputation of harboring mysterious magical powers that have been used by regents of Tibet to track down reincarnate Dalai Lamas over centuries. *(Courtesy Demton Khang Photographic Archive)*

ABOVE: The Dalai Lama, second from left, with India's Prime Minister Jawaharlal Nehru, third from right, and his daughter Indira, second from right, in 1956 in New Delhi, India. This visit to mark the 2,500th birth anniversary of the Buddha was believed to have firmed up his plan to eventually settle down in India. (*Courtesy Demton Khang Photographic Archive*)

LEFT: India's Prime Minister Jawaharlal Nehru, left, and His Holiness the Dalai Lama, center, ride on an elephant in India in November 1956. The head of state and spiritual leader of the people of Tibet was on a five-week goodwill tour of India during the celebration of the 2,500th anniversary of the birth of Buddha. (*AP photo*)

Receiving the Nobel Peace Prize in Oslo, Norway, in 1989. *(Courtesy Demton Khang Photographic Archive)*

The Dalai Lama with John Paul II at the Vatican in 1986. *(Courtesy Demton Khang Photographic Archive)*

The Dalai Lama offering prayers at Aligarh Muslim University in India. *(Courtesy Demton Khang Photographic Archive)*

ABOVE: In this photograph provided by the White House, President Bush, right, wearing a scarf presented to him by the Dalai Lama, meets with the Buddhist spiritual leader on November 9, 2005, in the private residence of the White House. *(AP photo/The White House, Paul Morse)*

LEFT: The Dalai Lama, center, is joined by actor Richard Gere, left, and composer Philip Glass at a news conference at New York's Guggenheim Museum on September 16, 2003. *(AP photo/Richard Drew)*

A view of Tengster village in Amdo province, where the Fourteenth Dalai Lama was born on July 6, 1935. *(Courtesy Demton Khang Photographic Archive)*

to parrot the party line, the people of Lhasa responded with even greater receptiveness than did Tibetans in Amdo. According to Smith, thousands came out to greet the delegation near the Jokhang temple. "I remember my younger brother later informing me about how overwhelmed and emotional he felt at having visited Tibet and Tibetans. I think the Chinese leadership seriously underestimated the feelings that the people of Tibet had toward me. I did not see the emotional response in personal terms but more as a rejection of all Chinese claims about having transformed Tibet after my departure," the Dalai Lama said. Norbu echoed his brother's views but went a step further. "Frankly, I have never been able to believe anything that the Chinese have said, since all their offers have followed Tibet's unjust and criminal annexation. You don't steal something and then sit down and negotiate how you would share it with the original owner," he said.

The Tibetans' response to the first delegation led the Chinese leadership to the realization that two decades of unassailable Chinese control over Tibet's culture, religion, and politics had produced less than satisfactory results, and it forced the Chinese leadership to rethink their strategy. Contrary to the picture of complete ideological indoctrination and cultural assimilation that the Communist cadres had projected from Lhasa and elsewhere to their bosses sitting in Beijing, Tibet continued to seethe below the surface with nationalist rage. Deng, who had had visions of settling this intractable issue on his watch by somehow convincing the Dalai Lama to return on Beijing's terms and using his presence to legitimize the Chinese takeover, developed serious doubts. So much so that in October 1980, a little over a year after the first delegation's visit, he described the Dalai Lama as a separatist. The change of language was not lost on the government-in-exile at

McLeod Ganj. "Essentially, Deng and the Communist Party seriously miscalculated the standing the Dalai Lama enjoyed across Tibet. They believed that the passage of two decades would have healed old wounds of the 1950s. They were completely wrong," Tempa Tsering, the Dalai Lama's brother-in-law and an important functionary of the Tibetan government-in-exile, said.

According to Smith's account, in April 1980 the Chinese leadership decided to send a high-level fact-finding mission to Lhasa, this time led by newly appointed party secretary Hu Yaobang. The nine-day mission between May 22 and 31 shook up Hu's notions that Tibet had achieved a perceptible degree of economic prosperity under China. Smith said Hu was shocked to see the poverty in Tibet.

The excerpts of Hu's speech quoted by Warren Smith, while indirectly contrite in tone, did not amount to a clear acknowledgment of the failure of Beijing's policies:

> *Our present situation is less than wonderful because the Tibetan people's lives have not been much improved. There are some improvements in some parts, but in general Tibetans still live in relative poverty. In some areas living standards have gone down. We comrades in the Central Committee, Chairman Hua as well as several vice-chairmen, were very upset when we heard about the situation. We feel that our party has let the Tibetan people down. We feel very bad! The sole purpose of our Communist Party is to work for the happiness of the people, to do good things for them. We have worked nearly thirty years but the life of the Tibetan people has not been notably improved. Are we not to blame?*

Hu ended on a rhetorical flourish, but he then followed up with quick reforms that included elimination of grain taxes and compulsory sales to state granaries. These measures had an immediate impact, for the first time giving Tibetans under Chinese rule access to grains they produced. Collectivization was ended, ensuring a greater freedom of movement for Tibetan farmers. The Chinese government also relaxed restrictions on the practice of religion and even sanctioned the use of some funds to rebuild some major monasteries. The calculation behind these actions was the belief that they would at least minimize, if not altogether eliminate, large-scale discontent among the Tibetans against the Chinese government. "I think the Chinese never cared to understand that they were unwanted guests in Tibet. Imagine a situation where guests whom you did not invite in the first place take over your household and take away all your freedoms and then relax a little bit in the foolish hope that the hosts would accept them. That is what happened in Tibet," Norbu said.

What the reforms in Tibet did was to achieve exactly the opposite result of what Beijing had hoped for. The Tibetans took whatever freedom came their way and used that little negotiating space to express their discontent even more forthrightly. That was evident when two more delegations from Dharamshala visited Lhasa toward the end of May 1980. One of the delegations was led by Jetson Pema Gyalpo, the Dalai Lama's younger sister, who was thirty-nine years old at the time. Her husband, Tempa Tsering, later said of the visit: "My wife spoke of ordinary Tibetans coming out in very large numbers and expressing a mixture of happiness and disappointment. She found that China had been lying and deceiving in its claims about the improving living standards. There was no education to speak of. For Buddhists education and learning is one of the most important aspects of life." The other delegation, led by Tenzin Namgyal Tethong, witnessed similar scenes. Going by the experiences of the first three delegations, Beijing decided to cancel the fourth promised by Deng.

"They thought the Tibetans were like those tamed chimpanzees in a circus who would perform for the benefit of the spectators. They found to their embarrassment that Tibetans were still fiercely independent-minded," Norbu said.

The disastrous results of the three visits by the delegations had their fallout. Beijing realized that bringing the Dalai Lama back was fraught with possibilities of lighting a short fuse to highly combustible Tibetan passions. One clear indication that all was not well in Beijing came when the government failed to respond to a formal letter from the Dalai Lama in March 1981 requesting to engage in serious negotiations. "I sensed then that Beijing was just not interested. The delegations' findings had only made them more stubborn," the Dalai Lama said.

Instead, Hu Yaobang presented to Gyalo Thondup a Five-Point Proposal at an informal meeting in Beijing on July 28, 1981. The proposal included the following points:

1. *Our country has already entered a new stage of long-term political stability, steady economic prosperity, and unity and mutual assistance among the nationalities. Since the Dalai Lama and his followers are smart, they should have confidence in this. If they doubt these changes, they can wait and see for a few more years.*

2. *The Dalai Lama and his representatives should be frank and sincere, and not beat around the bush. They should not bargain as if doing business. There should be no more quibbling about past history, namely the events of 1959. Let us disregard and forget this.*

3. *We sincerely welcome the Dalai Lama and his followers to return to settle. This is based on our hope that they will contribute to upholding*

China's unity and promoting solidarity between the Han and Tibetan
nationalities, and among all nationalities, and to make a contribution
to achieving the Four Modernizations.

4. *The Dalai Lama would enjoy the same political status and living*
   conditions as he had before 1959. The CCP will be able to
   recommend to the National People's Congress that he be reappointed as
   Vice-Chairman of the NPC Standing Committee. Also, through
   consultation, he can hold the position of Vice-Chairman of the Chinese
   People's Political Consultative Conference . . . But he should not return
   to Tibet. He should not concurrently hold positions in Tibet because
   young Tibetans have already taken office and they are doing their jobs
   well! Of course he can return to Tibet often to observe the conditions.
   His followers need not worry about their work and living conditions.
   These will only be better than before because our country has
   developed.

5. *When the Dalai Lama returns, he can issue a brief statement to the*
   press. He can decide the contents of the statement himself. He should
   give us notice of the year, month, date of his return. If he will arrive
   in Hong Kong and travel overland through Guangzhou, we will send
   a ministry-level cadre to the border to receive him and issue a press
   release. If he will arrive by air, we will organize a ceremony of proper
   scale to welcome him and issue a press release.

A closer reading of the proposals shows that while China wanted
the Dalai Lama to return, they did not want him to do so on his
terms. They essentially wanted the Dalai Lama cut down several
notches so that while they could trumpet his return, they could
also control and manipulate his presence.

In 1982 segments of the Chinese leadership still wanted the
Dalai Lama to return. A delegation of the Dalai Lama went to Bei-

jing that year to formally discuss the matter. At the back of the delegation members' minds was what Tempa Tsering described as the "disappointingly narrow" Five-Point Proposal of Hu Yaobang. They were also conscious of the overwhelmingly positive response they had received from ordinary Tibetans during the visits by the three delegations. The Tibetan interlocutors believed that those visits would compel China to recognize that the Tibetans in exile were negotiating from a position of strength. At the same time the delegation members were secure in the knowledge that in Deng Xiaoping's offer, apart from independence, all other matters were on the table for discussion. They went armed with the Dalai Lama's proposal, which asked that all Tibetan-inhabited areas be incorporated into a single administrative unit as well as be accorded the special status that had been offered to Taiwan. The delegation was disappointed when the Chinese insisted that the only basis for negotiations would be Hu Yaobang's Five-Point Proposal. That derailed the talks. Until 1984 the issues remained frozen as Beijing went about its own version of reform in Tibet. Then in 1984 the open-door policy to the region was implemented. The open-door policy made access to Tibet by foreign visitors, including journalists, much easier.

Plans were also in motion to integrate Tibet into China's peculiar free-market economy. Around the same time McLeod Ganj began to sense a discernible change in Beijing's attitude toward the Dalai Lama. Tibet Autonomous Region (TAR) party secretary Yin Fatang accused the Dalai Lama of treason even as, and quite surprisingly so, Hu Yaobang called him an opponent of economic development.

When the Tibetan delegation returned for the second round of talks in October 1984, it was clear to them that something had snapped between the two parties. They went ahead and rejected Hu Yaobang's Five-Point Proposal on behalf of the Dalai Lama and instead presented the Dalai Lama's proposal to create a demilitarized zone of peace in a reunified Tibet. "We believed that His Holiness's plan was a significantly new proposal which the Chinese should have considered. They did not," Tsering said.

According to Rabgey and Sharlho,

> *By this time, the Chinese clearly recognized that they faced serious problems in Tibet, but they did not regard the Dalai Lama as necessary to the solution. Rather, the Tibet issue was framed as primarily about the need for modernization and economic development. The Sino-Soviet rapprochement in 1986 gave further impetus to disengagement. With the elimination of the Soviet concern, the Dalai Lama was no longer seen as a low-cost solution to an outstanding strategic concern, but rather as simply a destabilizing factor in what turned out to be a quagmire of ethnic tension.*

Between 1986 and 1987 whatever hope remained of a possible solution vanished when Deng Xiaoping, once regarded as a highly unconventional thinker, attacked "bourgeois liberalism" in 1986 and followed up with the purge of Hu Yaobang in January 1987. What this effectively meant was that eight years spent deciding whether to talk to the Dalai Lama or not and if yes, what to talk about, were finally winding down without any gains being made.

After going through two decades of dislocation, loss of home, and statelessness, the Dalai Lama was not about to pack his bags in McLeod Ganj and return to Lhasa to offer himself as a willing victim of China's machinations. By this time he had gained considerable international stature individually and acquired a credible enough voice for the world to sit up and listen. It was one of the

most painful ironies of the Dalai Lama's life that his stature grew
in inverse proportion to Tibet's diminishing voice within China.
Notwithstanding the obvious problems of the integration of Tibet into China, it was quite clear to those who cared to pay attention that Beijing was set on a course that would necessarily mean
it had to hold on to its acquisition at any cost. Many in India
thought that China's predicament in Tibet was like that of a snake
that had captured a mongoose—it could neither swallow it nor
spit it out. Seizing Tibet was a case of China's biting off more
than it could chew. Those who chose to look beyond the Chinese
claims of stability in Tibet could see that the situation on the
ground was explosive. In the middle of 1987, McLeod Ganj was
receiving reports of mounting anger in Lhasa and elsewhere. Neither Mao's Cultural Revolution nor Deng's reform had worked in
Tibet to the degree that Beijing had claimed it had. The innate
pacifism of Tibetan Buddhism that the majority of Tibetans displayed was misconstrued as acceptance of Chinese rule. "China
could rule Tibet for the next thousand years and Tibetans would
not accept them in their hearts," Norbu said.

I 4

■

THE
NOBEL LAUREATE:
GANDHI'S SUCCESSOR

A week after the Dalai Lama appeared before the
U.S. Congress on September 21, 1987, Lhasa
exploded with its first major street demonstrations since 1959. Word reached the Dalai Lama quickly
about the seriousness of the events in Lhasa. The information he was receiving was far graver than what China
was letting on.

The Han Chinese in Lhasa and elsewhere increasingly became the target of attacks and lynching. There

were large-scale acts of arson against Chinese vehicles and buildings. As monks were rounded up and tortured inside police sta-
tions, Tibetans stepped up their attacks. For the next seventeen
months Tibet experienced what has so far been its longest spell of
political unrest and insurgency, eventually forcing China to impose
martial law in March 1989. The state of martial law remained in
force for nearly fourteen months. There was inescapable irony that
Tibet was coming under martial law during the fiftieth anniversary of the formal announcement of the Fourteenth Dalai Lama's
discovery.

Although no one quite saw the connection between the
two, three months later a pro-democracy movement, which had
been building silently across China, came to a boiling point in
June in the middle of Tiananmen Square in Beijing. The Tiananmen Square uprising gave the world the first real glimpse of the
fractures and inherent restiveness in Chinese society and underscored how fragile the hold of the seemingly unassailable Communist military machine could be. If the enduring image of a single
Chinese man standing defiantly in the path of battle tanks in the
square so powerfully captured the mood of the Chinese democratic movement, an unarmed Buddhist monk quietly campaign-
ing for his land's freedom for three decades became an equally
compelling symbol. At their core both campaigns are about individual freedom.

The events in China and Tibet had captured the imagination
of the Norwegian Nobel Committee in Stockholm as it considered the potential candidates for that year's Nobel Peace Prize. If
there ever was a perfect way for the awarding of a Nobel Peace
Prize to make a political point, it was staring them in the face.
They decided to honor the Dalai Lama that year. In doing so, the

committee was by its own admission trying to right a historical wrong. Mohandas K. Gandhi's omission from the list of the Nobel Peace Prize winners is one of the Committee's most inexplicable failures. What Albert Einstein is to science Gandhi is to political leadership. His philosophy of pacifist resistance against imperial subjugation altered political leadership as fundamentally as Einstein's Theory of Relativity did human understanding of the universe. It was not without reason that Einstein said, in his tribute to Gandhi after his assassination in 1948, "Generations to come would scarce believe that such a one as this [Gandhi] in flesh and blood ever walked on Earth." While Gandhi's followers argue with considerable conviction and weight that prizes, including the redoubtable Nobel, fall way short of acknowledging his accomplishments and greatness, his absence from the list of Nobel Peace Prize winners still remains incomprehensible.

The awkward realization of having failed to honor Gandhi was very much on Egil Aarvik's mind when he, as chairman of the committee, while introducing the 1989 Peace Prize winner in Oslo on December 10, said, "It would be natural to compare him with Mahatma Gandhi, one of this century's greatest protagonists of peace, and the Dalai Lama likes to consider himself one of Gandhi's successors. People have occasionally wondered why Gandhi himself was never awarded the Nobel Peace Prize, and the present Nobel Committee can with impunity share this surprise, while regarding this year's award of the prize as in part a tribute to the memory of Mahatma Gandhi," Aarvik said.

When I mentioned Gandhi to the Dalai Lama while discussing his own Nobel Peace Prize, the Dalai Lama folded his hands, closed his eyes, and momentarily fell silent. He seemed to be saying some prayer in his own mind, as if paying a very personal tribute to Gandhi. Then after a deep pause he said, "You see, someone like Mahatma Gandhi is not an ordinary phenomenon. I consider him an avatar and my inspiration, a role model. In moments of doubt about my own peaceful campaign for Tibet, I turn to Gandhi in my mind. Why did he not get the Nobel Prize? A great soul like Gandhi could not possibly be measured with a prize."

The Nobel citation read that the committee had

> decided to award the 1989 Nobel Peace Prize to the [Fourteenth] Dalai Lama, Tenzin Gyatso, the religious and political leader of the Tibetan people. The Committee wants to emphasize the fact that the Dalai Lama in his struggle for the liberation of Tibet consistently has opposed the use of violence. He has instead advocated peaceful solutions based upon tolerance and mutual respect in order to preserve the historical and cultural heritage of his people.
>
> The Dalai Lama has developed his philosophy of peace from a great reverence for all things living and upon the concept of universal responsibility embracing all mankind as well as nature. In the opinion of the Committee the Dalai Lama has come forward with constructive and forward-looking proposals for the solution of international conflicts, human rights issues, and global environmental problems.

"This year's Nobel Peace Prize has been awarded to H. H. the Dalai Lama, first and foremost for his consistent resistance to the use of violence in his people's struggle to regain their liberty," Aarvik said.

> Ever since 1959 the Dalai Lama, together with some one hundred thousand of his countrymen, has lived in an organized community in

exile in India. This is by no means the first community of exiles in the
world, but it is assuredly the first and only one that has not set up any
militant liberation movement. This policy of nonviolence is all the more
remarkable when it is considered in relation to the sufferings inflicted on
the Tibetan people during the occupation of their country. The Dalai
Lama's response has been to propose a peaceful solution which would go a
long way to satisfying Chinese interests. It would be difficult to cite any
historical example of a minority's struggle to secure its rights, in which a
more conciliatory attitude to the adversary has been adopted than in the
case of the Dalai Lama.

Pursuing the process of selection that resulted in the choice of him in
particular would involve trespassing what, to a Westerner, is terra
incognita, where belief, thought and action exist in a dimension of
existence of which we are ignorant or maybe have merely forgotten.

For a committee that predominantly honors excellence in sciences
and therefore rationalism, the choice of the Dalai Lama, the very
basis of whose being is mystical and therefore irrational, was not
an easy one. Committee members had to be careful while treading
the territory of reincarnation. On the one hand they could not be
seen to be openly endorsing a belief system that was in direct conflict with the reasons the prizes were created; on the other they had
to be tactful by not questioning the rationale behind that very belief system. Aarvik chose his words judiciously: "Like so much
else in the realm of religion this [reincarnation] is not something
we are asked to comprehend without reason: we encounter phenomena that belong to a reality different from our own, and to
which we should respond not with an attempt at rational explanation, but with reverent wonder."

At some level the idea of awarding the Nobel Peace Prize to a man who was supposed to be in his fourteenth reincarnation seemed as fantastical as awarding the Nobel Prize in Physics to German physicist Werner Heisenberg, the father of quantum mechanics, in 1932. As much as the belief in reincarnation stretched people's rational mind, so did Heisenberg's Uncertainty Principle strain the intelligence of some of the most brilliant minds of his time. For a twenty-six-year-old scientist to say, "The more precisely the position [of a subatomic particle] is determined, the less precisely the momentum is known in this instant, and vice versa," was as heretical to many scientists as the idea of reincarnated Dalai Lamas was mumbo jumbo to Chinese Communists. However, Heisenberg's principle was as scientific as it was spiritual. The notion that the subatomic world exists only because we care to observe it and then that the very act of observing a subatomic particle changes its position was so revolutionary that even the venerable Albert Einstein remarked, "God does not play dice with the cosmos." For the Norwegian Nobel Committee members in 1932, awarding the Physics Nobel to Heisenberg for his profound theory surely required as much of a leap of faith as honoring a reincarnate monk in 1989. In Heisenberg's case, the committee was honoring physics, no matter how incredible. In the Dalai Lama's case, it was honoring the philosophy of nonviolence and compassion, no matter how ineffective it might prove to be in countering injustice.

Interestingly, metaphysics and Buddhism have always been inextricably connected. Insomuch as Heisenberg's principle struck many as metaphysics rather than physics, the Dalai Lama and Heisenberg were in some strange way connected. Buddhist logicians of yore propounded what is known as the *ksanika* (point instant) theory, which is probably at the heart of the core Buddhist principle of impermanence. According to Vasubandhu, a fourth-century Buddhist scholar, "Motion consists of a series of immobilities [motion is discontinuous]. The light of a lamp is a common metaphor designation for an uninterrupted production of a series of flashing flames. When this production changes its place, we say that the light has moved, but in reality other flames have appeared in other contiguous places [page 99 of *Buddhist Logic*]." *Buddhist Logic* holds that every moment is discrete. According to *Buddhist Logic*,

> *We are faced in India by two different theories of a Universal Flux. The motion representing the world-process is either a continuous motion or it is a discontinuous, although compact, one. The latter consists of an infinity of discrete moments following one another almost without intervals. In the former case the phenomena are nothing but waves or fluctuations standing out upon a background of eternal, all-pervading undifferentiated Matter with which they are identical. The universe represents a legato movement. In the second case there is no matter at all, flashes of energy follow one another and produce the illusion of stabilized phenomenon. The Universe is then a staccato movement.*

So there was no need for Aarvik to create an extenuating circumstance that the Dalai Lama represented a reality "different from our own." The Dalai Lama came from a world where scholars over a millennium and a half ago had pondered some of the very questions that scientists such as Heisenberg faced in the early twentieth century.

In a different context, when I asked the Dalai Lama at a conference on the synthesis of science and religion in Bombay in the early 1980s whether he would have liked to pursue science, his response was quite telling. I started by asking him whether we were rapidly approaching a stage in human history wherein the dividing line between science and religion was fast vanishing. The Dalai Lama laughed from the core of his being and said, "Religion is science with faith. Science is religion in search of faith." Then I asked him if he would have liked to have been a scientist. He replied, "I greatly respect science. Perhaps I could have been a scientist, a physicist, but I became a metaphysicist. You see, science requires experimental proof. I do not conduct experiments. If I conduct experiments I would blow up the laboratory."

On a more mundane level, in his remarks at the time of awarding the Nobel Peace Prize to the Dalai Lama, Aarvik also spoke of why the world did not stand up in the face of Tibet's invasion and occupation by China in 1950. "Throughout its history Tibet has been a closed country, with little contact with the outside world. This is also true in modern times, and maybe explains why its leaders failed to attach due importance to formal de jure recognition of their country as an autonomous state. This, too, may be one of the reasons why the outside world did not feel any obligation to support Tibet, when the country in 1950 and the years that followed was gradually occupied by the Chinese, who—in direct opposition to the Tibetans' own interpretation—claimed that Tibet has always been a part of China," he said. He described the Chinese occupation as "the most pernicious crime that any individual or nation can be accused of, viz., a willful attempt to annihilate an entire people."

Aarvik noted something that reflected the reality of the 1960s, 1970s, and the early part of the 1980s. Those were still the frosty decades of the cold war when multilateralism was brittle and cracked easily under geopolitical pressure. Nations viewed one another with a great deal of suspicion and speculated on which side of the ideological divide the other belonged. In an atmosphere of intrigue, ideological rivalries, and military paranoia, a monk who spoke of compassion and tolerance despite having been driven out of his homeland by a militarist power was unlikely to find a receptive audience. Although from the time when Gandhi was assassinated in 1948, with peace and tolerance still secure in his heart, to the time when the Dalai Lama escaped in 1959, espousing practically the same philosophy, there was a gap of a little over a decade, the prevalent global political climate, both during Gandhi's time and the Dalai Lama's early years of exile, was openly hostile to pure pacifism. The world had barely emerged from the Second World War about a decade and a half earlier and it was divided right down the middle on which ideology to pursue—capitalism as championed by the West or Communism as advocated by the Soviet Union and China. Both sides were convinced theirs was a superior ideology, and they put their military might behind it. What also worked against the Dalai Lama in his early years was his age. A twenty-four-year-old Buddhist monk, chosen as a reincarnation through a bizarre process in an exotic country generally cut off from the rest of the world, was not about to ignite the world's imagination, caught as it was in vicious political, ideological, economic, and military rivalries. The Dalai Lama was still an obscure curiosity for the world and his cause was one in which no major nation had any immediate stake. His message of peace and compassion was muffled by the saber-rattling among cold war warriors.

"From his exile in India he now waged his unarmed struggle for his people with untiring patience. He has every justification for calling his autobiography *My Life and My People*, because the life of

the Tibetans is in truth his life. But political support from the outside world remained conspicuous by its absence, apart from a few
rather toothless UN resolutions that were adopted in 1961 and
1965. Throughout the '60s and '70s the Dalai Lama was regarded
as a pathetic figure from a distant past: his beautiful and well-
meaning philosophy of peace was unfortunately out of place in
this world," Aarvik noted quite accurately.

The Dalai Lama's acceptance speech was an exercise in humility.

*I feel honored, humbled and deeply moved that you should give this
important prize to a simple monk from Tibet. I am no one special. But, I
believe the prize is a recognition of the true values of altruism, love,
compassion and nonviolence which I try to practice, in accordance with the
teachings of the Buddha and the great sages of India and Tibet.*

*I accept the prize with profound gratitude on behalf of the oppressed
everywhere and for all those who struggle for freedom and work for world
peace. I accept it as a tribute to the man who founded the modern
tradition of nonviolent action for change—Mahatma Gandhi—whose
life taught and inspired me. And, of course, I accept it on behalf of the
six million Tibetan people, my brave countrymen and women inside
Tibet, who have suffered and continue to suffer so much.*

*The suffering of our people during the past forty years of occupation
is well documented. Ours has been a long struggle. We know our cause is
just. Because violence can only breed more violence and suffering, our
struggle must remain nonviolent and free of hatred. We are trying to end
the suffering of our people, not to inflict suffering upon others.*

*It is with this in mind that I proposed negotiations between Tibet
and China on numerous occasions. In 1987, I made specific proposals
in a five-point plan for the restoration of peace and human rights in*

*Tibet. This included the conversion of the entire Tibetan plateau into a
Zone of Ahimsa, a sanctuary of peace and nonviolence where human
beings and nature can live in peace and harmony.*

After winning the Nobel Peace Prize, the Dalai Lama's reputation
soared internationally as a spiritual leader who made sense not just
for Tibet but perhaps for the rest of the world. The prize was by
far the most potent recognition that he was a global force to
reckon with even though his cause was confined to a geographical
territory. For a short while the world thought with pardonable optimism that the Tiananmen Square protest in June combined with
the Dalai Lama's Nobel Peace Prize in December 1989 could together shake up the monolithic China. There was sincere anticipation around the world that at last China's old order was crumbling,
making way for democracy and a return to China's once glorious
past. Of course, the expectations were quickly belied as neither the
pro-democracy movement nor the Nobel Peace Prize for the Dalai
Lama made any real difference in the way the Chinese government
functioned.

China's reaction to the awarding of the prize was predictable.
They saw the prize as rewarding a "splittist" leader who was bent
upon fueling unrest in China and perpetuating serfdom and feu-
dalism in the guise of a religious tradition.

"As 1989 witnessed a new international anti-China wave, the
Nobel Peace Prize Committee in Norway, with clearly political
motives, awarded the 1989 Nobel Peace Prize to the Dalai Lama,
giving its strong support to the Dalai Lama and the Tibetan sep-
aratists. Since then, the Dalai Lama has traveled the world, advocating Tibet's separation from China," is how China reacted to the
Dalai Lama's receiving the Nobel Peace Prize. Really how long

and resentful institutional memory about the Dalai Lama in China can be was evident in a comment attributed to Zhang Qingli, Communist Party secretary of the Tibetan Autonomous Region, on August 14, 2006. Seventeen years after the Nobel Peace Prize, Zhang was quoted as saying by Jane Macartney of the *Times* of London from Beijing, "I still can't figure out how he was awarded the Nobel Peace Prize. What peace has he brought to the world?"

Personally, the Dalai Lama, while manifest in gratitude for the honor, did not see the prize as a political endorsement. "To be among the Nobel Prize winners is a truly great honor, but I do not consider it as the West's way of politically endorsing my cause. It did help me a great deal when I visited regions where I was not known. When a Nobel Peace Prize winner speaks, some people are bound to listen even out of curiosity. But I think the people were mainly drawn to me because I was representing a just cause and a philosophy that made sense," the Dalai Lama said.

"When the Tiananmen Square happened, I thought things are coming to a head in China. I saw genuine hope in it. With the Nobel Prize, which I did not consider as a personal triumph but more a recognition of the Tibetan cause, I thought things would begin to turn around. I was wrong, although the democracy movement has steadily grown in the country," he said.

On the seventeenth anniversary of the Tiananmen Square events on June 4, 2006, it was an open question how far the pro-democracy movement had progressed in China. Even as China's dramatic economic growth has enhanced its stature as one of the world's most powerful countries and a fast-emerging rival for the United States, its human rights record has remained seriously questionable. Its record in Tibet in particular has been of serious concern. According to Human Rights Watch, "The Chinese government's effort to eliminate support for Tibetan independence severely limits Tibetans' core human rights. Regulations limit the number of monks and nuns and impose secular control over the administration, activities, finances, and personnel of all monasteries. Personal testimonies tell of arbitrary detention, torture and ill treatment, and of judicial processes that fail to meet international standards."

If the Dalai Lama truly is Gandhi's successor, then he would recognize that pacifism is a painfully slow process. Gandhi and his fellow leaders took nearly three decades to dismantle the colonial grip on India. That freedom was won in completely different circumstances, where adversaries were sharply defined in terms of ethnicity, culture, religion, and language. No one could look at the British rulers in India and claim they were indigenous to India and shared its history. In the case of the ethnicity of China versus Tibet, culture and to some extent religion and language are often indistinguishable to the ordinary mind. This seeming lack of difference between the Chinese and Tibetan people is one of the most important factors that has influenced the way the world has approached the problem. Pacifism is also a continuing process that often does not really conclude in anything tangible. Many of the Dalai Lama's detractors have argued that there is a fundamental difference between what Gandhi had to deal with and what the Tibetan leader is dealing with. In the British colonialists Gandhi dealt with an adversarial establishment that had at its core some fair principles once one overcomes the fact they were subjugators. It was also an adversary that had mastered the art of appearing to be flexible, having colonized diverse parts of the world and learned to deal with people markedly different from themselves. The detractors argue that in the Chinese government the Dalai

Lama is dealing with an establishment that is not inherently fair and is not known to be flexible. So while Gandhi's pacifism worked because it was directed against an adversary astute enough in statecraft not to be blatantly and overtly unfair, the Dalai Lama's pacifism is unlikely to work because it is up against a regime that is fundamentally unfair. Of course, such logic is often simplistic and disregards the sheer force of history, which can often bend some of the mightiest empires.

While there are some obvious similarities between Gandhi and the Dalai Lama, the differences are quite overwhelming. Gandhi had the well-defined context of a country to operate in. He did not have to shoulder the burden of an ancient belief system. It was only toward the end of his life that he began to inspire an element of worship among some of his followers. Gandhi also had the support of a galaxy of powerful leaders, who were giants in their own right and helped him create perhaps the world's single biggest political movement. On Gandhi's leadership depended the destinies of over 300 million people. And most important, he was up against an imperial power in precipitous decline. The Dalai Lama, on the other hand, has no defined context of a country to operate from, although in his and other Tibetans' minds Tibet is a real geographical entity. The Dalai Lama is hamstrung by the demands of propping up an ancient belief system. He has been worshipped since he was a child. He remains the only leader of consequence for his cause, unlike Gandhi. The future of some 6 million people rides on the Dalai Lama, although a substantial number of them have resigned themselves to their fate of being under Chinese sovereignty. And most important, he is up against a political, military, and economic power that is steeply rising.

Gandhi justified violence in certain exceptional circumstances.

The Dalai Lama does not support violence in any circumstances. Although Gandhi and the Dalai Lama belong to two powerful faiths, Jainism and Buddhism, respectively, which originated around the same time (Mahavir, who was more or less the Buddha's contemporary, founded Jainism, whose core principle is extreme nonviolence), neither chose to turn his faith into a political weapon to sway public opinion. In many ways, however, the Dalai Lama can be considered Gandhi's successor insomuch as both represented an unconventional moral force.

"I sincerely believe that tolerance, compassion, and nonviolence eventually prevail," the Dalai Lama said.

15

∎

LIFE AFTER NOBEL

There was something ironic about an enlightened monk, who had presumably risen above worldly accolades, finding far greater popular acceptance precisely because of one such accolade. And that, too, coming from an institution whose founder had made a fortune by inventing dynamite. Nevertheless, what the Nobel Prize did for the Dalai Lama was give him a very visible and recognizable moral platform from which to operate. Over the last decade and a half after receiving the prize the Dalai Lama has firmly established himself as one of the world's most consequential voices in favor of peace and compassion as an alternative to violence and recrimination and as an instrument of change. Unfortunately for him his approach has not produced any gain for the Tibetan people in terms of autonomy, let alone independence. If anything, the sinicization of Tibet has progressed with worrisome speed. What China has done is practice a sort of demographic imperialism, systematically erasing any sense among the younger Tibetan population that they are a distinct people—an awareness that the older generation felt very strongly. This has been especially true of Tibetans born in the decades after the 1970s. The number of Han Chinese in Tibet has grown so large that they have overwhelmed the Tibetan population by sheer demographic and ethnic force.

An eighteen-year-old monk from Lhasa who was visiting the Dalai Lama as part of an officially allowed delegation in 1997 admitted that since he was born he had not known any reality other than having the Han Chinese as the predominant part of Lhasa's landscape. "I could have easily grown up thinking that Lhasa and Tibet were always predominantly Han Chinese had I not bothered to read about the struggles of His Holiness to protect our unique culture that thrived before the invasion. But there are not too many young Tibetans in the capital who bother to read history. In their minds things were always what they seem now—the Han Chinese being the predominant presence," said the monk, who did not want to be identified for fear of reprisals.

Between 1989 and 1992 the Dalai Lama's foreign travels intensified dramatically. Both the Dalai Lama and the Tibetan government-in-exile were conscious that it was imperative for him to travel in order to ensure that the world did not forget their cause. A highly learned monk who was a Nobel laureate to boot can expect regular speaking invitations on his calendar from many countries and international institutions. According to his official records, the Dalai Lama visited more than forty countries in that period, including the United States several times. That level of visibility was a matter of great concern for China. During his April 18, 1991, address to members of the U.S. Congress in the Rotunda of Capitol Hill, he said, "Here, I enjoy the freedom of speech, freedom of thought, and freedom of movement. This nation has always cherished these principles. However, when I was about 15, I lost those freedoms. Now I am 56 . . . 40 years later. The first nine years were not only without freedom, but also witnessed real terror and I was always surrounded by fear. Somehow I managed. Now after more than 32 years, although there is no longer that kind of terror or fear, I still remain a refugee. For the most part of my life, I never enjoyed this freedom or liberty. And the worst thing is that thousands and thousands of my Tibetan brothers and sisters have not only lost these freedoms, but they have suffered tremendously, something really unthinkable. Besides this suffering, there is also a lot of destruction. For the present Tibetan generation, we are passing through the most difficult and darkest period in our history.

"Sometimes, when I look at this negative side, I feel very sad. But then on the other hand, if there is a challenge, then there is an opportunity to utilize our human intelligence and determination. It seems to me that the Tibetan nation is not only a civilized one, but also one that possesses genuine inner strength. So, this is a good opportunity to face the challenge. I think after 40 years, after so much destruction, after so much human misery and suffering, the Tibetan spirit was never lost. It is still kept very firmly," the Dalai Lama said.

The more the Dalai Lama traveled, the more he was able to keep Tibet throbbing in the international consciousness. In a world where even conflicts have to jockey for television ratings, having a charismatic, albeit exotic, proponent for a cause is a most important element of the struggle. Although Tibet never really captured the world's imagination other than during its early years in the immediate aftermath of the Dalai Lama's flight, it has managed to interest and attract high-profile supporters because of the sheer force of the Dalai Lama's personality, and they in turn have helped Tibet stay alive in the West.

During the three years after he won the Nobel Prize, the Dalai Lama met heads of state, foreign ministers, important religious leaders such as Pope John Paul II, academics, and members of the media in Europe, Australia, North America, and Central America as part of a conscious effort to draw the attention of the world to his campaign. "We recognized that the only weapon we had was His Holiness's tremendous ability to convince the world to see our side of the issue. In many parts of the world which he visited Tibet was not even known by a lot of people. For a campaign that is decidedly peaceful and nonviolent, staying alive in the world's memory is a tough job. The Dalai Lama has done that job with outstanding resolve and results," said Tenzin Geyche Tethong, the Dalai Lama's private secretary, who has worked with him closely for decades.

The combination of the Tiananmen Square uprising followed soon after by the Nobel Prize being awarded to the Dalai Lama was bound to anger the Chinese leadership and push them to become more recalcitrant than ever before on the subject of Tibet's future. A top Indian government functionary, who was in active diplomatic service in 1992, said of the effects of the two events on China: "If I understand the Chinese mind, and I think I do, then the Tiananmen Square uprising and the [awarding of the] Nobel Prize to the Dalai Lama were seen [by Beijing] as part of a grand Western conspiracy to interfere in [China's] internal affairs. When the two happened practically together, I told some of my colleagues at the foreign ministry in Delhi that whatever prospects existed for the reasonable resolution of Tibet's status were muddied forever."

He said that as a monolithic political entity the Chinese government has a very long institutional memory and it holds grudges for a long time. "You can conclude . . . that if and when China chooses to address the question of Tibet, it would do so entirely on its own terms, and not because the world or the Dalai Lama wanted it to."

At the local level, the people of McLeod Ganj, both Tibetan exiles and Indians, saw the Nobel Prize as a matter of personal triumph. Ashok Sharma, a tea vendor on the street leading up to the Dalai Lama's bungalow, said, "I am told this is a very big prize. Guruji [the Dalai Lama] has brought honor to our community. I feel as if I have won the prize because we are from the same village." Migmar, a Tibetan refugee, had a similar response: "Since His Holiness won the prize fighting for our cause I feel we all have a small part of the honor."

On the thirty-third anniversary of the March 10, 1959, Lhasa uprising, it was clear to everyone that honors such as the Nobel Prize, while helpful in focusing the world's attention, were of no real consequence. In his annual address the Dalai Lama struck an optimistic note in keeping with his overall optimism about life in general. "I am more optimistic than ever before about the future of Tibet. This optimism stems from the determination of the Tibetan people inside Tibet and also from the dramatic changes that have taken place everywhere in the world, particularly in the erstwhile Soviet Union. I feel certain that within the next five to ten years some major changes will take place in China," he said.

"The collapse of totalitarian regimes in different parts of the world, the breakup of the Soviet empire and reemergence of sovereign, independent nations reinforce our belief in the ultimate triumph of truth, justice, and the human spirit. The bloody October Revolution of 1917, which controlled the fate of the Soviet Union for seven decades, came to an end in the bloodless, nonviolent August Revolution of 1991. We know from history that the mightiest of empires and military powers come and go. No power remains sacrosanct for ever. This is particularly true in this modern age when the power of communications is so effective. It is, therefore, quite clear that China cannot remain unaffected by what is happening inside and outside the country," he said.

"The present Chinese leadership today has two choices. The first one is to start an enlightened political process for a smooth transition toward a fully democratic society and allow the countries they have forcibly annexed and occupied to become free and equal partners in a new world order. The second choice is to push the country to the brink of bloody political struggles, which in a country populated by a quarter of humanity would be a great tragedy. On our part, there will be no lack of willingness or sincerity, should the Chinese government show a genuine interest in finding a solution to the Tibetan problem. Even though the Strasbourg Proposal, which I made more than three years ago, is no longer valid, we are committed to the path of negotiations. This willingness is amply demonstrated in my proposal for an early visit to Tibet. Regrettably, this proposal was turned down by the Chinese government," he said.

"With increased awareness of the real situation in present-day Tibet, there has been growing world concern and support for our cause. I was very encouraged by the genuine interest and sympathy shown by political leaders I met during my travels in the past year. We consider these favorable changes in the attitude of governments not to be anti-Chinese, but pro-justice and truth," he said.

When the Dalai Lama speaks, the Chinese do care to listen and monitor even if only to dismiss the substance of what he is saying. Apart from the Dalai Lama's own comments, the Chinese had also noted that the International Year of Tibet was celebrated in over thirty-six countries.

In his address the Dalai Lama also referred to the question of Inner Mongolia and East Turkestan, saying he hoped both would be "reunited in full freedom in our respective countries."

It is not clear whether it was out of rhetoric or genuine belief that the Dalai Lama also referred to preparations for a fully democratic Tibet. He spoke about an official document entitled "Guidelines for Future Tibet's Polity and the Basic Features of Its Constitution." The document said that the present Tibetan administration would be dissolved the moment he and Tibetans in exile return to Tibet, and that he would hand over all his traditional political power to an interim government. "The interim government, it explains, will be responsible for drawing up a democratic constitution under which the new government of Tibet will be elected by the people. It assures that there will be no political recrimination against those Tibetans who have worked in the Chinese ad-

ministration. In fact, because of their experience, the Tibetan officials of the existing administration in Tibet should shoulder the
main responsibility," he said.

How unfounded the Dalai Lama's optimism was became
painfully obvious barely six months after he struck a high note
during his traditional address to the Tibetans in exile. China was
paying attention to every word he uttered and had its own response ready. Part of the Chinese strategy has been not to let anything the Dalai Lama says about Tibet go unchallenged. A Chinese
diplomat in Delhi once said, "We believe in countering the Dalai
Lama everywhere and every time. He must not think that he can
run away with his propaganda because a few Hollywood actors fall
for his tricks."

16

■

UNYIELDING
CHINESE AND
UNCOMPROMISING
TIBETANS

In September 1992 the Information Office of the State Council of the People's Republic of China issued a white paper entitled "Tibet: Its Ownership and Human Rights Situation." The document was a clever mix of selective historical realities and classic Chinese obfuscation. Most of what it stated then remains its official position up to the present. If that is a measure of how unyielding China is, it is also a reflection on how in over a decade nothing really moved for the Tibetans. The choice of the word "ownership" is instructive of how, for China, Tibet was and has remained a question of proprietorship.

In a section entitled "Ownership of Tibet" the paper said,

Tibet is located in southwest China. The ancestors of the Tibetan race who lived there struck up links with the Han in the Central Plains long before the Christian era. Later, over a long period of years, the numerous tribes scattered on the Tibet Plateau became unified to form the present Tibetan race. By the Tang Dynasty (618–907), the Tibetans and Hans had, through marriage between royal families and meetings leading to alliances, cemented political and kinship ties of unity and political friendship and formed close economic and cultural relations, laying a solid foundation for the ultimate founding of a unified nation. In Lhasa, the capital of the Tibet Autonomous Region, the statue of the Tang Princess Wen Cheng, who married the Tubo tsampo, king of Tibet, in 641, is still enshrined and worshiped in the Potala Palace. The Tang-Tubo Alliance Monument marking the meeting for this purpose between Tang and Tubo erected in 823 still stands in the square in front of the Jokhang Monastery. The monument inscription reads in part, "The two sovereigns, uncle and newphew, having come to agreement that their territories be united as one, have signed this alliance of great peace to last for eternity! May God and humanity bear witness thereto so that it may be praised from generation to generation."

The Tibetan response to these claims was swift:

According to Tibetan annals, the first king of Tibet ruled from 127 BC, but it was only in the seventh century AD that Tibet emerged as a unified state and a mighty empire under Emperor Songtsen Gampo. With his rule, an era of political and military greatness and territorial expansion started that lasted for three centuries. The King of Nepal and the Emperor of China offered their daughters to the Tibetan Emperor in marriage. The wedding to the Nepalese and Chinese princesses were of particular importance, because they played important roles in the spread of Buddhism in Tibet. Chinese propaganda always refers to the political implications of Songtsen Gampo's wedding to the Chinese imperial princess Wen Cheng, conveniently ignoring the Tibetan ruler's other wives, particularly his Nepalese one, whose influence was, if anything, greater than that of her Chinese counterpart.

Tibetan ruler Trisong Detsen [reign: 755–797] expanded the Tibetan empire by conquering parts of China. In 763, China's capital Chang'an [modern-day Xia'n] was invaded and China had to pay an annual tribute to Tibet. In 783, a treaty was concluded which laid down the borders between Tibet and China. A pillar inscription at the foot of the Potala Palace in Lhasa bears witness to some of these conquests. The peace treaty concluded between Tibet and China in 821 is of particular importance in illustrating the nature of relations between these two great powers of Asia. The text of this treaty, both in Tibetan and Chinese, was inscribed on three stone pillars: one was erected in Gungu Meru to demarcate the borders between the two nations, the second in Lhasa where it still stands, and the third in the Chinese capital of Chang'an. Passages quoted from the pillars in the white paper are inaccurate and out of context, and aimed at creating the impression that some sort of "union" resulted from the treaty. Nothing is further from the truth, as is clear from the following principal passage of that treaty: "Tibet and China shall abide by the frontiers of which they are now in occupation. All to the east is the country of great China; and all to the west is, without question, the country of great Tibet. Henceforth, on neither side shall there be waging of war nor seizing of territory."

It is hard to see how China can, in its White Paper, interpret these
events as showing that "the Tibetans and Hans [Chinese] had, through
marriage between royal families and meetings leading to alliances,
cemented political and kinship ties of unity and political friendship, and
formed close economic and cultural relations, laying a solid foundation for
the ultimate founding of a unified nation."

In fact, the historical records, both Tibetan and Chinese, contradict such an interpretation and refer to separate and powerful empires.

Notwithstanding the Tibetan contention the white paper said, "In the mid-13th century, Tibet was officially incorporated into the territory of China's Yuan dynasty. Since then, although China experienced several dynastic changes, Tibet has remained under the jurisdiction of the central government of China."

The Yuan dynasty (1271–1368), according to the white paper, had come about as a result of a change of title from the Khanate established in north China in the early thirteenth century by the legendary Mongol warrior Genghis Khan. "In 1247 Sagya Pandit Gonggar Gyamcan, religious leader of Tibet, met the Mongol Prince Gotan at Liangzhou [present-day Wuwei in Gansu, China] and decided on terms for Tibetan submission to the Mongols, including presentation of map and census books, payment of tributes, and the acceptance of rule by appointed officials," the document said.

"The regime of the Mongol Khanate changed its title to Yuan in 1271 and unified the whole of China in 1279, establishing a central government, which, following the Han [206 BC–220] and Tang dynasties, achieved great unification of various regions and races within the domain of China. Tibet became an administrative region directly under the administration of the central government of China's Yuan Dynasty," the white paper said.

The Tibetan version of the same events is diametrically opposite.

> *The Mongol ruler Genghis Khan and his successors conquered vast territories in Asia and Europe, creating one of the largest empires the world has ever known, stretching from the Pacific to eastern Europe. In 1207, the Tangut empire north of Tibet fell to the advancing Mongols, and in 1271, the Mongols announced the establishment of the Mongol Yuan Dynasty to rule the Eastern part of the Empire. By 1279, the Chinese Song dynasty in southern China fell before the advancing armies and the Mongols completed their conquest of China. Today, China claims the Yuan Dynasty to be its own dynasty because, by doing so, it lays claim to all Mongol conquests, at least in the eastern half of the Mongol Empire.*
>
> *Prince Goden, grandson of Genghis Khan, dispatched an expedition to Tibet in 1240 and invited one of Tibet's leading religious hierarchs, Sakya Pandita Kunga Gyaltsen [1182–1251], to his court, thus establishing an enduring Tibetan-Mongol relationship. Here began the unique cho-yon [priest-patron] relationship. Kublai Khan, who succeeded Goden Khan, embraced Tibetan Buddhism and adopted Drogon Choegyal Phagpa, nephew of Sakya Pandita, as his spiritual mentor. This cho-yon relationship resulted in Kublai adopting Buddhism as his empire's state religion, and Phagpa became its highest spiritual authority. In gratitude, Kublai Khan offered his Tibetan lama political authority over Tibet in 1254, conferring various titles on him.*
>
> *It is undeniable that Mongol Emperors spread their influence over Tibet. But, contrary to the assertion made in the Chinese White Paper that, "In the mid 13th century Tibet was officially incorporated into the*

territory of China's Yuan Dynasty," none of the Mongol rulers ever made
any attempt to administer Tibet directly; Tibet did not even pay tax to the
Mongol Empire, and it certainly was never considered part of China by
the Mongol emperors.

"The Chinese resort to history only to distort it. If you stretch history that far back, China will be on as unsound a footing as they say Tibet is. As we have demonstrated time and again, and so have many independent historians and scholars, China has twisted history to suit its purpose. The most important point to bear in mind is the situation as it obtained in the early twentieth century. If you go by that the Chinese claims make no sense," Tempa Tsering said.

The official Tibetan position as well as that adopted by many independent legal scholars is similar.

The Chinese Communist Government claims it has a right to "ownership"
of Tibet. It does not claim this right on the basis of its military conquest
in 1949 or alleged effective control over Tibet since then or since 1959.
The Chinese Government also does not base its claim to "ownership" on
the so-called "Seventeen-Point Agreement for the Peaceful Liberation of
Tibet" which it forced upon Tibet in 1951. Instead, China's alleged legal
claim is based on historical relationships primarily of Mongol or Manchu
rulers with Tibetan lamas and, to a lesser extent, of Chinese rulers and
Tibetan lamas. The main events relied on by the Chinese Government
occurred hundreds of years ago: during the height of Mongol imperial
expansion, when the Mongol Emperors extended their political supremacy
throughout most of Asia and large parts of Eastern Europe; and when
Manchu Emperors ruled China and expanded their influence throughout
East and Central Asia, including Tibet, particularly in the 18th century.

It is not disputed that at different times in its long history Tibet came under various degrees of foreign influence: that of the Mongols, the Gorkhas of Nepal, the Manchu Emperors of China and the British rulers of India. At other times in Tibet's history, it was Tibet which exercised power and influence on its neighbors, including China. It would be hard to find any state in the world today that has not been subjected to foreign domination or influence for some part of its history. In Tibet's case the degree and length of foreign influence and interference was quite limited. Moreover, relationship with the Mongol, Chinese and Manchu rulers, to the extent they had political significance, were personal in nature and did not at any time imply a union or integration of the Tibetan state with or into a Chinese state.

However fascinating Tibet's ancient history may be, its status at the time of the Chinese invasion must, of course, be judged on the basis of its position in modern history, especially its relationship with China since 1911, when the Chinese overthrew the foreign Manchu rule and became the masters of their own country. Every country can go back to some period in history to justify territorial claims on neighboring states. That is unacceptable in international law and practice.

The Tibetan response claimed that the white paper paid scant attention to Tibet's modern history before 1949. The Tibetans argued that from 1911 till 1951, when the Chinese occupation was complete, there was no evidence of Chinese authority or influence in Tibet that can support China's claim. "In fact, the preponderance of the evidence shows precisely the opposite: that Tibet was to all intents and purposes a sovereign state, independent of China. This conclusion is supported by most legal scholars and experts on the subject," the official Tibetan position said.

According to the International Commission of Jurists' Legal

Enquiry Committee on Tibet, "Tibet demonstrated from 1913 to 1950 the conditions of statehood as generally accepted under international law. In 1950, there was a people and a territory, and a government which functioned in that territory, conducting its own domestic affairs free from any outside authority." The commission noted that from 1913 to 1950, foreign relations of Tibet were conducted exclusively by the government of Tibet. Official documents, the commission asserted, showed that the countries with whom Tibet had foreign relations treated Tibet in practice as an independent state.

In the committee's view forty years of independence for Tibet is "clearly sufficient" for Tibet to be regarded as a country by the international community. They pointed out that many member countries that belong to the United Nations have been regarded as countries even though they had "enjoyed a similar or even shorter period of independence." A problem, probably specific to the China-Tibet issue, that the committee highlighted was that China had "selectively" rewritten Tibet's ancient history in order to justify its claim of "ownership."

"There can be little argument that on the eve of China's military invasion, which started at the close of 1949, Tibet possessed all the attributes of independent statehood recognized under international law: a defined territory, a population inhabiting that territory, a government, and the ability to enter into international relations," it said.

The committee said Tibet's population of six million at the time of the Chinese invasion constituted the Tibetan people, "a distinct people with a long history, rich culture and spiritual tradition."

It said that neither the Tibetans nor the Chinese have histori-

cally considered the Tibetans as Chinese people. Chinese historical annals described those outside the Great Wall as "barbarians."

Another significant point the committee used to strengthen its
case was that the government of Tibet had its own taxes, currency,
postal system, and postage stamps. It also had a small army. "The
Tibetan form of government was a highly de-centralized one, with
many districts and principalities of Tibet enjoying a large degree
of self-government. This was, to a large extent, inevitable due to
the vastness of the territory and the lack of modern communication systems," it said.

The committee challenged the Chinese claim that "no country ever recognized Tibet," asserting that in international law,
recognition can be obtained by "an explicit act of recognition or
by implicit act or behavior." Treaties, negotiations, and diplomatic
relations are "forms of recognition," the committee said. "Mongolia and Tibet concluded a formal treaty of recognition in 1913;
Nepal not only concluded peace treaties with Tibet, and maintained an Ambassador in Lhasa, but also formally stated to the
United Nations in 1949, as part of its application for UN membership, that it maintained independent diplomatic relations with
Tibet as it did with several other countries including the United
Kingdom, the United States, India and Burma."

The Chinese white paper specifically spoke of "a feudal serfdom characterized by the dictatorship of upper-class monks and
nobles." It said, "The broad masses of serfs in Tibet eagerly
wanted to break the shackles of serfdom. After the peaceful liberation, many enlightened people of the upper and middle classes
also realized that if the old system was not reformed, the Tibetan
people would never attain prosperity."

The Tibetan response to these sensitive charges has been quite categorical.

> *China has always justified its policy in Tibet by painting the darkest picture of traditional Tibetan society. The military invasion and occupation has been termed a "liberation" by China of Tibetan society from "medieval feudal serfdom" and "slavery." Today, this myth is repeatedly rehashed to justify China's own violations of human and political rights in Tibet, and to counter all international pressure on Beijing to review its repressive policies in occupied Tibet.*
>
> *Traditional Tibetan society was by no means perfect and was in need of changes. The Dalai Lama and other Tibetan leaders have admitted as much. That is the reason why the Dalai Lama initiated far-reaching reforms in Tibet as soon as he assumed temporal authority. The traditional Tibetan society, however, was not nearly as bad as China would have us believe.*
>
> *The peasants, whom the Chinese White Paper insists on calling "serfs," had a legal identity, often with documents stating their rights, and also had access to courts of law. Peasants had the right to sue their masters and carry their case in appeal to higher authorities.*

The purpose of this historical hairsplitting by China was to keep the Tibetan government-in-exile permanently on the defensive. China's frequent references to some admittedly abhorrent practices, which were by no means unique to Tibet in those times, was part of a strategy to keep reminding the world that perceptions that the Tibetan Buddhist clergy was a progressive leadership were a myth and had it not been for Beijing's military intervention the institution represented by the Dalai Lama would still be oppressing working-class Tibetans. As the Tibetan rejoinder underscored, under the old regime there were practices in Tibet that were highly exploitative, but they did not constitute the core philosophy of what the Dalai Lamas and even most of the so-called ruling elite stood for. Like the ruling classes everywhere, including in Europe and China, the elite in Tibet too were guilty to a degree of riding roughshod over the dispossessed and the powerless. However, the political and religious order in Tibet was nowhere close to as oppressive as the Chinese would have the world believe. To the extent that China's white paper put the Dalai Lama's government on the defensive, the strategy succeeded, but those who understood history recognized that the document was one more in a series of China's attempts to confuse the fundamental issue of Tibet's sovereignty.

17

■

MURDERS IN
THE MONASTERY

On a cold February night in 1996, as fog
descended on the Dhauladhar mountains,
seventy-year-old Lobsang Gyatso, a close
confidant of the Dalai Lama, prepared to sleep. Living
barely a few hundred yards away from the Dalai Lama's
quarters, Gyatso and two younger monks had no reason
to suspect that the night ahead hid savage and mortal
danger. At some time during the night, between five and
eight men reportedly slipped into their room and at-

tacked them with unnerving brutality, stabbing each of the three
monks fifteen to twenty times. According to the Indian police,
there was a ritualistic pattern to the wounds, in the way they cut
across the bodies. The walls of the room were splattered with
blood. One police officer familiar with some of the shadowy practices of the darker sub-sects of Tibetan Buddhism said the murders were aimed at sending a clear message to the Dalai Lama's
secretariat that this was not a random act of violence but an action probably motivated by some deep-seated resentments and an-
imus within the Tibetan exile community.

If the Chinese white paper and the Tibetan rejoinder under-
lined the complex historical, religious, and political forces that
were at play between China and Tibet for centuries, a remorselessly
executed triple murder in the heart of the government-in-exile's establishment laid bare fault lines under the seemingly tranquil edi-
fice of the Tibetan government-in-exile.

The triple murder shattered the pristine serenity of the commune and cracked open shocking rivalries among competing Buddhist sects and sub-sects for the control of Tibetan affairs. The
murders also underscored that despite the impression of enlightened harmony so eloquently personified by the Dalai Lama, there
were fissures that could potentially threaten his unassailable supremacy. The Indian police suspected that the murders were carried out by the followers of Dorje Shugden, an obscure three-eyed
deity whose worship the Dalai Lama had proscribed in 1996. The
followers of the deity tend to be doctrinaire and are generally in-
tolerant of any dilution of their dogmas. When I first met the
Dalai Lama the murders were fresh in the minds of the Tibetan
exile community and had rocked their notions of civility in political and spiritual discourse.

The Dalai Lama was shaken. "This is not the way to express disagreement. There are clear reasons why I was compelled to take the extreme action of banning the worship of Dolgyal [Dorje Shugden]. I believe such a practice can turn Tibetan Buddhism into spirit worship. Tibetan Buddhism is a profound tradition. Such spirit worship reduces Tibetan Buddhism to a set of strange beliefs. Propitiating Dolgyal is greatly harmful to the Tibetan cause as well as my life personally," he said.

The origin of Dorje Shugden can be traced back to the time of the Fifth Dalai Lama in the middle of the seventeenth century. The Great Fifth, as he is popularly known, had a contemporary Buddhist master named Dragpa Gyaltsen, who was regarded by many as the spiritual equal of the Dalai Lama. Of course, this claim has been strongly rejected by the Dalai Lama's supporters. The rivalry between the Great Fifth and Gyaltsen is said to have reached a point where the Dalai Lama's chief minister had the rival master murdered. Such claims are impossible to prove one way or the other, but they highlight the inherent tensions among various cults and sects of Tibetan Buddhism for centuries. Gyaltsen reincarnated as Dorje Shugden, according to Tibetan belief.

Shugden followers consider the Dalai Lama's unquestioned sway over Tibetan affairs problematic. The Shugdens consider themselves to be the true guardians of Tibetan Buddhism and condemn the Dalai Lama as a traitor. However, the explanation offered by the Dalai Lama himself and his advisors flies in the face of what the Shugdens claim. One of the Dalai Lama's main contentions is that the cult is too openly commercial and offers rewards in return for cash, a claim denied by the Shugdens.

Dr. Robert Thurman, one of the world's leading authorities on Tibet and Tibetan Buddhism and a close friend of the Dalai

Lama's, was quoted by *Newsweek* magazine in its April 28, 1997, issue as saying, "I think there's no doubt that Shugden was behind
the killings. The three were stabbed repeatedly and cut up in a way
that was like an exorcism." In a separate interview with this author
Thurman reiterated that comment, adding, "There are serious
questions about the way Shugden operates."

The disagreement between the Dalai Lama and his followers
and the Shugdens is as much spiritual as it is political. The Shugdens insist on doctrinal purity in Buddhist practice and argue that
the Dalai Lama has diluted Tibetan Buddhism by broadening its
core base. Although the worship of Dorje Shugden remained
largely underground, in 1991 a senior monk, Kelsang Gyatso, established a new order called the New Kadampa Tradition, based
in England. The Dalai Lama's followers found it strange that while
on the one hand the Shugdens spoke of doctrinal purity, on the
other hand they turned their system into a commercial enterprise
insomuch as they were making money from selling some of their
teachings. The Shugdens have consistently denied those allegations, claiming that their system is legitimate and that they are
genuinely concerned about Tibet's independence, unlike the Dalai
Lama, who is willing to settle for much less. The Shugdens also
accuse the Dalai Lama of selling out Tibet in settling for autonomy rather than complete independence.

Soon after the murders, death threats were issued against fourteen members of the Dalai Lama's secretariat. Indian investigators
questioned five Shugden followers who they believed knew about
the plot against the monks but were not actual participants in it.
The investigators said the real culprits may have left India. There
was also speculation at the time that the murderers were Chinese

agents who were carrying out a plan to play one sect against another, but such allegations were never proved.

The Kashag's (the Tibetan government-in-exile Cabinet's) position on the sordid affair was quite categorical. While claiming that the prospects of Tibetan freedom had improved over the years under the Dalai Lama's leadership, the Kashag's official statement said, "Obstructive factors of various kinds, emanating from beings of both the form and formless realms, continue to hinder our efforts.

"His Holiness the Dalai Lama has investigated these obstructions and their causes for many years. One of the findings of his investigations is that depending on the spirit, Dolgyal, otherwise known as Dorje Shugden or Gyalchen Shugden, conflicts with Tibet's two protector-deities [Nechung and Palden Lhamo] as well as the protector-deity of the Geluk-pa tradition, Pledge-holding Dharmaraja [Damchen Choegyal]. The inclination of this spirit is to harm, rather than benefit, the cause of Tibet," the Kashag said.

Tibetan Buddhism has two types of deities and spirits, the transcendental beings and the worldly beings. The transcendental beings are necessarily considered to be in the same category as exalted Buddhas in whom people can take refuge. The worldly beings are more like servants who perform certain services in return for ritual offerings. The Geluk-pa tradition proscribes worshiping the latter type because they are considered less evolved.

"Understanding this, His Holiness the Dalai Lama himself made a complete break with the Dolgyal in 1976. Since then, His Holiness has regularly explained to the Tibetan people why depending on the Dolgyal was inappropriate. Many lamas, abbots, geshes, as well as the general Tibetan public, both lay and ordained, heeded his advice and stopped propitiating Dolgyal. As a result, the Tibetan situation has taken a turn for the better," the Kashag said.

During the preparatory ritual for an empowerment (a form of Buddhist teaching given to remove impediments) on March 21, 1996, the Dalai Lama said, "Recently I have conducted a number of prayers for the well-being of our nation and religion. It has become fairly clear that Dolgyal is a spirit of the dark forces. Therefore, during the Hayagriva invocation last year, I specifically mentioned Dolgyal by name and an incantation was made to ward him off." His Holiness continued: "I wonder if any among you here today continue to propitiate Dolgyal and still feel comfortable receiving this Hayagriva Empowerment. This is the reason why I suggested yesterday that it would not be appropriate for those who propitiate Dolgyal to attend this empowerment. When the protector concerned is disloyal to it commitments, the person concerned becomes disloyal in turn. As I said yesterday, this gives rise to a breach of commitments which carries with it a definite threat to the life of a lama."

"If any among you here are determined to continue propitiating Dolgyal, it would be better for you to stay away from this empowerment, get up and leave this place. It is improper for you to continue to sit here. It will not benefit you. On the contrary it will have the effect of reducing the life span of Gyalwa Rinpoche [the Dalai Lama], which is not good. However, if there are any among you who hope that Gyalwa Rinpoche will soon die, then you can stay," he said.

"The biography of His Holiness the Great Fifth Dalai Lama contains a reference to discord between him and Tulku Dragpa Gyaltsen [whose spirit is alleged to have become Dolgyal]. The matter is made very clear in the Great Fifth's Extensive Collection of Secrets [Sangwa Gyachen]. On the basis of this evidence, the Thirteenth Dalai Lama imposed restrictions on Dolgyal," he said.

Calling himself a "successor to the Great Fifth Dalai Lama" as well as pointing out a unique karmic relationship with the Thirteenth Dalai Lama, the Dalai Lama said it was his duty to carry out their legacy. "This is not a matter of what is in the Dalai Lama's interest, but what is in the interest of the Tibetan nation and religion," he said.

The Dalai Lama argued that propitiating spirits was a practice followed in pre-Buddhist Tibet, a clear reference to the shamanistic rituals and nature worship that prevailed in the country when Buddhism reached Tibet in the seventh century. Propitiating spirits can be quite akin to witchcraft, whose many rituals are quite dark in nature. "However, when Guru Padmasambhava was helping to establish Buddhism in Tibet in the eighth century, he recruited some spirits such as Nechung, the state oracle, to protect the Buddhist doctrine. Due to his high spiritual attainments, he was able to neutralize bad influences, and bind them by oath. Propitiating spirits, therefore, is not a Buddhist practice itself, but a means to help sustain spiritual practice. Over the centuries the practice of propitiating spirits has instead become widespread as a means to achieve fame, fortune and the general well-being for this life, concerns that run counter to general Buddhist outlook," he said.

I had an occasion to discuss some of these points with the Dalai Lama. I asked him how worshiping Dorje Shugden could imperil his life. "You should not think that dangers to my life come only from someone armed with a knife, a gun, or a bomb. Such an event is extremely unlikely. But dangers to my life may

arise if my advice is constantly spurned, causing me to feel discouraged and to see no further purpose in living." He also said
that because of his good karma over his past many lives, he did
not perceive any personal danger to his life.

The Dalai Lama's official position on the subject is quite clear.
"Propitiating Dolgyal does great harm to the cause of Tibet. It
also imperils the life of the Dalai Lama. Therefore, it is totally inappropriate for the great monasteries of the Geluk tradition, the
Upper and Lower Tantric Monasteries and all other affiliated
monasteries which are national institutions ever to propitiate Dolgyal. The public should be thoroughly informed so that they can
gain a clear appreciation of the situation themselves. However,
everyone is completely free to say: 'If the cause of Tibet and the
Dalai Lama's life are undermined so be it. We have religious freedom. We are a democracy. We are free to do as we please. We will
not change our tradition of propitiating Dolgyal.' "

It is hard to establish the extent of following that Dorje Shugden commands among Tibetan exiles as well as among the Tibetans in Tibet. But scholars say that while Buddhism remains the
prime philosophy among Tibetans, many also continue to maintain their ancient beliefs. One follower of the deity in McLeod
Ganj, a young man in his thirties, said, "I do not see any contradiction in following Dorje Shugden and respecting His Holiness
at the same time. Both have a place in my heart."

18

■

THE DALAI LAMA:
THE MAN

L ife in exile has accentuated the Dalai Lama's role as a man of worldly affairs much more than his primary calling as a monk and a mystic. He has had to spend much more time on the affairs of the state-in-exile than he might have been required to had he remained in Lhasa in an independent Tibet. When he was chosen to be a reincarnate lama at three, it was ordained for him that he would no longer be able to explore life as a regular, normal man. And being the Dalai Lama is not just about having to practice celibacy. The rigors of the Buddhist order are overwhelming. Although the Buddhist monk order is quite flexible in that it allows those who join the freedom to disavow it anytime, the case of the Dalai Lamas has been historically different. They are chosen for life quite like the pope. There is no instance of a Dalai Lama giving up his exalted but highly regimental life midstream, except the Sixth Dalai Lama, who took up a life of decadent pleasures with gusto and largely disregarded his canonical duties. Tibetans argue with convenient but faultless logic that the Sixth Dalai Lama was born to test their faith in Buddhism, and he performed that role admirably.

Unlike his predecessors, with the possible exception of the Thirteenth Dalai Lama, Tenzin Gyatso's life has been sharply defined by three distinct roles—those of a man, monk, and mystic. Even the Thirteenth Dalai Lama was forced into exile twice during his lifetime, but the length of his exile from Tibet was nothing compared to that of his successor. "His Holiness recognizes that the circumstances of his life in exile demand that his role as a man is equally important [to his role] as a monk, if not more," Tenzin Geyche Tethong, his private secretary, said. "But it would be a mistake to believe that one is at the cost of the other."

A major function of the Dalai Lama the man is his duty as the Tibetan head of state. It is a role he does not particularly enjoy but is required to perform under the Tibetan system of governance. He could easily have chosen to perpetuate the overarching supremacy of his institution without most Tibetans raising any concern. But his instincts were strongly democratic and in any case the circumstances in which he operated made it essential for him to evolve a democratic system of governance. On January 26, 1992, the Dalai Lama issued "Guidelines for Future Tibet's Polity and the Basic Features of Its Constitution," in which he categorically declared that he will not hold an official position in the government of a future Tibet since he thinks that he will be "in a better position to serve the people as an individual outside the government." The document was the culmination of a process of democratization that he began in 1961 when he first promulgated a democratic constitution. Barely two years after he had gone through his life's most harrowing political persecution, it took a lot of courage and conviction for the Dalai Lama to create a document that expressly made his own role superfluous.

"Although it is difficult to predict the future, all human beings who wish to achieve happiness and avoid suffering must plan for the future. As a result of the Chinese occupation, Tibetans in Tibet are deprived of their basic human rights; this tragic situation cannot be permitted to continue for long," the Dalai Lama wrote.

"Tibet has a recorded history of over 2,000 years, and according to archaeological findings, a civilization dating back to over 4,000 years. In terms of geographical features of the country, as well as in terms of race, culture, language, dress and customs, Tibet is a distinct nation," he said.

He explained the circumstances which brought to him the responsibility of being a head of state in his teens. "Under Tibet's kings and the Dalai Lamas, we had a political system that was firmly rooted in our spiritual values. As a result, peace and happiness prevailed in Tibet. However, by the middle of this century, Chinese occupation forces marched into Tibet through its eastern border regions of Kham and Amdo. Soon after, the Chinese intensified their military repression in Tibet, driving our political situation to a crisis point. In the face of this, I had no alternative but to comply with my people's request to assume full responsibility as the head of state of Tibet, although I was then only sixteen," he said.

"Personally, I have made up my mind that I will not play any role in the future government of Tibet, let alone seek the Dalai Lama's traditional political position in the government. There are important reasons why I have made this decision. There is no doubt that Tibetans, both in and outside Tibet, have great hope in, and reverence for, me. From my side too, I am determined to do whatever I can for the well-being of my people. The fact that I am in a position to do this is due to my karma and prayers over past lives. However, in the future I will not hold any official position in the government. I will most likely remain a public figure who may be called on to offer advice or resolve some particularly significant and difficult problems which could not be overcome by the existing government or political mechanisms. I think I will be in a better position to serve the people as an individual outside the government," he said.

"Moreover, if Tibet is to survive as an equal member of the modern international community, it should reflect the collective potential of all its citizens, and not rely on one individual. In other words, people must be actively involved in charting their own political and social destiny," he said.

"It is, therefore, in the interests of the Tibetan people, both long- and short-term, that I have come to this decision, and not because I am losing interest in my responsibilities. There is no need to worry on this count," he wrote.

The 1992 guidelines suggested that in the event Tibet became free its interim government would be headed by a president "who will assume all the political powers presently held by me."

At much lower levels of responsibility the Dalai Lama is

known to enjoy a lot of activities that men of his age and even younger than him enjoy. "Gardening is my passion. I feel thrilled when a plant that I planted flowers. I feel as if I created something even though I know that I did nothing more than water that plant," he said. He is an avid follower of news and current affairs programs on television. "BBC is my favorite channel. It was my favorite during the age of the radio as well. It has the reputation of being unbiased," he said.

"I enjoy all those beautiful documentaries on BBC, especially their travel shows. I like to travel. I see the travel show by Michael Palin [a successful British actor who hosts a popular travel show]. Maybe I could become his assistant and travel the world," he said.

"If I were not chosen the Dalai Lama, I could have become anything—a watch repairer, a filmmaker, a writer, or even a politician. But China thinks I am already a politician," he said and laughed.

The conflict that he has been at the heart of has considerably shaped the man. Although he is not given to angry outbursts or open shows of anger, the Dalai Lama admitted that the campaign for Tibet does bring out negative thoughts in him from time to time. "I used to get angry but not anymore. Anger achieves nothing other than making you feel ugly," he said. Asked how his life might have turned out had there been no conflict over Tibet, he said, "I don't know. For sure, I have learned a lot because of the conflict. I have learned how to deal with the larger world and world leaders. Therefore I don't think I can say it has been all bad."

Preserving Tibetan culture outside Tibet has been one of the Dalai Lama's most important contributions. Within four months of his exile in 1959 the Dalai Lama established the Tibetan Institute of Performing Arts (TIPA). Tibetan Buddhism would have fewer problems surviving outside Tibet than Tibetan culture. Unlike religion, culture needs a specific context. "One of my biggest worries was that Tibetan culture would become extinct after the Chinese invasion. We had to find a way to preserve it. Therefore I established TIPA," the Dalai Lama said.

TIPA preserves and promotes three important branches of traditional Tibetan arts—opera, dance, and music. In fact, preserving the Tibetan opera known as Lhamo is one of the principal responsibilities of TIPA. Each year the institute organizes a nine-day Shoton Opera Festival. The institute also encourages artists who can play Tibetan instruments such as the *fule*, *dranyen*, and *piwang*. Both the dranyen and piwang are stringed instruments. Tibetan dance forms vary from region to region. Lhasa, for instance, prefers a more quick-footed style compared to Kham's more elaborate and complex movements. The Dalai Lama himself plays no instrument. "I can make some noises with drums, you see. As for dancing, you would run away if I danced," he said. TIPA also offers residency to aspiring Tibetan artists who can live and work on the institute's beautiful campus.

Another equally important priority for the Dalai Lama has been the education of exiled children. "I must say Nehru played a great role in helping us start several Tibetan schools," the Dalai Lama recalled. Early in his exile the Dalai Lama founded Tibetan Children's Village (TCV), which is a residential school system. TCV schools mainly teach the curriculum approved by the Indian government but they also teach courses in Tibetan language and culture. Students from these schools are now among the top performers in the country.

"Because many Hollywood celebrities are drawn to my brother, many in the West believe that the Dalai Lama leads a glamorous life," Norbu said. "Nothing could be further from the truth. On his own he has never sought celebrities. It has always been the other way around. But more important, his main preoccupation has been dealing with serious survival issues. I know for a fact that he believes education is the most important thing for Tibetan children, whether they are in exile or in Tibet. He also believes equally passionately in preserving Tibetan culture."

Having attained the equivalent of a PhD in Buddhist studies in his early twenties, the Dalai Lama has frequently talked about education as a "liberating influence." "If you are educated your mind can never be colonized. As a refugee community living outside our occupied homeland, it is important that we keep our minds free. For that education is very important," the Dalai Lama said.

19

THE DALAI LAMA:
THE MONK

Tenzin Gyatso is no ordinary monk, notwithstanding his protestations to the contrary. Ordinary monks do not get recognized as the world's conscience keeper. Nor do they win the Nobel Prize. They also don't get courted and feted by heads of state, movie stars, and scientists with equal exuberance. And they certainly don't inspire people to fall at their feet in abject reverence. The Dalai Lama is not an ordinary monk, no matter how genuine his self-effacement is. It is true that he sincerely believes that there is nothing extraordinary about him, but the world, at any rate a significant part of it, thinks otherwise.

As far as Buddhism goes, its clergy has not historically been known to exercise even a fraction of the control over society that the Dalai Lamas have done over Tibetan society. Buddhist monks in India, Thailand, Sri Lanka, Japan, and other countries are at best a marginal presence. In exceptional cases such as Sri Lanka, a Buddhist country, the clergy do exercise political clout, but that is more by default than by design. By and large, monks are symbols of a world that is beyond everyday humdrum existence. However, in Tibetan Buddhism monks have always enjoyed considerable sway over society, and the Dalai Lama, of course, has been re- garded as the ultimate arbiter of Tibetan destinies. In many ways there was no separation between church and state in Tibet. Church was state and state was church. Since Buddhism is not a congrega- tional religion in the sense of Christianity or Islam, this peculiar convergence between church and state has generally remained non- controversial even though from time to time the supremacy of the Buddhist clergy has been seriously questioned. The amalgamation of religion and politics or church and state in the Tibetan context appears to be a mutation, considering Buddhism was born of its founder's disenchantment with the world that he was born to rule. It is debatable whether there would be any Buddhism had Sid- dhartha chosen to inherit his father's empire and responded to the calling that was his by birth. In the Buddha's universe there was no state, only church insomuch as the Sangha could be called a church. That claim too is dubious, since the Buddha never founded any specific church. The Sangha was more like a spiritual school than a deliberately created institution that would rival or usurp the powers of a secular administration.

In Tibet, since the inception of Lamaism in 1391 and up to 1875 when the Twelfth Dalai Lama died, the Dalai Lamas were automatically anointed rulers. The separation of church and state is essentially a modern concept; it did not matter back then whether the Dalai Lama as a monk would also double up as a politician or an administrator. That situation changed significantly with the Thirteenth Dalai Lama, who pioneered many democratic reforms, so that by the time the current Dalai Lama came along the institution was on the verge of a fundamental shift. His exile hastened the process of democratization since the Dalai Lama recognized that life as a monk, even as a Dalai Lama, would be very different outside Tibet.

As a monk who is supposed to have mastered knowledge of all that Buddhism offers, the Dalai Lama is considered a scholar of the highest order. Known for his passion to seek a common ground between the Buddhist practice of meditation and science, especially neuroscience, the Dalai Lama has over the last two decades reached out to scientists across the world. "I believe Tibetan Buddhism has a lot to offer to scientists studying the human brain and what meditation could do to help it attain levels of awareness that one cannot ordinarily do," he said.

The latest example of the Dalai Lama's keen interest in connecting Buddhist meditation techniques with neuroscience was manifest when he received an invitation from Neuroscience 2005, the Society for Neuroscience's annual conference, in November 2005. The conference is considered one of the most important events on the calendars of neuroscientists across the United States. "The Dalai Lama has long been interested in science and has maintained an ongoing dialogue with leading neuroscientists for more than fifteen years. His talk is expected to bridge the cultural gap between neuroscientists and Buddhist practitioners by pointing to the methods of observation and verification that lie at the heart of both science and Buddhism. He is expected to discuss the study of meditation, a practice of mental discipline that Western neuroscience has shown to change neural states in circuits that may be important for compassionate behavior and attentional and emotional regulation," the conference organizers said.

"Buddhist masters over the centuries have been known to attain a level of neural control through meditation that scientists now find baffling. I think there is a lot to learn from Buddhist meditation techniques," the Dalai Lama said. Quite in keeping with his humility, he played down his own meditation abilities. "I am still learning. I am nowhere near some of the past masters," he said. However, his aides said when the Dalai Lama goes into meditation he is known to attain the same level of heightened awareness that he credits to some of greatest past masters. "Because of his preoccupations with the Tibetan question, the world does not get to know much about his life as a monk, but I know for a fact that His Holiness has attained the highest level of awareness as a monk," said his private secretary, Tenzin Geyche Tethong.

The Dalai Lama's involvement with the neuroscience establishment predictably upset some neuroscientists. The Society for Neuroscience's invitation to him prompted some scientists to initiate a protest. Jianguo Gu, a neuroscientist at the University of Florida, organized a petition against the Dalai Lama's lecture. "I don't think it's appropriate to have a prominent religious leader at a scientific event. The Dalai Lama basically says the body and mind can be separated and passed to other people. There are no scientific grounds for that. We'll be talking about cells and molecules and he's going to talk about something that isn't there," Dr. Gu, a scientist of Chinese origin, said. His being Chinese had nothing to do with his opposition to the Dalai Lama's involvement in a scientific conference, Dr. Gu said, although he cancelled his presentation at the meeting. "I'm not against Buddhism," Dr. Gu said. "People believe what they believe but I think it will just confuse things."

The scientists' petition said: "Inviting the Dalai Lama to lecture on the neuroscience of meditation is of poor scientific taste because it will highlight a subject with hyperbolic claims, limited research and compromised scientific rigor."

The protesting scientists argued that inviting the Dalai Lama was like inviting the pope to talk about "the relationship between the fear of God and the amygdala [a part of the brain]." They said, "It could be a slippery road if neuroscientists begin to blur the border between science and religious practices."

But Carol Barnes, the president of the Society for Neuroscience, countered saying: "The Dalai Lama has had a long interest in science and has maintained an ongoing dialogue with leading neuroscientists for more than fifteen years, which is the reason he was invited to speak at the meeting. It has been agreed that the talk will not be about religion or politics. We understand that not every member will agree with every decision and we respect their right to disagree."

A particular area of interest for neuroscientists is what is known in Buddhism and Hinduism as *ekagrata*, or single-point meditation. This is a technique that Buddhist monks, including the Dalai Lama, use to concentrate their attention on a single object or a single thought or a single emotion or the tip of the nose or the space between the eyebrows or simply the Creator for several hours uninterruptedly. Those who practice this meditation say that what they essentially do is suppress the "psychomental flux."

Conversely, meditating monks can shift their attention about seventeen times in the time it takes to snap one's fingers. Both are extraordinary claims that defy current scientific wisdom, which holds that not only can you not hold your attention on a single object for that long, but you also can't switch your attention that quickly. Despite the skepticism, some neuroscientists have been investigating whether there is a biological basis to such fantastic claims.

"I have always maintained that we need a scientific basis for our claims, but then there is a lot that science does not explain or understand. I greatly respect science and scientists and we need to work together on seeking those answers," the Dalai Lama said.

In November 2004, a team led by Richard Davidson, a psychologist at the University of Wisconsin, Madison, published findings of their research in the journal *Proceedings of the National Academy of Sciences* suggesting that networks of brain cells were better coordinated in people who meditate. The research included Matthieu Ricard, a Buddhist monk at the Shechenm monastery in Nepal, who has a PhD in molecular biology from the Pasteur Institute in Paris. The researchers found that the differences they observed in the brains of those who meditate could explain the heightened awareness experienced by meditating monks.

"Meditation is really like emptying your body and soul of everything to reach a level of pure consciousness. I feel the human brain has many unexplored areas. Buddhist monks in Tibet and India have sought to explore those areas for centuries. But my interest is more immediate. Can we use meditation as a technique to bring about a sense of calm and peace in the world? That is the question I want to explore along with scientists," the Dalai Lama said. Asked how often he engages in single-point meditation, he laughed and said, "My single-point meditation these days is Tibet's freedom. I do try to meditate every day. I do that during predawn hours."

Having to live three competing and often conflicting lives as a man, monk, and mystic often presents the Dalai Lama with a difficult choice about which role takes precedence over the other two. Quite clearly, though, he draws his primary identity from being a Buddhist monk. Apart from his well-known scholarship in Buddhist studies, which is generally not known to people with whom he interacts on a daily basis, the most visible feature of his life is external. A part of the Dalai Lama's international success is attributable to his being a monk, and not in the least to superficial but enchanting details such as his ochre robes and other colorful trimmings that surround the ceremonies he is often involved in. If for a moment you separate him from his sartorial details and the mysticism they exude and imagine him in the regular clothes that heads of state are wont to wear, it would strike you that some of his appeal would be diluted. The power of exotica to the Western eye is unquestionable. His appeal, quite like the land that he symbolizes, is visual first and everything else later. Of course, it would be foolish to explain his success only from the standpoint of exotica but insomuch as it helps him to draw attention immediately, it is important. If the Dalai Lama were standing next to President George W. Bush, for instance, it is almost inevitable that the eye would first travel to the Buddhist monk. Not that he consciously chooses to draw attention through his robes or other exotic aspects of his persona or his culture's peculiarities. On the contrary, he is hardly aware of such trivialities. Standing out accentuates his appeal even more. In that respect too he is quite similar to Gandhi, whose appeal to the Western eye was visual first and everything else later. The tiny loincloth that Gandhi wrapped around his frail body and the bamboo stick he carried for support made him a recognizable icon of the early twentieth century. Gandhi without his loincloth and the Dalai Lama without his ochre robes would somehow look out of place.

Costumes have always been one of the most compelling differentiators in human history. In every religion the priestly class or the clergy has been painstaking in evolving a dress code that sets them apart from the rest of the crowd. All these details add up to create an aura about this particular class of people, just as with royalty and warriors. In Hindu and Buddhist traditions the significance of the ochre, saffron, or orange robes is that they represent the color of fire, which is also considered the color of purity. These cultures believe fire to be pure. By implication, those who wear the colors that denote fire are considered pure.

"I have not known any other clothes, although in Tibetan culture men, like women, like fine clothes. Since I have always worn ochre robes, it has come to be my favorite color. I also like white and other colors but I can't wear them. I sometimes wonder what I might look like in a three-piece suit," the Dalai Lama said.

20

■

THE DALAI LAMA:
THE MYSTIC

At the root of the mystical aspects of the Dalai Lama's life lies the way in which Buddhism came to Tibet and evolved within the specific context of the nation's already existing religious practices and rituals. The Dalai Lama as a mystic is as much a product of Buddhism as he is a product what Tibet was before Buddhism arrived.

By their very definition mystics dwell in an uncharted world. The world of Tibetan mysticism in particular is one of the most intriguing. Bonism, shamanism, animism, Tantrism, and Buddhism live in each other's shadow, making it hard to tell where one ends and the other begins. Because of its spiritual and intellectual underpinnings, Buddhism stands out from the rest, but it too has its own mysterious practices, known as Tantra. Stories abound about Tantric practitioners who can travel hundreds of miles in a second, possess telepathic powers, and command extraordinary sexual prowess. The veracity of these claims is hard to establish. Nevertheless, Tantric phenomena are part of Tibetan mysticism. The popular Tibetan response to skepticism about such fantastic claims is refreshingly open-ended. They exist if you believe. They don't exist if you don't believe.

One of the main contentions of Sakyamuni, or the Buddha, was that nonattachment to the material world was a primary condition to attaining enlightenment. He defined enlightenment, insomuch as it could be defined, as consisting of "neither fullness nor emptiness, being nor nonbeing, substance nor non-substance." While enlightenment could not be defined specifically, the process of seeking it could be explained and defined. The one seeking enlightenment needs an environment that fosters purity of thought, word, and action. Such purity needs an ecology to grow to its full potential. That in turns necessitates monasticism and monasteries.

A minority among those who have followed the Buddha's teachings have attained enlightenment. They were known as arhats, or the "worthy ones." The concept of arhats created a spiritual elite in the sixth century, and the rest of the society was essentially excluded from pursuing goals loftier than what their mundane struggles imposed on them. These learned men did not care to share their knowledge with others and believed in knowledge for the sake of knowledge. Their school came to be known as Theravada; it is a more conservative and purist strand of Buddhism. The lack of compassion and consideration toward others in this strain of Buddhism prompted other followers of the Buddha to introduce Mahayana, or the "bigger vehicle," a more inclusive school of Buddhism.

As a differentiator, the Mahayana Buddhists created a system of bodhisattvas, who were regarded as beings higher than arhats. Bodhisattvas are those who could have led the life of enlightenment if they chose, but decided instead to postpone attaining Nirvana in order to help others. Their motivating force was compassion toward others. The Dalai Lama is considered a bodhisattva who has of his own volition chosen to be of assistance to whomever he can.

Even within Mahayana Buddhism, which is a more liberal version of pure Buddhism, attaining enlightenment is quite a grueling process, and because of its inherent intensity most people are filtered out. According to the Mahayana school, Nirvana can be achieved over many lifetimes. Tantrism, on the other hand, is a kind of shortcut to Nirvana, ensuring that one can attain enlightenment in one's lifetime. The first Tantric texts reached Tibet in the eleventh century and began diluting the more purist forms of Buddhism that had arrived earlier. On the turnpike to enlightenment, Mahayana is for those who do not care to buy a monthly pass. They choose to slow down and drop in a few coins at every tollbooth. Tantrism, on the other hand, is for those who want to use an easy express pass. One has to slow down a little at the tollbooths, but one need not stop.

Tibetan Buddhism is a derivation of Mahayana Buddhism with a generous dose of Tantrism. Tantric techniques include making and contemplating mandalas, fasting and other forms of penance, saying prayers and mantras in meditation, and performing rituals. These practices require a learned teacher, and hence the teacher-student relationship in the monasteries is very important.

The introduction of Buddhism to Tibet in the seventh through the eleventh centuries was met with serious resistance from the adherents of the Bon religion. Nature worship, spirit worship, and shamanistic rituals were all part of Bon. The focus was on propitiating spirits found in trees, mountains, springs, and lakes. Shamans and other practitioners of such worship were part of the society's royal structure that sought blessings of nature spirits, both out of belief and because it was politically expedient. Priests and shamans routinely presided over royal ceremonies. While the motivation behind the decision to involve shamans and priests in royal proceedings was more political than religious, by the time that King Songtsen Gampo introduced Buddhism in the seventh century, Bon already had deep roots in the system of governance. It was necessary that Buddhism and Bonism be harmonized in order for Tibet to retain religious equilibrium. In the eighth century Indian Buddhist master Padmasambhava, locally known as Guru Rinpoche, played a significant role in incorporating the Bon pantheon of deities into Tibetan Buddhism.

Rather than treating them as antagonists, Padmasambhava converted the Bon deities into protectors of Buddhism known as Dharma Palas, or "Defenders of the Dharma." This accounts for the presence of the fierce-looking deities in Tibetan Buddhism, including Yamantaka whose ferocious image the Dalai Lama was reported to have seen during his meditation just before Mao's death.

In keeping with their fantastic belief system, Tibetans believed that Padmasambhava was born eight years after the death of the Buddha and was more than a thousand years old. They believed it was because of his mastery of Tantra that he was able to prolong his life. Padmasambhava enlisted the help of the adherents of Bon to subdue demonic forces while building Tibet's first Buddhist monastery, Samye.

On the more sinister side, Tantric practitioners are said to employ magical means to destroy their enemy. According to the *Hevajra Tantra*, for instance, they can cast a spell on enemy soldiers who can then be decapitated in one stroke. The two authors also say that Tantric masters could cause such a high fever in the enemy's body that it would vaporize. For those who claim such devastating powers, leaping from peak to peak would be a relatively minor accomplishment.

Sexual symbolism is an intrinsic part of Tantra, which sees the cosmos as a living entity full of sacred rituals and spells, secret formulas, and baffling diagrams and drawings. Female energy is considered an integral part of Tantra. The Dalai Lamas of the past are known to have practiced Tantra. It is especially true of the Sixth Dalai Lama, who was a colorful, bohemian, indulgent, and, some would say, even decadent figure. There is a famous quote by him where he says, "Never have I slept without a sweetheart. Nor have I spent a single drop of sperm." This paradox was supposed to represent the Positive Sexual Yoga where in the male and female energies converge but there is no ejaculation.

Tibetans who traveled to India in search of Buddhist knowledge also discovered yoginis, or female tantric masters, engaged in esoteric disciplines with their female disciples. Yoginis were fiercely independent women who fraternized with men who were willing to be initiated. This coming together also led to the spread of Tantric Buddhism. The Dalai Lama believes that women are more adept at secretive practices while men are better at the more public forms of Tibetan Buddhism.

An interesting fallout of the fusion between Buddhism and Bonism was that many of the supernatural powers that the Bonists once ascribed to shamans and priests were now being extended to lamas, including the Dalai Lama. No wonder then that my childhood apocrypha about the Dalai Lama included stories that he had powers to destroy the entire Chinese army through these techniques. Perhaps my neighbor was better informed than I gave him credit for. If ordinary lamas could leap from peak to peak, the Dalai Lama could surely atomize an entire army. Such powers were more in the realm of fables than reality. It also begs the question why none of the Tantric masters in Tibet unleashed those powers on the invading Chinese army.

I asked the Dalai Lama if he believed that lamas could leap from peak to peak. He laughed aloud, perhaps the loudest I have heard in all my interactions with him. "That means I can return to Tibet anytime, you see. I just have to leap over a few peaks. That's all," he said, pausing and turning serious. "Tantric knowledge is a serious responsibility. I know people believe that Tantric masters have great powers. What is important is not being able to do magical things but doing things that help people," he said.

The Dalai Lama is not given to talking about some of the more magical and mystical details of life. One conclusion one could draw is that he does not really believe in them since he has grown up in a modern age and naturally tends to be more scientific and rational in his outlook. But that conclusion is too obvious and simplistic. The matter demands a more complex and more accurate assessment. Considering that he has kept up his faith in

the core Tibetan Buddhist belief of reincarnation, which from a
scientific standpoint is in itself more incredible than lamas leaping from peak to peak, it is possible that he believes in ideas that
to a rational mind defy all explanation. Background conversations
with many in the Tibetan government-in-exile revealed that the
Dalai Lama has consciously chosen to distance himself from the
controversial practices of Tantric Buddhism since he does not
want to convey to the world the impression that he represents a
dark faith that is prone to violence, black magic, sorcery, witchcraft, bizarre sexual practices, and even ritual suicide. Mysticism of
the kind underscored by Tantra could work for a practitioner
whose ideas and objectives are far less lofty than what the Dalai
Lama stands for. Since Tibet's leader represents the reformist
branch of Tibetan Buddhism, he would never do or say anything
to undermine his credibility with his growing international con-
stituency. For that reason he has deliberately focused on the more
cerebral and philosophical areas of Tibetan Buddhism.

What sets the Fourteenth Dalai Lama apart from his predecessors in matters mystical is that he lives in a world where science
and technology dominate human endeavor. Notwithstanding his
rational outlook on life, it is conceivable that during a different
period of history, untrammeled by the forces of modernity, Tenzin Gyatso too might have had to pursue some of the very practices and rituals that he has been compelled to play down or reject
altogether, as in the case of spirit worship by the followers of
Dorje Shugden. The circumstances of his life in exile and the pro-
tracted nature of his political fight have ensured that he remains
trapped in what Hindus and Buddhists call *samsaric*, or phenome-
nal or worldly preoccupations, where karma overrides everything

else, rather than being able to seek *nirvanic* objectives, which are beyond karmic demands and compulsions.

The Dalai Lama himself is not particularly troubled by the fact that he has had to fundamentally alter the institution that he embodies. "Everything changes according to time. The institution of the Dalai Lama too should change. In my current role it is my duty to do what I am doing," he said.

He does not see himself as someone torn between three competing and contradictory roles. In fact, he does not even recognize the distinction. The Dalai Lama does not necessarily share the view that he is a figure of great consequence in both Tibetan and world history. Tibetans explain this self-effacement as a very Buddhist attitude. Living without revealing one's existence is one of the key concepts that the Buddha spoke of. At a very personal level his rising international celebrity does not really excite him. He is more amused by it.

■

21

PART SOCRATIC,
PART ROCK STAR,
PART EASTERN
WISE MAN, MOSTLY
BUDDHIST MONK

Time magazine's much-coveted annual list of the one hundred most influential people in the world is mostly a publishing business gimmick, but at some level it is still a barometer of the American mood. The 2005 list included the Dalai Lama in the heroes and icons list along with Bill Gates. The spectrum from the fabulously rich to the fabulously spiritual was clearly designed to help interest a larger readership. Nevertheless, his inclusion underscored how the Dalai Lama has managed to etch himself in the Western consciousness with his deceptively simple philosophy of compassion. The growing Western fascination for the man with no personal wealth, no state, and no power can be explained in a variety of ways. The glibbest explanation would be that the West is a guileless prey before the beast of Oriental mysticism. A cuddly monk in ochre robes with a charming sense of humor and unfettered laughter, who talks about loving everyone—what is there not to like about him? But as one explores why the Dalai Lama has the "It" factor in the West, even more than in Asia where he is deeply respected but not followed as avowedly other than among Tibetans, layers unravel.

In many parts of America the Dalai Lama is seen as a modern-day sage who works his intellectual scythe to trim down the wild growth of human complexities and turn them into neatly manicured gardens. To them the Dalai Lama is like the Socratic figure at the public square who dispenses wisdom, the full measure of which dawns on them long after he has receded back into his mystical world. Despite that reputation he does not speak in conundrums, nor does he attempt to sweep you off your feet with epigrams. In some way he is like the karate master in the movie *Karate Kid* who seems like an eternal pushover but packs a quietly powerful punch, which when delivered invariably leaves you shaken to the core. Being a Buddhist master of the highest order, he is as reflective as he is in the moment, and erudite yet free of pleonastic bombast. There are no epiphanies in Buddhism, only continual manifestation of life's many features. As with the Buddha, the

Dalai Lama's answers to life's many questions are seemingly commonplace but, in fact, quite deep. "You are your own refuge," the
Buddha once said. "Hatred or lack of compassion makes you feel
tense, weak, and unclean in your own mind," said the Dalai Lama.

I happened to attend two major events in the United States
where the Dalai Lama was the chief attraction—in Bloomington,
Indiana, at his brother's institute in August 1999, and in San Francisco, in September 2003. During his visit to San Francisco, one
of the Dalai Lama's engagements was a lecture on "nothingness"
at the University of San Francisco. Close to six thousand people,
mostly university students, came to listen to him. The atmosphere
was like a rock concert, only much more nuanced. I spoke to several students to find out what had drawn them at their young age
to a figure like the Dalai Lama, whose glamour quotient, though
quite high, was not of the type they would naturally identify with.
"I was raised a Catholic but am no longer one. When I try to compare the pope [John Paul II] with the Dalai Lama and go beyond
the obvious but superficial similarities such as both being celibate
monks wearing robes and inspiring reverence among their flocks, I
am left with a clear impression that the Dalai Lama is far more
universal in his message than the pope. He is very comfortable in
his own skin, being what he is without wanting to convert you to
his religion or point of view. I feel that if Tenzin Gyatso was not
a Buddhist master he would have been a cool rock star whose lyrics
would be squeaky clean and his music awesome," Megan (she used
only her first name), a nineteen-year-old literature student, told
me. The one common thread running through my conversations
with scores of students was that they found the Dalai Lama "very
cool and accessible." Craig, another nineteen-year-old student, put
it in a language closer to his peer group: "This man is not full of

BS like others. He says, like, this is what life is, man. It can suck but there is a way out. He does not ask you to go to the church or temple or whatever. He just says be compassionate. That works for me. When I see him I feel like saying hey, what's up, dude, without the fear of being excommunicated."

In Bloomington the event was more specifically Buddhist as it involved Kalchakra initiation. Kalchakra initiation is a form of mass teaching by the Dalai Lama. Most of the thousands of people in the audience were already practitioners of Buddhism in some form or the other. However, there was also a large number of the curious and the undecided. Paul Miller, who said he was a thirty-five-year-old company manager from London, was both curious and undecided and "very Protestant." "As I hurtle toward my middle age I am searching for something more inspiring than Protestantism. I find my Christian faith has too many dos and don'ts. I know Tibetan Buddhism too has its tenets, but they are nothing compared to what I grew up with. What attracts me to the Dalai Lama is that he speaks a largely cerebral language, which does not smack of any organized religion. He is like those Greek philosophers who break life down to simple yet profound interpretations," he said.

A Buddhist monk from Thailand said he was there to "learn from the master himself." "I have been a monk for ten years and have waited for this opportunity all my life. Although I have read Buddhist scriptures all my adult life, listening to the Dalai Lama's interpretations illuminates the concepts totally differently," he said. His perspective on why the Dalai Lama had managed to break through the barriers and reach Westerners with no previous connection to Buddhism was incisive. "His amiability and accessibility are the main factors. He maintains no distance between his supposedly supremely enlightened self and the uninitiated. He makes it all look so simple and uncomplicated. He never commands. He always gently nudges you to think about what he has to say. That has to do with the fact that Buddhism is not a proselytizing philosophy," he said.

The Dalai Lama described his own success with characteristic self-effacement. "I tell you what you already know. You just want to hear it from someone else," he said. We had a detailed conversation about the subject of religion versus spirituality. I asked him whether he made a distinction between the two. "You do not have to be religious to be spiritual. Religion often demands a certain discipline, it imposes certain rules. It is about following particular religious belief. Spirituality on the other hand is a sort of consciousness about something much larger than you. It is about understanding the essence of everything around you," he said.

Asked whether he would call himself religious or spiritual, he said, "I do not define myself. I suppose I am more spiritual, perhaps more introspective. I believe inner awareness comes from introspection rather than prayer or meditation."

I reminded him about my interaction with him in the 1980s when I asked him if the world was entering a stage where the dividing line between science and religion is getting blurred. His response was religion is science with faith, while science is religion in search of faith. "I said it in the 1980s. It is too soon to change that opinion. [Laughs.] Science and religion converge in many ways. We just need to look for a common ground," he said.

Among the questions that he is frequently asked is whether he thinks a spiritual journey is a lonely journey. "In the material world a lot of things are connected. A certain work or job started by one person can be finished by another person. That is not so in spiritual life. In the Buddha Dharma we believe no one can achieve spirituality on your behalf. It has to be done by the individual."

Another question I was very keen to ask him was what he thought of the Buddha's teaching "One is one's own refuge, who else could be the refuge?" "That in a sense sums up what Buddhism is all about. As I said about one's spiritual quest, eventually it is up to the individual. That is what the Buddha means when he says one is one's own refuge.

"Spirituality is beyond any religion. Therefore to that extent it helps everyone; but if people want to practice their own religious belief that is fine with me. I am for anything that fosters compassion for and understanding of fellow sentient beings."

His views on proselytizing were unambiguous. "I do not approve of conversion of any kind. Religious belief or spiritual quest is a matter of individual choice or volition. It cannot be imposed on anyone. I repeat what I said earlier: one cannot be religious or spiritual on someone else's behalf. I do not believe in exclusionist religions. Religion is not about excluding anyone. To say that my God is superior to your God is dangerous and pernicious. That is imposition of one's narrow beliefs on others," he said.

In that context I asked him if he thought more people in the world should turn to Buddhism. "That goes against my thinking. I would be happier if the world becomes more compassionate. Love and compassion are not functions of a particular religion. I believe the foundation of all spiritual practice is love. Buddhism is just one of the many ways to seek the truth. I am against people rushing to change their religion," he said.

Buddhism, he said, "is a way of leading a virtuous and compassionate life. It is a way of understanding the world around you in a rational practical manner. It is a way of comprehending life. I am not saying it is the way."

The most refreshing aspect of his philosophy, which goes against all institutionalized, congregational, and canonical religions, is his view about the necessity of religion in one's life. "I do not believe so, although a religion can help people discover answers to difficult questions. In Buddhism we believe we have to find our own answers. We take what is given and work with it. Religion is not necessary for a person to become decent, honest, compassionate and loving. You don't have to be a Christian or a Muslim or a Hindu or a Jew or a Buddhist to be decent, honest, compassionate, and loving. These qualities are irrespective of any religion," he said.

One of the key features of Buddhism is "nothingness" or "voidness." The Dalai Lama's lectures on the subject have been widely attended around the world. While a lot of people understand the concept in its broad sense, many people still have problems coming to terms with its essence. It is at once purely metaphysical yet utterly practical.

Reality, according to Buddhism, may be singular in its purest essence but it does not have any intrinsic value or identity that can be ascertained through one particular method. "The fact that reality is devoid of any intrinsic value is what the Buddha called voidness or nothingness. That is one of the core reasons why Buddhism does not support unquestioning faith or fanaticism. To argue that reality can be pursued by a single proposition is flawed," the Dalai Lama said during one of his many discourses on nothingness.

He said there are different truths on different levels. "Truth is relative. It depends on the context. The question whether there is absolute truth is a tricky one. By absolute truth I mean something that is enough in itself and independent and exclusive of everything else. I personally don't think there is absolute truth. We have what we call 'interpretable truths,' which are situation or people specific. The Buddha had different teachings for different people under different circumstances. There are those who draw their beliefs on the basis of a Creator. There are those who don't. The only absolute in Buddhism is absolute negation that there is one single absolute truth," he said.

The Buddhist concept of interpretable truths is in direct conflict with Christianity and Islam, both of which are strong on absolutes. Both religions present themselves as the divinely revealed word of God and anything outside those revelations ought to be rejected. At the Kalchakra initiation in Indianapolis, I asked Paul Miller what he thought of the Dalai Lama's definition. "That is precisely the point. Buddhism is not dogmatic. It does not claim any monopoly on truth. I think interpretable truth is a very scientific way of looking at things," he said.

The Dalai Lama said he has always stood for many religions and many truths. "Pluralism of religious belief is a great strength. No one religion should be presented as the only religion. But the difficult side of many truths is that there is a real danger of nihilism. One must not become a nihilist," he said.

His assertion that religion is not a precondition to being a decent, honest, and compassionate human being is a key reason that he is able to reach out to people from varied belief systems and to those without any specific belief system. The Dalai Lama said he never spends any time trying to analyze his appeal to the Westerners in general and Americans in particular. "I don't think I have any personal charisma or appeal. It is partly because Americans are open-minded people. It could also be because Buddhism is not religious. It is more like an intellectual discourse on life, like psychology perhaps. It offers a strong possibility of being in disagreement. Talking about my personal success, I don't think I am successful as an individual but as a Buddhist monk. It could also be because I am good-looking [laughs]," he said.

The Tibetan government-in-exile does not keep any record of how many people the Dalai Lama has initiated into Buddhism through Kalchakra ceremonies. Expanding the flock is not an item on the government's or the Dalai Lama's agenda. But it is conceivable that over the past twenty years that he has traveled extensively throughout the world, hundreds of thousands of people have become Buddhists primarily because of his lectures and discourses. "Although Buddhism is older than most other major philosophies with the exception of Hinduism, it retains that modernist edge. That is the main reason why many people are drawn to it. You must not confuse Buddhism with the Sangh or the order of Buddhist monks. Buddhism does not demand renunciation or ascetic life as a condition to following the philosophy. The order of monks is just one aspect of Buddhist life," he said. There are far more useful aspects of Buddhism which have been recognized and addressed only in the past five years.

In September 2003 neuroscientists and psychologists gathered at the Massachusetts Institute of Technology (MIT) at a conference on "Investigating the Mind." The Dalai Lama was one of the distinguished attendees. His presence intrigued many, but those who know Tibetan Buddhism and have heard the Dalai Lama's lecture about metaphysics and the extraordinary limits to which the human brain can stretch understood what he was doing there.

The conference's main purpose was scientific—to "identify

the common ground between two powerful empirical traditions: Tibetan Buddhism and behavioral science." "Buddhism offers profound insights into human consciousness and human behavior. It is true that some of the language Buddhist masters have used may not sit well with the modern scientific terminology and nomenclature, but essentially what they talk about are precisely the questions that scientists are now trying to answer," the Dalai Lama said.

The Dalai Lama's success in the West has as much to do with what he is and what he represents as it has to do with the West's quest for something new. When he first traveled to the United States in 1978, he was completely unknown to Americans. His supporters had a tough time attracting even a couple of hundred people to attend his speaking engagements. Attempts to get the networks to interview him were met with incredulity. "They did not understand whether the Dalai Lama was human or animal," the Dalai Lama said, laughing.

Now his lectures routinely attract tens of thousands of people. According to Jeffery Paine, author of the celebrated book *Re-enchantment: Tibetan Buddhism Comes to the West*, the number of Buddhist followers in the United States has grown faster than any other religion or philosophy.

In a newspaper article, Paine commented on the Western fascination with Tibetan Buddhism:

> *The story begins, in a sense, with the celebrated Catholic writer Thomas Merton and his fateful voyage to the Indian Himalayas in 1968. Before Merton's visit, he had assumed the Dalai Lama was a pompous ecclesiastical bureaucrat, and he considered Tibetan Buddhism to be a backward, superstitious faith suffused with too much black magic and*

even sex. Like earlier Westerners, Merton had misinterpreted the religion's paintings of copulating beings, not realizing they symbolized the union of the human and the divine. In fact, those Westerners were not entirely mistaken about the sensuality they saw. Unlike other kinds of Buddhism, the Tibetan variety accepts the passions and the emotions and transforms them to fuel the difficult transition toward what Buddhists call compassionate wisdom. Tibetan is at once the most mystical and the most earthy of all Buddhisms.

According to Paine, Merton discovered the "two-sided nature" of Buddhism.

"The Tibetan Buddhists are the only ones, at present," Merton noted, "who have attained to extraordinary heights [in spiritual achievement]." Merton was exploring if the essence of Tibetan Buddhism could be extracted to help restore religion in America to its former vigor. Merton became practically the first American to decide to devote his days to studying Tibetan Buddhism—although a freak fatal accident that very year cut prematurely short both his resolve and his life. (To Merton's perplexity, one lama, who intuited that the scholar might die soon, attempted to teach him Tibetan pre-death exercises.)

One reason that Tibetan Buddhism was received with unusual openness among certain sections of American society was that there were people in the early 1970s who were searching for something out of line with the accepted wisdom of the day. Paine describes such people as "countercultural types," such as poet Allen Ginsberg, who accepted the early Tibetan lamas and their ideas with extraordinary enthusiasm. Such Americans, Paine, said, "expected those lamas to remake them into American versions of wise Eastern sages. Beyond the counterculture, many others—including liberal, well-educated Americans who had outgrown their faith of origin and were uncomfortable with anything theological—began to demand satisfactions reminiscent of the ones once provided by religion." For them Tibetan Buddhism held the promise of something quite out of the ordinary. That Tibetan Buddhism presented a dogma-free alternative full of stimulating metaphysical concepts, with the freedom to argue, and yet retained its exotic value was a very powerful draw. Here was an Eastern philosophy that came with the label "theology-free," and for the renegades and rebels of the era that was an irresistible appeal. The early lamas were quick to recognize the pervasive thirst for something different among a class of Americans who were smart, intelligent, and culturally influential. What they offered was a version of Tibetan Buddhism that was easy to understand and did not demand the regimentation of the monastic life.

By the time the Dalai Lama paid his first visit to the States, the lamas who preceded him had already laid the ground for him. The difference between him and his predecessors was that he carried with him the enormous sanctity enshrined in his person by the centuries-old institution of the Dalai Lama. When Rutgers University announced it was hosting his lecture titled "Peace, War and Reconciliation," on September 25, 2005, a virtual scramble ensued to book tickets for the event. Weeks before the event the university had sold more than 25,000 tickets for his appearance at Rutgers Stadium, which seats 41,000.

Popular British actor and travel show host Michael Palin summed up what most people feel about the Dalai Lama's appeal: "What struck me most of all was how delightfully easy and comfortable we all felt even though he is a charismatic man with a charisma without condescension. He is also an authoritative man with an authority without intimidation. These things rarely come together. People in positions of power usually want to let you know where their power lies and that you must respect them. This didn't seem to enter into him . . . He has a tremendous sense of humor," said Palin, whose travel programs, including *Pole to Pole* and *Around the World in 80 Days*, enjoy a cult following worldwide, and who was also part of the Monty Python group.

"In my travels I have come to the conclusion that his view of the world is the view that I also share. The natural order of the man is not conflict, it is not aggression, and it is not the desire to fight. It is actually the desire to understand, compassion for others, and simply empathy for others, which he amply embodies. I think His Holiness really embodies the other way of looking at things—that the pursuit of happiness is important, gentleness is important," said Michael Palin, adding that "empathy for our fellow human beings is the only way we are actually going to survive in this world, and it is the only way forward."

22

SEX, SEXUALITY, HOMOSEXUALITY, AND CELIBACY

"Sex" is a nine-letter word in Buddhism—it is spelled *sublimate.* The vow of poverty and the vow of celibacy are two pillars of Tibetan Buddhism. Celibacy was chosen for the Dalai Lama even before he knew anything about human physiognomy. He had no say in the matter. By the time he reached puberty his life was so completely taken over by affairs of the state and religion that he had no time to discuss more intimate questions that a boy that age would naturally have.

Tibetan Buddhism is perhaps the only major faith where celibacy is enforced on monks from childhood.

I asked him if in his younger days he thought about sex. "Like a normal man I too was curious about sex. Of course, I took the vow of celibacy. Once you do that you learn to sublimate your desires," he said.

"My role as the Dalai Lama does not allow me time or opportunity to think about sex, let alone consider my own sexual desires. Sex is often a result of an idle mind. Of course, in my, what you might call, more manly years I too could have strayed but I managed not to," he said.

Did he think about sex in private moments? "I am a curious person. I am sure I did but that was a long time ago. Besides my training as a monk has prepared me not to be distracted by it," he said.

While celibacy is a cherished virtue and a requirement for Buddhist monks, Buddhism does not consider sex to be a sin. It merely considers it an obstacle to the pursuit of spiritual goals. "I do not believe in sins the way many other religions do. Sex is most certainly not a sin even if I believed in sins. It is a natural aspect of life. Most people enjoy it. Some, like me, choose not to pursue such pleasures," he said.

Why are Buddhist monks required to be celibate? "I think the insistence on celibacy comes from the idea that sex can lead to an attachment to another person and even children and that does not work for monastic life. When you have chosen to be a monk, to serve other people, it is important that you are not distracted by personal attachments. The insistence on celibacy is not because Buddhism considers sex a sin, but it is in the light of the consequences of sex," the Dalai Lama explained.

The Dalai Lama has quite obviously grappled with the question of homosexuality and has had to cultivate a response that is not in line with the almost conditioned response of rejection by other Buddhist monks who condemn it outright. Asked for his view, he replied deliberately and with nuance. "It certainly does not produce another human being but does that make it wrong? I don't know. I see it as another way of seeking physical pleasure."

Does he think homosexuality is against nature or does he think it is deviant behavior? "As I said it is another way of seeking physical pleasure. Can seeking pleasure be against nature? It is not for me to define what another person's physical pleasure should be," he said.

During one of his visits to the United States he was asked about his views on homosexuality. At first he condemned it and then he said something that he reiterated in my interviews. "If the two people have taken no vows [of chastity], and neither is harmed," he said, "why should it not be acceptable?" Coming from a Buddhist monk this answer is as revolutionary as the pope supporting abortion rights. Clearly though, the Dalai Lama has not resolved vis-à-vis his private world where he really stands on the subject, even though he has outwardly accepted homosexuality as a preference that some people make. His approach to homosexuality has been that of the path of least resistance. He does not seem entirely convinced about it, but he is understanding enough not to demonize it or view it as ungodly. He is not judgmental about it, although in his early years it is possible that he was raised to reject the practice if not condemn it altogether.

Asked whether he has missed out on physical pleasures, he said, "I do not think about those subjects. It is very possible that I would have enjoyed physical pleasures, but the fact is that I chose not to pursue them. It has worked for me. It may not work for everyone."

The subject of if and how young men who join the Sangha really manage to sublimate their desires has not been seriously studied. It is quite likely that there are tensions that arise when one curbs a powerful natural urge. Many young monks in McLeod Ganj, most of them in their late teens and early twenties, said the regimen of their life in the monastery was strict enough for them not to stray. However, some of them did concede that they had been tempted to compromise on celibacy. One young monk, who did not want to be named, said, "I know I will never be a Dalai Lama. His Holiness talks about being an ordinary monk. We all know that is not true at all. Someone like me is an ordinary monk. I admit that I am tempted from time to time but I somehow fight it off. I am interested in Buddhist studies but celibacy is not so important." Another monk had somewhat more adventurous views. "It is time for the Sangha to accept that you don't have to be a celibate to be a Buddhist monk. How can you proscribe something that brings you into this world in the first place? Would there be Buddhism without the Buddha? And would there be the Buddha if his parents were celibate? I really wonder." Such views are not widespread. If they are, they are certainly not articulated this easily. Both of the young monks I spoke with had recently joined the Sangha and were understandably overwhelmed by the demands of their new life.

Related to the question of celibacy in Buddhism is the rather sparse presence of women in monastic life. "It is an individual choice. There is no bar on women joining the Sangha. Women are treated as equal to men and in many ways are even superior to men," the Dalai Lama said.

"From the standpoint of the highest levels of Buddhist traditions, the highest yoga Tantra, there is no distinction between the two. There are some points such as when a man looks down upon a woman, there is bound to be his downfall. But when a woman looks down upon a man it is not necessary that there will be a downfall for that woman. That often makes men envious, what you call jealous, you see," he said.

An interesting aspect of interviewing the Dalai Lama is that his aides instruct you to ask any question without any inhibition. "His Holiness likes to be grilled. He enjoys tough questions. That keeps his brain sharp," his private secretary, Tenzin Geyche Tethong, said. So I asked the Dalai Lama if women ever made a pass at him. "If they did, I did not know. I do not look at a fellow human being in sexual terms or physical terms," he said.

Of interpersonal human relationships, he said, "I see two types of relationships. One is based on sexual or physical attraction where the primary motive is physical gratification. I do not bring any judgment to bear on such relationships, but they are essentially between two objects. The second type is not predominantly physical or sexual but based on deeper appreciation for each other's qualities and attributes. Such relationships work better because they are free from the tensions of physical attraction."

Do Dalai Lamas strike up personal friendships? "Sure, I have many friends all over the world. I do not believe in protocol. I believe in love and compassion. My friendships are generally without expectations. There are many great friends from whom I have learned a great deal," he said.

23

THE LAST
DALAI LAMA?

There is a popular Tibetan prophecy that says there will be seventeen Dalai Lamas. After the seventeenth the institution would either end or it would no longer be necessary for a Dalai Lama to exist. Notwithstanding the prophecy, Tenzin Gyatso is seen by many as possibly the last Dalai Lama. The fact that according to the Tibetan belief system it is entirely up to him whether to reincarnate or not does not stem the tide of speculations over what might become of one of the world's most mystifying traditions.

The Dalai Lama himself is quite ambiguous on this debate. His ambiguity is understandable given that the debate goes to the very heart of Tibetan Buddhism and in many ways any conclusions that are arrived at could determine the very survival of the Tibetan cause. Over the centuries the Dalai Lamas have been viewed as the embodiment of everything Tibetan. Quite paradoxically the Fourteenth Dalai Lama has come to embody Tibet even more than any of his predecessors despite the fact that he has operated in a modern context, lived outside his homeland for the better part of his life, and held genuine belief in democracy and in minimizing his own role in Tibetan government. It is hard to prove or disprove whether all the stories surrounding the near magical process of discovering the Dalai Lamas are in fact true or are cleverly crafted myths used primarily to lend the person of the Dalai Lama the weight of mysticism that would help him control an ancient land of guileless people. Although the establishment surrounding the Dalai Lama did represent enormous financial, territorial, cultural, political, and religious power, those were not the real reasons that the Tibetan elite perpetuated the institution of the Dalai Lama for centuries. Certainly, those were compelling enough arguments in favor of perpetuating the Dalai Lamas. But more than those, the institution was the result of a genuine belief among ordinary Tibetan people that several aspects of the Buddha reincarnate in different people. If the Dalai Lama ended up having unassailable authority as a result of those beliefs, it was considered merely an unintended consequence. Since the Dalai Lamas have traditionally been discovered in sections of Tibetan society

far removed from the elite, there is some case to be made in favor
of the argument that the institution is not an altogether cynical
ploy created by the elite to perpetuate their rule through a proxy.

A very senior Tibetan official, who bound me to the condition
of not revealing his name, said, "On the face of it the mystery surrounding the Dalai Lamas seems like a device to hoodwink the innocent people of Tibet. In fact, the Chinese believe that the Dalai
Lamas are nothing but clever manipulators and scamsters aided by
the power-hungry elite to rule over Tibet without giving them any
chance to experience democracy. But as you begin to scrutinize
[the institution of the Dalai Lama] more carefully, you realize that
it is anything but that. A majority of the Dalai Lamas has been
quite devoid of any lust for power. In the case of the current one
it can be said without any exaggeration that he would have walked
away from his formal position a long time ago. Unfortunately for
him, because he is the most recognizable face of the Tibetan cause
he is not permitted the luxury of indifference to the details of formal power. I can say without any risk of contradiction that the
Fourteenth Dalai Lama is the most democratic Dalai Lama in
history. He has no interest in formal power, nor in control of any
sort."

For Thubten Jigme Norbu, the debate on whether his younger
brother is the last Dalai Lama is irrelevant. "I don't think so. That
will depend on Tibet. If it is up to Tibet and Tibetans, it is guar-
anteed that he is not the last Dalai Lama. If there is Tibet, there
must be a Dalai Lama," he said.

One December morning, after he had finished his meditation
and Buddhist studies, I sat down with Tenzin Gyatso to discuss
whether he believes he could be the last Dalai Lama. I was told he
had been awake since three in the morning, often his usual time to

get up and start the day. He looked as fresh as the flowers in his courtyard. By the time I met him at 9 a.m. he had already put in six hours of intense work. "You see, the Dalai Lamas reincarnate for a specific purpose. As long as sentient beings need them they come back. So you see it is an open question," he said in response to my question.

Many people fear that his death would essentially end the Tibetan struggle since the next Dalai Lama would take quite some time to rise in stature and influence. "There are ways out of this. You see the next Dalai Lama can be named in my lifetime." The importance of that statement in the limited context of Tibet and Tibetans is enormous. It is the equivalent of the pope resigning in his lifetime to make way for a successor. What he said implied a break in the mystical tradition of finding reincarnate Dalai Lamas. "It does, but the cause is larger than the person of the Dalai Lama. I am sure there are many worthy leaders around," he said.

"If I were to die now I have told the Tibetan people it is up to them to decide whether they want another reincarnation. If they do, it will happen. If they believe there is no need for the Fifteenth Dalai Lama, then it will not happen. Reincarnation is about continuing your work from the previous life. If they think my work is important and relevant, I will reincarnate."

Must the Dalai Lama reincarnate as a man? "It can be a woman or a man. The institution of the Dalai Lama must change according to the times," he said.

He said he did not have any successor in mind. "I have not. I am still quite young but you see, death does not respect age," he said.

Although the prospects of the Dalai Lama returning to Tibet in his lifetime seem bleak at their best, I asked him how in his

judgment the institution of the Dalai Lama would change if he
were allowed to return and were granted a role within an autonomous set-up. "I have always said I want to devote my life to
Buddhist studies and remain a simple monk. If an autonomous
Tibet becomes a reality, I would like to disengage from secular duties. I am not interested in political power. I am not interested in
power. Tibetans are very capable people. I would like to make myself available in any role that they choose for me."

We then went on to discuss death and whether he thought
about it. "Not particularly. Death is a part of life. Death is inevitable. Thinking about it does not change that reality. It is no use
being anxious about death. Dying in a way is like casting off or
changing old clothes."

Does he fear death? "Why should we fear something that is inevitable and part of our life? Calmness is the answer to death. The
calmer you are closer to your end, the easier it would be."

He had an interesting explanation of why many people fear
death. "People fear death because they think they are going into
something unknown. They fear death because they have to leave
their attachments behind. They fear death because they think it is
painful. It is true that the process leading to death can be often
painful, but death itself is not painful. We become anxious about
death because we do not know when it might happen or where or
how. Death is an extremely important experience because the state
of our mind at the time of death can decide the quality of our future rebirth," he said.

The belief in reincarnation always intrigued me from the
standpoint of death. If one reincarnates, one does not really die.
I asked him if he had a sense of death from his previous lives. Of
course, he laughed first. "Reincarnation works at several levels. It

is not as if one reincarnates fully as the last person. There are aspects of that person you reincarnate as. I do not claim any supernatural powers. I do not have any supernatural powers. I have fleeting memories of the past that come and go."

Reincarnation poses another question. Does it make the one who reincarnates feel invincible? "No one is invincible," he said. "The human body is not invincible. Everybody grows old and everybody eventually dies. I face the same physical challenges that you do. The other day I had an intense stomachache. Some time ago I had conjunctivitis. I fall ill as well."

A large number of skeptics who want to support the cause of Tibet on the ground of historical fairness feel awkward throwing their lot behind a tradition of reincarnation. They believe reincarnation is improbable and are disinclined to support a cause that has at its heart a belief system that is so fantastic and bizarre. "There are so many things in this universe that we find hard to accept. Treat reincarnation as one of them. It is not for me to convince the world whether reincarnation is real or not. That does not influence basic human qualities such as love and compassion. You do not have to believe or disbelieve in reincarnation to believe in love and compassion. And also in the reality of Chinese annexation of Tibet. Nothing is bizarre in this world," he said.

I asked him if he has specific memories of his previous births. "It is never specific, although there are times when I have a strong sense of having been here before. I do not think much about these things," he said.

It is widely believed that at this stage of his life—the Dalai Lama turned seventy-one on July 6, 2006—China is waging a battle of attrition against him and the cause. The Dalai Lama knows that the nation of China will far outlast any individual life. The

Chinese strategy seems to be to wait for the Dalai Lama to pass away. Those who support this way of thinking argue that once the current Dalai Lama dies, the Tibetan cause as it is understood and espoused by many in the West will also die. Somehow the flawed notion that Tibet is the Dalai Lama and the Dalai Lama is Tibet has gained so much currency in the last decade that many well-meaning supporters have not bothered to look beyond Tenzin Gyatso or the institution of the Dalai Lama. The Dalai Lama himself is acutely aware of this weakness and has done everything he can to promote the cause rather than the person. But his compelling personality and all the exotica that come with being a reincarnate "living Buddha" often overshadow the substance of the larger issue of Tibet. In a sense the Dalai Lama no longer remains just a powerful figure of reverence and inspiration for the Tibetan people. He has gone far beyond that narrow definition and has emerged as a voice of sanity for the entire world. That stature is a double-edged sword.

While it helps enormously in keeping the issue alive, it also distracts attention from the Tibetan cause since he is no longer seen as belonging to just one cause.

As the world grapples with profound questions of faith and belief and as the world worries about the clash of civilizations, the Dalai Lama's message of love and compassion comes across as un-encumbered by any religious dogma. In his own mind the Dalai Lama makes no distinction between his struggle for justice in Tibet and his message for the rest of the world. He believes that those who are fascinated by what he has to say about life automatically enlist themselves in support of the Tibetan cause. "Tibet is not just about being an independent country. It is about a valuable belief system that is being destroyed by China. So when you support what I have to say you also support that belief system and therefore Tibet," he said. He is very aware that Tibet is not just an esoteric idea but a real, geographical entity with real people with real problems.

"For him one of the biggest challenges has been how to ensure that the outside world, particularly the West, does not lose sight of the Tibetan people's very real problems. For us there is nothing exotic about our way of life. It is not a fad. It is an everyday reality. Ordinary Tibetan people's human rights and freedoms have been routinely violated for no reason other than that they believe in something different from what the Chinese believe. To know that Lhasa is no longer Tibetan but Han Chinese is such a devastating thought for us. While His Holiness's celebrity helps a great deal, it can also deceive the Westerners into thinking that everything is fine with our world. It is not. His Holiness is deeply concerned about that," Tempa Tsering, his brother-in-law, said.

Notwithstanding the irony of that thought, he said that the Dalai Lama remains the "most potent weapon" for the Tibetans inside and outside Tibet. "Whether Tenzin Gyatso is the last Dalai Lama or there will be more is not nearly as important as having such a potent symbol for us. He does not just articulate the Tibetan people's problems; he speaks of an alternative to a world order that creates problems such as Tibet. If you follow his philosophy to its logical conclusion you would realize that most political and religious conflicts in the world would cease," Tsering said.

24

TWILIGHT YEARS

The Dalai Lama has entered the outskirts of the twilight of his life. While age may be irrelevant to anyone believing in the mystical reincarnation of the Dalai Lamas, Tenzin Gyatso's advancing years are fraught with serious practical implications for the future of Tibet. The fact that he embodies everything that is lofty and powerful about the cause of Tibet has been the single most decisive factor in keeping the issue alive throughout the latter part of the twentieth century. Yet such an indistinguishable merger of the cause and the leader may not help the future of Tibet in the long term. If anything, it significantly compromises Tibetans' ability to negotiate and resolve the dispute in a manner that he would approve and they would find acceptable.

There are strong and diverse views among the supporters of the Tibetan cause on how to resolve the seemingly intractable dispute, but those of four very eminent men are compelling enough to be featured in this book. During the course of the research for this biography I met over two hundred people in India and the United States. Thubten Jigme Norbu, the elder brother of the Dalai Lama and the first incarnate lama in the family who went on to become the abbot of the powerful Kumbum monastery; Professor Robert Thurman, one of the most eminent scholars of Tibetan Buddhism, a personal friend of the Dalai Lama, his most vocal advocate, and the first American to be ordained a Buddhist monk; Dr. Orville Schell, one of the world's foremost China and Tibet scholars; and Richard Gere, Hollywood star and genuine student of Tibetan Buddhism constitute a highly eclectic group of people who have been influential players in the cause. Between Norbu, Professor Thurman, Dr. Schell, and Gere they represent a diversity of views with one common thread—a deep concern for the future of Tibet. While Norbu's lifelong association with the cause is natural and in some ways inevitable, the other three personalities have remained wedded to Tibet out of a sense of deep conviction, although they have no personal stake in the future of Tibet other than the calling of their conscience.

In 1926, at the age of four, he was chosen as the reincarnation of an important lama by the prestigious Kumbum monastery in the province of Amdo. The simple peasant family of Thubten Jigme Norbu was more than pleased that there was a tulku in their family. Little did they know that about a decade later they would be blessed with the ultimate reincarnation.

As the elder brother of the Dalai Lama, Norbu has learned to live in his brother's shadow without a trace of sibling rivalry or jealousy despite his own considerable accomplishments, including becoming the abbot of the Kumbum monastery in his twenties. The age gap of thirteen years between Norbu and his brother gave Norbu the distance necessary to deal with such an enormous presence in the family's midst.

Unlike his brother the Dalai Lama, Norbu believes that the status of Tibet is strictly nonnegotiable. At the same time he knows that the Dalai Lama has overwhelming forces of history to balance when he deals with the over-five-decades-old dispute.

Having lived more than fifty of his eighty-four years outside Tibet, Norbu may have come to terms with the loss of his homeland, but he has certainly not let the pain of having been dislodged from his roots die.

Norbu believes that the autonomy of Tibet within China is not the solution. "No, I do not, but I also know that you cannot get anything more from the Chinese. The status of Tibet must be Tibet, nothing else. If we don't achieve that I think in the future there will be no Tibetans in Tibet. Period. In two generations there will be no Tibetans in Tibet. See what is happening in Inner Mongolia. There are four million Mongols but you cannot find ten Mongols together in the capital," he said.

While the Dalai Lama says he remains optimistic about Tibet and believes ordinary Chinese people's wish for democracy would eventually help resolve the Tibetan dispute, Norbu equivocates. "At this moment I cannot say anything. Only a few Chinese out of a billion say that [they want democracy]. I am not confident about that."

He believes India's role remains crucial. "India should recognize His Holiness's government. That is crucial. That will help. Once that happens then the situation will change. Doors will open up," he said.

What about the United States? "I don't think the United States can do anything because the United States is interested in green paper [dollars] and how much Mr. Coffee they can sell. They are not concerned with Tibetans' suffering. They are concerned with trade," he said. Having dealt with the Americans for fifty years, including a few years spent helping the Central Intelligence Agency mount an armed uprising in Tibet in the 1950s, Norbu's pessimism about the U.S. role is surprising.

Asked if he thinks an armed uprising can help, Norbu said, "One billion Chinese, six million Tibetans—what can anyone do? Even if the Chinese say come cut our throats, who is going to do that? The Tibetans will get tired and the Chinese will still be there." Nevertheless Norbu still maintains that the Tibetan people must ask China to leave Tibet.

A sense of resignation seems to have taken over Norbu's mind. Asked if he would like to visit Lhasa, he said, "No, what for? I went in 1980. I regret that. What would one do there? The Chinese do not let you move around freely. The few Tibetans who meet you cry about the state of affairs. I am a human being. I feel a lot of pain."

If the Chinese were to offer Tibetans a deal under which Tibet's identity would be preserved, would Norbu accept living within China? "If the Tibetan people rule themselves it is fine. If the Chinese are the masters then it is a joke," he said.

A lot of supporters of Tibet's independence have been at a loss to understand why some 500 million Buddhists around the world are not openly supporting freedom for Tibet. "We do not have good contact with fellow Buddhists. It is possible that together they might help if we tried," Norbu said.

Norbu said he is aware of a growing movement among Tibetans against the Dalai Lama's middle-path approach. He also knows that his brother is unlikely to waver from his position. "I don't think so. I asked him what the middle path or the middle way is. You might talk about it in philosophical terms but when it comes to the status of Tibet, how do you argue the middle path? But then this is his way and we must respect that. He is not an ordinary man like me."

Asked if he was hopeful about Tibetan culture hundred years from now, he said, "If Tibet is kept as Tibet its culture will survive. If Tibet does not become independent and Tibetan culture has to be preserved outside then it will probably become like a museum. There will be stories like once upon a time an old man who lived here built such and such museum."

Norbu also counts on the Tibetans inside Tibet to precipitate a crisis to resolve the issue. "Tibetans are a very peaceful people. However they must see that the Chinese in Tibet are not very comfortable. They should not buy Chinese goods. They should ask the Chinese to leave Tibet on a regular basis. Tibetans will never say they are one with the Chinese," he said.

Asked what would have happened had the Dalai Lama stayed on in Tibet despite the Chinese invasion, Norbu said, "The Chinese had already said they would wipe out everything in five years. Perhaps he too would have been wiped out. Probably he would have been put under house arrest. They would have said come and live in Beijing and not Lhasa."

Does Norbu support the Dalai Lama's return to Tibet? "It is unrealistic for him to return like that. You never know what his presence in Tibet could do. It would electrify the Tibetan people and traumatize the Chinese."

D r. Orville Schell has a benign professorial bearing that restores one's faith in the noble profession of teaching. As a leading scholar of Chinese history and Tibet, Schell could be forgiven a little bit of vanity, but dealing with one of the world's greatest ancient civilizations has given him a sense of detachment from his personal accomplishments.

An author of fourteen highly regarded books and scores of important essays and articles, an advisor on Emmy Award–winning documentaries, and dean of the Graduate School of Journalism at Berkeley, Schell chooses to conduct himself with a great deal of self-effacement.

He described the Tibet issue as "relatively quiescent" and apprehends that it could well become irrelevant. In a wide-ranging interview he discussed the leadership of the Dalai Lama, the future of the institution of the Dalai Lama, and the narrowing options before him.

"I would have to say that hope has sprung eternal on this question. The last two delegations by Lodi Gyari [the Dalai Lama's special envoy] to China raised some hope and expectations, but having watched this for a very long time it is very unclear whether this means any major movement or a shift in China's attitude toward Tibet. In many ways the subjects of Taiwan and Tibet are as frozen as any issue that China confronts and it's a shame and counterintuitive that it should be so because in actuality both these problems can be solved very simply without any deleterious effect to either side, in fact to a great positive effect. I think China's strategy very often is to yield a little bit here or a little bit there but not to actually make major shifts on issues like these. So I am not optimistic that we are a whole lot closer now than we were ten, fifteen, twenty years ago. We may have been much closer in the early 1980s," Schell said.

Asked if he thought China is waging a battle of attrition, essentially waiting for the Dalai Lama to die, he said, "The trouble with the system that China now has is that it is very difficult to move in a deliberate and radically new way on anything. The whole path of reform has been a tiny little piecemeal experiment that has become the de facto reality. In a certain sense the problem with Tibet is more symbolic than real, a little bit like Taiwan. So it is harder for China to move symbolically to clear major policy shifts and easier to move on piecemeal practical questions. I don't think this leadership feels capable of making such a shift. It is one of the great mysteries of China's political system how resistant it is to fundamental change and less resistant to superficial changes, which in aggregate add up often into something major, but that's not Tibet's problem. So they are hoping that the Dalai Lama would simply die. What they fail to appreciate, however, is that he is their best hope to bring about some sort of reconciliation and to keep Tibet peacefully within the sovereign boundaries of China. They don't fully understand the negative consequence of what they are doing to themselves."

The death of the Dalai Lama at this stage could mean two things. "There are two consequences. When he dies no one will replace him that we can see. He is a person very high on the periodic table of leadership. I do think that the entire movement will have a very difficult time staying together. On the other hand it is possible that things could blow up in Tibet at some point and there will be no one to calm it down. This is one of the great roles he could play before such a thing happens," Schell said.

On the possibility of the Dalai Lama's anointing a successor in his lifetime, he said, "It is possible but it is a long shot. However, it is not going to have the mystery of ritual credentials that this Dalai Lama has as a result of the old system in Tibetan society. Apart from the force of his own personality this whole mythology of reincarnation is very powerful for people outside of China."

As a conflict in terms of its global significance, he said, "You never know when these things blow up, if the economic situation in China takes a bad turn or something like that. Right now though, it is not a major international issue. But it is a major international moral issue. So there is great capital for China to win by doing the right thing on that front. I don't think it is going to lose all that much by continuing the status quo which is exactly the dilemma that the Dalai Lama finds himself in. There is no place to get a finger hole in a new way. He wants to talk. They don't want to talk. End of story."

The inherent pacifism of Buddhism precludes violence as an instrument of change. "Buddhists are never capable of fighting against Leninists from a distance. I mean fight in a nonviolent way against the forces of violent repression by China the way it happened in India under Gandhi against the British colonial rulers, but they will never allow a force like Gandhi to emerge in Tibet. Buddhism and all the Dalai Lama represents is ill equipped to deal with the kind of controlled society that China specializes in, and that marginalizes the Dalai Lama's government-in-exile. On the other hand one would be loath seeing [the Dalai Lama] change in a sense that he would become a Leninist who believes that the end justifies the means. That is exactly the problem that China confronts. To play their game is to be defeated and not to play their game is losing as well. Here the lack of international resonance is also not helping," Schell said.

The inevitable question of what the Dalai Lama's options are prompted a mixed response. "The Dalai Lama has done as good a job as he possibly could given the parameters of his own principles. It's the paradox of life that sometimes might trumps principles and morality. One wishes it were otherwise but it isn't always. I can't think what else he can do. In many ways he is an exemplar of absolutely the opposite of what China is all about. The problem is that China has so polluted itself with its own propaganda in regard to Tibet and Taiwan that it is very hard for [China] to think in a very revolutionary way and solve Tibet, something we can do in five minutes. Nothing would be lost and everything would be gained. China would become a truly great power in the eyes of the world, cosmopolitan, sophisticated, which might be emulated in ways that even the United States cannot be emulated."

The solution, he said, is for the Dalai Lama to go back. "Let the Dalai Lama go back as a cultural figure, given real political autonomy. Defense and foreign policy can be in Chinese hands. Do experiments the way Canada does with Quebec or the way Britain does with Scotland. This will have a very salutary effect on Hong

Kong and Taiwan. It could do a one country, two systems that is real."

Schell sent this proposal to the standing committee of China's politburo. He said he knows for a fact that its translation was distributed among the higher-ups in the party. "I think they know it but there is something blocking the way, probably the military. We don't really know the conservatizing effect and power of whole blocks of Chinese institutional society, the security bureau, the People's Liberation Army, the party, and so on. I think people are aware of this but evidently no leader or block of leaders feels compelled or strong enough to launch a new policy initiative," he said.

As things stand now Schell agrees that it is a dead end. "Yes, but you never know. Look at what happened to Eastern Europe or Russia. I don't think China is right now going to implement a well-ordered, well-articulated reform program with the goal of making Tibet a more autonomous or independent entity with the Dalai Lama playing some considerable symbolic role. They are going to pass out little scraps to a few delegations here and a few delegations there. That keeps everybody quiet and shuts everybody up and it keeps the status quo."

In Schell's assessment the question of Tibet is not territorial but psychological. "It is certainly not economic. To a minor extent they imagine it being strategically important. I think it has to do with the humiliation of China being dismembered in the nineteenth century. There is no reason for the Communist Party to govern unilaterally other than for nationalistic reasons. Communism is dead. It is a Leninist form of capitalism. It is their one claim to fame and to continue on this one-party system is what has made China whole. Tibet is a very important piece of it," he said.

I suggested that perhaps the Dalai Lama could do something radical like showing up in Lhasa surreptitiously, the way he had left it in 1959. "It is an exciting idea, almost like a Hollywood movie. I am sure he would laugh his deep-throated chuckle at the idea. Although doing something like that does not sound like him, I cannot say it would not delight me if he did something like that. He is not that kind of person. He is not a provoker. But then that is about the only thing he could do—something utterly shocking. Maybe hop on a horse and go the same way he came out. Right now he plods around the world doing events for fawning Westerners. They love his spiritual cuddly side and he feels powerless to help his own people," he said.

As the Dalai Lama's exile has become stretched to several decades the institution itself could come under strain. On its future Schell sounds pessimistic. "I don't see how it will work in the context of his life in exile. The truth is that there is a receptor side within Tibet which is very worshipful and devout. I think it would be very very hard to continue, and the Chinese know this. That's a tragedy. They don't quite understand that it is a loss to them. It could be a loss to them in terms of their ability to make something commendable out of Tibet."

It is hard to decide whether Robert Thurman is an academic with a monk's soul or a monk with an academic's intellect. Widely regarded as one of the world's most respected scholars of the Tibetan and Sanskrit languages, he was ordained a Buddhist monk in 1964 by the Dalai Lama. About one and half years later he gave up the life of a novice and returned to the world of academia "because in that position I could not expect to teach people since as an American Buddhist monk, and perhaps the first one to be so ordained, I was seen as somehow defective, a bit of an oddity.

"Even today, when the cause of Tibet generally and the Dalai Lama particularly is so well known, there is no real understanding of the position of a monk in a Western society," Thurman said in an interview. During his visit to McLeod Ganj in August 1997 I too happened to be in town. Thurman was then working on a documentary and was traveling with a group of people, many of them in complete awe of him. [The Dalai Lama's] secretariat suggested that I speak to Professor Thurman. Thurman's minder looked at me quizzically and after some rumination said, spreading his four fingers and thumb like a fan, "Five minutes. That's all he can grant you. It could be pretty late tonight. Shall we say 11 p.m. in the coffee shop?"

The coffee shop in question was at Hotel Surya—barely thirty feet away from the edge of the steeply declining mountain it sat on—where both Thurman and I were staying. It is a hotel from whose windows you can see the Dalai Lama's official bungalow with some effort. That night I quickly discovered that the good professor himself was nowhere near as self-absorbed as his staff had projected him to be. If anything, he was professorial in a monkish sort of way—curious to engage his interlocutors but not too worried whether he would convince them as to his point of view. The five minutes stretched to a good hour and a half. We spoke about a wide range of subjects, from the future of Tibet to Buddhism and why he gave up the life of a renunciate.

We began with his views on whether the Tibet of the Dalai Lama's vision could be realized through his nonviolent campaign. "It must be realized through a nonviolent campaign. The Dalai Lama says, and I agree with him one hundred percent, the only

way to peace is peace. In the Indian context he is following the tradition of Mahatma Gandhi and in the U.S. context Martin Luther
King. While Gandhi and King operated within their own nations,
the Dalai Lama has charted a new territory. Since he is not in his
own homeland and is in exile, he is doing it in the international
context.

"Very much like the ridicule that Gandhi faced from the
British or King faced from many in America, the Dalai Lama's
steadfast insistence on pursuing nonviolent ways too has been
laughed at by many like Henry Kissinger or Deng Xiaoping. However, I think that is the right way to go," Thurman said.

Thurman believes that the Dalai Lama is in a "unique" position, unlike other comparable religious or spiritual leaders, to
change the way the world thinks and operates. "Most religious
and spiritual leaders do demand that we accept their way of life as
the only way of life. The Dalai Lama does not. What he offers is
something so basic and yet so profound. Love and compassion are
not the preserves of a particular religious philosophy. You don't
have to be a Buddhist or even religious to practice what he talks
about," he said.

While it is important for the world as a whole that the question of Tibet is resolved in accordance with the wishes of the
Dalai Lama and Tibet, Thurman said what the Dalai Lama stands
for is of great value outside Tibet as well. "Of course, China needs
to urgently settle the issue. His Holiness has now lived the better
part of his life outside the land he is so attached to. However, it
is equally important to recognize that the Dalai Lama now is a
man of international consequence. What he stands for is good not
just for Tibet but for the rest of the world," he said.

Thurman also sees great merit in the basic principles of Tibetan Buddhism and its relevance to the non-Buddhist world. "Tibetan culture is based on a set of principles from the heart of the Buddha's movement—individualism, nonviolence, educationalism, altruism, and egalitarianism. All this is worthy of preservation not just for the sake of Tibet but for the sake of the rest of the world," he said.

In his book *Inner Revolution: Life, Liberty, and the Pursuit of Real Happiness*, Thurman writes: "The tradition of nonviolence, optimism, concern for the individual, and unconditional compassion that developed in Tibet is the culmination of a slow inner revolution, a cool one, hard to see, that began 2,500 years ago with the Buddha's insight about the end of suffering. What I have learned from these people has forever changed my life, and I believe their culture contains an inner science particularly relevant to the difficult time in which we live."

Thurman said that Tibet was not an individual nation-state question but something that goes far beyond that. "It is not about a people yearning for freedom from an invading state. It is about a very valuable society struggling to keep its centuries-old tradition of intellectual evolution alive." He said that while he was hopeful that the problem would be resolved soon, "and during His Holiness's lifetime," it was hard to put a time frame to it.

McLeod Ganj is a sort of wannabe Tibet. In the town's two-street bazaar chances are that Hollywood star Richard Gere would walk past you unobtrusively.

Gere, who is among the most high profile supporters of Tibet and a keen student of Tibetan Buddhism, visits here every year for about three weeks to continue with his "learning of the soul."

Since his first meeting with the Dalai Lama in 1982, he has become the most vocal Hollywood campaigner against the Chinese "repression and genocide" in Tibet and the "systematic annihilation" of its people and culture. He holds forth on Tibet and Tibetans passionately and upholds India as Tibet's "best friend" in the world.

Gere spoke to me in an interview at Kashmir Cottage, the residence of the Dalai Lama's younger brother overlooking endless miles of pine trees enveloping the pre-Himalayan Dhauladhar mountains.

Gere's attraction to the Tibetan cause came by way of Tibetan Buddhism. He said he was attracted to it by its "fearlessness." "You are not afraid of questioning anything in Buddhism. Most philosophical systems start with a series of givens and build an argument on that. In Buddhism there are no givens. That is the only way you can find the root ground of consciousness. It is a very practical system which is emotionally and intellectually sound. It speaks to all ages. It speaks the basic truth about the mind."

He said he espouses Tibet because it is "a valid cause." "They are people who need friends. There are very few people who stand up for the Tibetans. The movement has been nonviolent. I think all nonviolent movements should be supported in all possible ways. There is repression and genocide taking place there. Those who have access to the media should talk about it," he said.

Gere first met the Dalai Lama in 1982 in Dharamshala. "I had been a student of Zen Buddhism before that. I did not know much about Tibetan forms at all. I was very nervous about meeting him. But he made me feel comfortable at once. That is the sign of a great and humble man. He introduced himself as an ordinary human being and nothing else. He did not know who I was, but

his brother had told him I was an actor. He asked me when I act
angry in movies, do I actually feel angry or when I act [as if I am]
crying do I actually cry. Then he told me that the illusory nature
of the emotions that an actor has is almost identical to the illusory emotions that a normal person has. He said when I fake anger
as an actor it is no different from a normal person. I know it is a
performance and you don't. That fascinated me," Gere said.

One of the frequently heard criticisms is that for Hollywood
Tibet is just a fad, one that has lasted longer than other fads but
one that will pass eventually. Asked if his involvement makes a difference in the way Tibet is perceived internationally, he said, "No,
I don't think so. It is not us but the person of His Holiness that
changes people's minds. Every time we have facilitated His Holiness's meeting with anyone, there is a change in people's minds. He
is the key. When you know you are in the presence of a great man,
a great mind, and a great soul, you can't help but be touched and
influenced."

On when he thinks the Tibet issue may be resolved, Gere said,
"I don't think there is a realistic timetable. When you are playing
with combustible situations in China, especially now, no one
knows what is going to happen. I suppose it is as combustible now
as Eastern Europe was, and as spontaneous and all-inclusive too.
No one had any idea that everything would fall apart in one year.
It is possible in China too. Unfortunately, China has seen what
happened in Eastern Europe and Russia and has guarded their situations very carefully. The military presence in Tibet is extremely
high. The control of information is extremely tight. I can't go to
Tibet anymore. I can't even transit through Beijing just because I
am a friend of Tibet's. Now am I calling for the violent overthrow
of any country? Of course not. I speak the truth and am involved

with any human rights group or any group that is looking for justice."

What does the Dalai Lama ask Gere to do for Tibet? "We talk about it constantly. We talk about what is a good strategy that would help the cause. We discuss specific things too."

25

■

GEOPOLITICS DEVOURS TIBET'S DESTINY AGAIN

Nearly five decades after he was forced to flee Tibet in the face of its annexation by China, the Dalai Lama remains as distant from an independent Tibet as he was then. He has spent the past twenty-five years touring the Western world to campaign for Tibet's independence through peaceful means. He has been courted by powerful world leaders and feted by Hollywood celebrities. He has drawn in a legion of new followers through his spiritual teachings

and bestselling books such as *The Art of Happiness.* He has even won
the Nobel Peace Prize. Yet Tibet has moved no closer to resolution—and it appears to be losing ground in its struggle.

Tibet, whose fate has for the past century been determined by
external forces, is yet again caught between major geopolitical
shifts. In the late nineteenth and early twentieth centuries, Tibet
was an unwilling and in some ways even unsuspecting part of the
Great Game played by the colonial British rulers in Central Asia.
Although the Great Game between British India and Tsarist Russia mainly focused on control of Afghanistan, which the British
saw as a stepping-stone for Russian imperial ambitions in the Indian subcontinent, the colonial rulers were quite interested in Tibet because of its strategic location.

The British interest in Tibet began in the late eighteenth century. Initially they were more interested in trade, but it was clear
to Tibetans that the British colonials typically began their expansion using trade. Many expeditions were sent to Tibet in search of
trading posts either inside its borders or along it. The most ambitious of these expeditions took place in 1903 under the colorful
imperialist Sir Francis Younghusband, who eventually escalated his
diplomatic mission to a military invasion of Tibet. The British im-
perialists, who saw themselves as natural inheritors of power in
South Asia and regions beyond, were not amused to hear a rumor
that the tsar of Russia had struck a secret deal with the rulers of
Tibet, namely the Thirteenth Dalai Lama.

In the mid-twentieth century, Tibet's destiny fell prey to Chinese machinations. Now, in the early twenty-first century, it is being decided by the growing courtship between China and India,
the world's two most populous countries with the two fastest-
growing economies. The traditionally frosty ties between the two

nations, laden with barely concealed mutual suspicions and acrimony, are rapidly making way for a cordial relationship of enormous global significance. The fact that 2006 was officially celebrated as a "Friendship Year" is a measure of how far the two Asian giants have traveled since their first war in 1962. The two countries have elevated their bilateral ties to an unprecedented economic, political, and military level, and in the process have reduced the Tibetan cause to a mere sideshow. Even at the best of times Tibet was never an issue of national foreign policy or political discourse in New Delhi, although through the decades it has always attracted considerable fringe support of the Indian intelligentsia, as well as that of Indian people generally. Now that New Delhi and Beijing are working to fundamentally alter their relationship, it is more likely that the issue of Tibet will recede further into the background. The thaw between India and China, coupled with China's ongoing efforts to remake Tibet in its own image, makes prospects for independence appear dim.

During his life in exile, the Dalai Lama has grown from a young monk in his twenties into one of the world's most compelling voices for peace. India has been the most ardent supporter of the current Dalai Lama, allowing him to form his government-in-exile on its soil. Nevertheless, India has also had to balance its own economic, territorial, and military interests in the face of a powerful Asian neighbor that is separated from India by Tibet. India's bitter memories of a humiliating defeat at the hands of China in 1962 have long lost their intensity. And the two countries have lately attempted to put their relations on an even keel, an effort driven mainly by economic interests. As the world's most populous countries, they recognize the importance of maintaining peace as they seek to be the preeminent powers in Asia.

A series of recent events, starting with the Indian prime minister's visit to China in June 2003, along with the reciprocal visit of Chinese premier Wen Jiabao in 2005, could jeopardize Tibet's struggle for independence. During Indian prime minister Atal Bihari Vajpayee's 2003 visit, India reiterated its recognition of the Tibetan Autonomous Region as a part of the People's Republic of China. On its own, that recognition would not have been considered significant. But China reciprocated by accepting the northeastern region of Sikkim as a part of India, although Sikkim has been a part of India since 1975. By April 2005 China had changed its official map to show Sikkim to be part of India. That is a very significant concession on the Chinese side in the context of strained Sino-Indian ties. The softening of mood on both sides—as so clearly underscored during the Jiabao visit—is not a happy augury for Tibet.

As long as India and China held to their stubborn positions on territorial disputes along their long-shared border, there was a chance that New Delhi could use the Dalai Lama as leverage simply because of his presence in India. Now that the two adversaries have begun to talk about disputed territories of about 12,700 square miles (20,439 kilometers) along India's northwestern border with China, chances are that the Dalai Lama's presence will no longer be seen as a bargaining chip.

In another sign of cooperation, India and China concluded their first joint military naval exercises in November 2003. This was followed by the first-ever visit of a high-level Indian army delegation to Tibet. This symbolic visit clearly signaled that both sides are willing to let bygones be bygones.

The India-China rapprochement, which gained momentum under the pro-Hindu Bharatiya Janata Party's government until

2004, has intensified under the coalition government led by the Congress Party, which came to power after parliamentary elections. This continuity underscores a national consensus about dealing with China and, in a sense, further erodes the operating space for the Tibetan government-in-exile. That India-China relations are no longer confined to just polite rhetoric between two uncomfortable neighbors was highlighted early in 2006. The leaders of the two Asian giants, which together account for more than 30 percent of the world's population, began the year 2006 by exchanging exceptionally warm pleasantries and making a pledge to consolidate what India's president A.P.J. Abdul Kalam called "the deep historical and cultural association that our two ancient civilizations have." China's response was equally sanguine, as its leaders noted the "new stage of development" with the decision to establish a Strategic and Cooperative Partnership for Peace and Prosperity and a statement that their relations were set to grow in an "all-round and in-depth way."

The geopolitical impact of a Sino-Indian embrace will be enormous for the world in general, and for the United States in particular. Although historical rough edges and strong individual ambitions to acquire global superpower status may yet prevent a seamless convergence of India and China, there is enough common ground between the two nations for them to forge a partnership that could seriously prevent the United States from running away with the global agenda. In a development unthinkable even a decade ago, the two countries have begun working together to ensure their energy security.

On December 20, 2005, their state-owned oil corporations, China National Petroleum Corporation (CNPC) and India's Oil and Natural Gas Corporation (ONGC), jointly won a bid to acquire 37 percent of Petro-Canada's stake in Syrian oilfields for $573 million.

The two rapidly rising economies' already robust and growing appetite for oil and gas is causing dramatic shifts in the world energy balance and prompting major concerns in Washington, which has for decades considered controlling global oil to be its natural right. It is hardly surprising that the Bush administration is making major concessions in its nuclear proliferation control regime to accommodate India's civilian nuclear program.

The United States has recognized that while individually China and India may not be close to challenging its supremacy, together they have enough muscle to act as a bulwark against American unilateralism resulting from its status as the singular superpower. It is in that context that the dramatic upswing in Sino-Indian relations ought to be viewed.

The warming bilateral ties between India and China, partly driven by a powerful utilitarian instinct on both sides, have been barely noticed as a story of consequence by the world media. It could not be that media commentators do not understand the significance of this development; perhaps it is because they believe that the two uncomfortable neighbors will not be able to go the distance because of the inherent suspicions and overarching ambitions—especially in China's case, since it sees itself as the next superpower.

The growing Sino-Indian collaboration is also a story that has not attracted international media attention in terms of its implications. The U.S. media has reported on how China and India are aggressively shopping around for oil fields, but has not quite covered the underlying theme of how this shift could affect the overall geopolitical balance.

"In 2006, the Chinese side is ready to work together with the Indian side to take the Year of China-India Friendship as an opportunity to carry forward the traditional friendship between our two countries; strengthen dialogues, exchanges, and cooperation in all fields and at all levels; continuously deepen the contents of the bilateral relations; and push forward the China-India Strategic and Cooperative Partnership in an all-round and in-depth way," Chinese president Hu Jintao said of the collaboration.

It is rare for the Chinese leadership at any level, let alone at the highest level, to communicate such effusive views about relations with another country. That these views are about India, China's potential rival on the world stage, a country with which it has fought a war and which is home to the Tibetan government-in-exile, makes the expression even more extraordinary.

One of the least examined consequences of the Sino-Indian rapprochement is its impact on the future of Tibet. Every step that India and China take together is a step away from Tibet's independent future. Tibet as a cause is in serious danger of losing its potency, and the growing communion between India and China is serving to erode that potency even more.

If the two countries can prospect for oil and gas together, the chances of Tibet surviving as a cause are bleak. Even though the Dalai Lama remains in good health at seventy-one, he is aware that time is not on his side. If he wants any degree of resolution of the Tibet question within his lifetime, his options are becoming increasingly narrow in view of the India-China camaraderie.

Unfortunately, in the 2006 Friendship Year between the two Asian neighbors, Tibet is unlikely to be an obstacle. The policy seems to be that neither side will talk about Tibet with any degree of seriousness or conviction. If only Tibet were sitting on as much oil as Iraq!

What began with a rhetorical flourish at the onset of 2006 had by May managed to acquire very specific and tangible gains, as made evident during a visit of India's defense minister Pranab Mukherjee, when the two nations decided to strengthen their strategic and military ties. Mukherjee and his Chinese counterpart, Gen. Cao Gangchuan, signed a memorandum of understanding (MoU) that "provides a formal basis for the defense and military exchanges that have been taking place between the two countries in the last few years." The MoU focused on the following areas:

- Holding of joint military exercises and training programs in the field of search and rescue, anti-piracy, counterterrorism, and other areas of mutual interest. Each side will invite senior military officers of the other side to witness designated military exercises.
- Frequent exchanges between the leaders and high-level functionaries of the defense ministries and the armed forces of the two countries. Both sides will work out an annual program of exchanges.
- An annual Defense Dialogue, hosted alternatively by the two sides, to review progress in the defense exchanges, make suggestions for the future, and exchange views on international, security, and strategic issues.
- Establish a mechanism of study tours for each other's senior- and middle-level officials in order to facilitate better understanding of the foreign, defense, and national development policies of the host side.

- Participation in seminars and discussions on themes to be mutually agreed upon.
- Exchanges in other mutually agreed fields to be decided through consultation.

Indian officials described the MoU as "a major confidence build-ing measure in the defense field," which will contribute toward "building up greater understanding and trust."

By the middle of the year India-China relations had acquired enough traction for India not to rock the boat by raising the issue of Tibet in any significant bilateral forum.

Indian political and diplomatic sources say that with India's economy growing at a fierce pace of 8-plus percent annually, its government has no option but to nuance and even soften some of its pet foreign policy angularities, particularly with a country like China. "Shibboleths of the twentieth century must be discarded. They are no longer current and serve no purpose. India and China have to forge long-term economic, military, and political ties. It is possible that in the process Tibet would get squeezed out. It is tragic, but the country has to put its own interests before anything else," said a senior Indian diplomat, requesting anonymity. He also said that supporting Tibet may get India some "brownie points," but overall it no longer makes sense for the country's foreign pol-icy administrators to "harp on" Tibet in every diplomatic inter-course with China.

The diplomat further cited the example of the United States, saying that the superpower, "even while making some pretty stan-dard noises about human rights and Tibet," had "seriously engaged China in a constructive relationship."

In this context, the April 2006 visit to the United States of

Chinese president Hu Jintao was fascinating. Making his first state visit to Washington, Hu quite tellingly chose to begin his engagement by first meeting with Microsoft founder Bill Gates in Seattle. He also visited the Boeing plant there. By the time he arrived in Washington, D.C., many observers say he had more or less concluded the substantive part of his visit. In this atmosphere of pragmatism and utilitarian self-interest, diplomats say it makes little sense for India to remain so wedded to Tibet that in the process it ignores unprecedented economic opportunities that arise out of engaging China.

This show of pragmatism is not just restricted to India. Even the Tibetan government-in-exile, sensitive to the delicate nature of its ongoing rounds of talks with Beijing, issued an extraordinary directive to Tibetans in the United States and elsewhere not to protest during Hu's U.S. visit: "Under the wise guidance of His Holiness the Dalai Lama's Middle-Way policy, we have been striving for a genuine autonomous status for all the Tibetan people through negotiations. This policy has been adopted democratically by the Tibetan people in and outside Tibet, as well as by the Assembly of Tibetan People's Deputies. In order to achieve this, the envoys of His Holiness the Dalai Lama have undertaken five rounds of talks with the concerned officials of the People's Republic of China since 2002. At present our effort to bring about negotiations has reached a critical stage of whether we are able to sustain it or not," the Tibetan government-in-exile said in a statement prior to the visit.

The statement made a strong appeal "with utmost importance and emphasis to all the Tibetans and Tibet Support Groups to refrain from any activities, including staging of protest demonstrations, causing embarrassment to [the Dalai Lama]." It said, "This appeal is not only to create a conducive atmosphere for negotiations but also not to cause embarrassment and difficulty to His Holiness the Dalai Lama, whose visit coincides with President Hu Jintao's visit to America. If protests are held, this will give the impression that no Tibetan or Tibet Support Group is taking notice of and carrying out His Holiness the Dalai Lama's instructions issued in the recent March 10 statement."

There was speculation in some quarters that given the rare convergence of visits by Hu and the Dalai Lama to the same country, not to mention that the country being visited happened to be the United States, the two leaders might have at the very least exchanged views away from the media glare, if not met secretly. However, sources within the Tibetan government-in-exile strongly denied the suggestion. The denial notwithstanding, many watchers of the Sino-Tibetan imbroglio wondered what such a meeting might mean for the future of Tibet. To counter any burgeoning hope, the realists within the community pointed to Hu's stint as Communist party chief of the TAR in 1988. They also highlighted the fact he was in charge of Tibet during the time when the people had stepped up their demand for independence. He'd cracked down on Tibetan resistance groups and had reportedly caused many deaths. At the same time, though, he was also credited with having liberalized cultural life in Tibet.

In an unrelated development that could have a bearing on the future of Tibet, there were reports that Taiwanese president Chen Shui-bian had sent a secret message to the Chinese leadership to bring about a thaw in bilateral relations. The message was said to be the first issued at the highest level of contact between the two countries in five years. Incidentally, the Dalai Lama has enjoyed enormous respect and popularity in Taiwan, which he has visited amid effusive reception and over objections from China.

Meanwhile, China has fashioned the region in its own image, including altering Tibet's demographics by moving Han Chinese people into Tibet. According to estimates, Tibet is now home to about 6 million indigenous Tibetans and 7 million Han Chinese. Beijing is also strengthening its hold over Tibet through economic activities. One powerful example of this is the construction of a railroad linking mainland China and Lhasa, which is bound to make it easier for China to bring in military personnel and civilians. The Beijing-Lhasa rail became operational in July 2006, after four years of construction. The 500-mile (1,127-kilometer) rail link is quite an engineering feat considering that much of it has been built on permafrost. There are sections on the railroad, the world's highest, that are 14,764 feet (4,500 meters) above sea level.

The project's critics have questioned the wisdom of building such a rail link since its cost has far outweighed its economic benefits. They say that the project's main motivation is political rather than economic since it would help speed up the integration of Tibet into China. Prime minister of the Tibetan government-in-exile Samdhong Rinpoche believes the railroad, whose test runs were scheduled to begin in July, would bring tremendous negative influences on Tibetan culture and its fragile ecosystem, but he is not opposed to it as it would open up huge possibilities for growth of trade in Tibet.

"This railroad has serious ramifications," says Khedroob Thondup, a former parliament member of the Tibetan government-in-exile. "It will create an even larger influx of Han people

into Tibet. It will speed up the transportation of military personnel and supplies into Tibet. The railroad will also create a serious
imbalance in the already fragile ecosystem."

In an article on the popular Tibetan Web site www.phayul.com,
Thondup said, "The Tibetan plateau, spanning 4 million square
kilometers, is the highest and largest plateau on earth. It is home
to over 5,000 higher plant species and over 12,000 species of vas-
cular plants, 532 different species of birds, and 126 identified
minerals, and has rich old-growth forests. It is also the source of
many of Asia's major rivers whose tributaries are the lifeblood of
millions of people in the Asian continent. Research figures show
that rivers originating from Tibet sustain the lives of 47 percent
of the world's population. Thus the environment issue has a huge
global significance that warrants international attention."

Andrew Fischer, an economist who specializes in Tibet and the
author of *State Growth and Social Exclusion in Tibet*, was quoted by
ABC Australia radio as saying, "The railroad, I don't think, makes
any sense economically speaking. Last year they announced that
they need to put an extra six or seven billion yuan into the railroad
to complete it, so we're looking at a project of over thirty billion
yuan [about US $3.7 billion] essentially."

Fischer said what he was worried about "is that right now
what we're seeing is a boom, because there's a lot of employment
and so much money rushing into the province, related to that one
single project. But once that project is completed, you . . . you'll
most likely see a bust . . . the government will be challenged to
maintain subsidies, subsidize investment at such a high level without that project being there, and then you have a drop-off in employment and so forth."

China has invested far too much in Tibet to just walk away

from it under international pressure led by the Dalai Lama. The Beijing-Lhasa railroad is just one compelling example of that. The more China spends on Tibet, the less likely it is to leave.

Given these developments, the only viable option Tibetans have is precisely defined autonomy within China, ensuring self-rule and unambiguously stating what areas of government the Tibetans would control. Contentious areas would involve nearly every major issue, from judicial and legislative powers to cultural and religious affairs. Experts are looking at several models of autonomy, including the "one country, two systems" model followed by China in Hong Kong. China's quest for economic growth and geopolitical clout will compel it to contain, if not eliminate, conflicts within its territory.

Tibet is potentially the most troublesome territory for China because of the Dalai Lama's powerful advocacy of the right to self-rule. The Dalai Lama has consistently said that "any relationship between Tibet and China will have to be based on the principle of equality, respect, trust, and mutual benefit. It will also have to be based on the principle which the wise rulers of Tibet and China laid down in a treaty in AD 823." This treaty still remains carved on the pillar that stands in front of Jokhang, Tibet's holiest shrine.

The treaty reads: "Tibetans will live happily in the great land of Tibet, and the Chinese will live happily in the great land of China." That sentiment has long been overrun by the unassailable control that China exercises over Tibet. Going by the change of demographic map, the treaty should perhaps now read: "The Chinese will live happily in the great land of China as well as Tibet. As for Tibetans, they can live by the side of the Chinese, uncertain of their future."

During his early years in exile, the Dalai Lama favored independence. But in the past fifteen years, he has come to recognize its impracticability. He knows his options are limited because of China's stranglehold on Tibetan affairs, and the world's waning attention. Recently he has been advocating the middle-path philosophy. While this would guarantee that Tibet would retain its distinct political, social, cultural, religious, economic, and linguistic identity, it also means abandoning the idea of complete independence from China.

As time goes by, the Buddhist master's negotiating space is getting narrower. As his middle-path approach fails to yield the kind of outcome that would satisfy younger Tibetans in exile, there are signs of defiance among them; some of the young leaders in India are openly advocating that Tibet secede from China rather than settle for autonomy.

26

■

HOTHEADS VERSUS
MIDDLE WAY

April 27, 1998, was an oppressively hot day in New Delhi. The yellow haze of pollution that hung over the city made the sunlight seem unnaturally subdued. Outside Jantar Mantar, an eighteenth-century observatory that is among the city's most popular tourist destinations, sat a group of Tibetans looking sullen and angry. But fifty-year-old Thubten Ngodup seemed particularly outraged. Ngodup said he saw no option but to inflict violence on himself to make a point about how frustrated young Tibetans were becoming that the Tibet question was not getting resolved fast enough. Ngodup had in fact said he would have no qualms about immolating himself to "fuel the movement onto a new trajectory." What sounded like angry rhetoric turned out to be much worse as he carried out his threat.

Although there has been no other incident of immolation since Ngodup burned himself on that April afternoon in India's capital, there is still plenty of anger and disenchantment at the "utter failure" of the Dalai Lama's middle-way approach. The Tibetan Youth Congress (TYC) is the most vocal group of young Tibetans advocating independence for Tibet rather than autonomy within China as favored by the Dalai Lama. Ironically, the TYC was founded in October 1970 with an inaugural address by the Dalai Lama. Among its founders were Tenzin Geyche Tethong, private secretary to the Dalai Lama, and Lodi G. Gyari, the Dalai Lama's special envoy to Washington, both of whom strongly support the Tibetan leader's middle-way approach.

The TYC, which claims twenty thousand members worldwide, has said it does not support the Dalai Lama's middle-path philosophy, although it holds him in great esteem as their leader. The younger and more hotheaded elements among the exile community have made considerable political gains in recent times. The 2006 parliamentary-in-exile elections saw the rise of many young representatives who support the independence of Tibet. "The middle-path approach of His Holiness the Dalai Lama has not worked and will not work in dealing with Communist China," said new deputy Serta Tsultrim, thirty-two, who edits a Tibetan-language newspaper and advocates Tibetan independence. Another young deputy, Karma Yeshi, said, "What's needed is independence."

A rare incident highlighting the simmering dissension occurred during the April 2005 visit of Chinese premier Wen Jiabao to India. During an engagement at the Indian Institute of Science in Bangalore there was a security breach when Friends of Tibet general secretary Tenzing Tsundue climbed a two-hundred-foot tower and managed to interrupt the meeting by raising anti-China slogans. The protest was seen to be aimed at the Dalai Lama's middle-way approach.

TYC vice president Lobsang Yeshi was then quoted as saying that the point of the protest was "to send a clear message to the Dalai Lama and his government-in-exile that the younger generation is not pleased with the Tibet policy being pursued by him."

The middle-way approach was the result of a resolution passed by the Tibetan government-in-exile on March 10, 2004. "The Tibetan administration would like to appeal to all Tibetan organizations to support the middle-way approach and work towards creating an atmosphere conducive for dialogue," the resolution said. "We, at the moment, are committed to the middle-way policy for resolving the Tibetan issue through nonviolence. When we initiate any activity for the cause of Tibet, it is very important that our actions do not go against the very policy and approach we're committed to."

Notwithstanding the outrage among their ranks, there is clear recognition among the young Tibetan exiles, who advocate an armed uprising, that they are up against a mighty adversary that now ranks among the great powers of the world. As so graphically explained by Thubten Jigme Norbu, even if the Chinese were to willingly offer their lives to an armed uprising by the Tibetans, the sheer numbers are so overwhelmingly against the latter that it makes absolutely no sense to even attempt a revolt. The Dalai

Lama's only choice is to craft a compromise for autonomy, however unpopular this decision may be with the younger generation of Tibetans.

The Dalai Lama remains steadfastly committed to nonviolence. "Sure, a nonviolent campaign can take a lifetime," he says. "We have the great model of what Mahatma Gandhi did for India. While violence may work under a certain circumstance, it would invariably engender violence in return at some point. A lot of young people speak in anger about the Chinese having destroyed many monasteries. If you resort to violent methods because the other side has destroyed your monastery, for example, you then have lost not only your monastery, but also your special Buddhist practices of detachment, love, and compassion. I justify violence only in very extreme cases. For instance, if there was only one learned lama or a true practitioner of Tibetan Buddhism alive and his life was in danger and his death could destroy all hope of keeping intact our knowledge, I might agree to the elimination of our enemies through violent means," he said.

"It is obvious that we cannot compete with the Chinese in military or diplomacy, nor in money and size. They have everything but no justice. Our whole faith, on the other hand, is in truth and justice. Tolerance is an important virtue of bodhisattvas [enlightened beings]. I call it disarmament from within. Tolerance frees you from the shackles of seeking revenge or carrying out a counterattack," he said.

It is an open question whether the Dalai Lama's demise at this stage will light a short fuse to the combustible rage in certain quarters of the young exile leadership. If the extent of the Congress's membership is any measure, there may be a fair number of members who might be willing to take the extreme step of an armed uprising. At the same time, though, there is enough realization within the leadership that they simply do not have the numbers or means to make any perceptible impact on China through any form of insurgency. Even if one were to set aside the complete improbability of conducting any insurgent movement from their base in India, the hotheads are hamstrung by their own innate limitations as a group. In the absence of any credible measure of the popular mood within Tibet it is nearly impossible to speculate on how native Tibetans would respond to any external stimulus to embark on a full-fledged armed struggle.

Indian intelligence sources, who occasionally track prospects of Tibetan resistance on Indian soil, say so far they do not fear organizations such as the TYC mounting an armed insurgency. "These are very peaceful people. They have no history of violence in India. We do not think there are any serious plans under way to start an armed insurgency, but we still keep an eye on them from time to time," said one intelligence source in New Delhi. Interestingly, the source also said they would find it difficult to characterize self-immolation as an act of terrorism or insurgency. Under Indian law, the source said, such acts would be viewed as suicide, which is outlawed. "But we do not see this as an act of rebellion," the source said.

Asked if he feared that some renegades in the movement might take the extreme step of suicide bombing or committing acts of terrorism, the source said, "You can never say about individuals, but if history is any guide these are people who do not like violence at all. Besides, their number is not so large as to constitute a serious threat of that nature."

Several background conversations within the government-in-exile indicated that while they recognize that some serious disagreements over the models for a future Tibet exist, they were not such that young Tibetans would stage an armed rebellion. "His Holiness commands enormous respect and wields great influence with the Tibetan community outside and inside Tibet. We do not think our youths would disrespect the Dalai Lama's wishes to the extent of committing violence," said a senior functionary of the government-in-exile.

But sentiment among young Tibetans who are not members of the TYC and who do not claim any political affiliation is one of exasperation. Many of them say they do not believe in violence as their first choice, but argue that they have been pushed into a corner where there is no option but to fight back. In 2003, then–TYC president Kalsang Godrupka Phuntsok told Jehangir Pocha of the Web site www.inthesetimes.com, "You cannot give up the independence of Tibet. Anyone who tries this is making a mistake. The negotiations mean nothing. The Chinese cannot be trusted. They are just playing with [the Dalai Lama], buying time and waiting for him to die." He also advocated what he called "targeted, victimless violence" against the Chinese, which included destroying economic targets such as bridges.

While such views may not be widespread, they do prevail among a section of the young Tibetans who would be the future inheritors of any post–Fourteenth Dalai Lama political movement. There are other pro-independence supporters in the exile community who believe in a different approach. An eleven-day "March for Tibet's Independence" from Charlottesville to Washington, D.C., ended on June 11, 2006. Among the marchers was Jigme Norbu, the Dalai Lama's nephew (son of elder brother Thubten Jigme Norbu), who said, "This walk has demonstrated once again Tibetans young and old want nothing less than to rule their own free country and to assure Tibetans inside of Tibet their wish for independence will be realized."

It is not known how young Tibetans in Tibet look at the question of armed insurgency, but reports filtering into the exile community in India via newly arriving refugees suggest that many of them lack the motivation to even consider it. Since all young native Tibetans were born into a Tibet already dominated by the Han Chinese, they have no perspective on life without the pervasive Chinese influence. Their exposure to the Dalai Lama and what he stands for is limited. They have little, if any, access to news and information about the struggle waged by the exile community. However, some refugees, many of them young monks in their late teens or early twenties, point out that many Tibetans are quite angry about the Chinese occupation. While many of them see and approve of the modernizing impact of the Chinese presence, at the same time they do not like the idea of their Tibetan identity being systematically erased. More than the question of identity, what takes precedence is the urge among ordinary Tibetans to improve their lot in life. According to an AFP news report dated September 10, 2003, there is change taking place in Tibet. The wire service quoted Melvyn Goldstein, an anthropologist who has researched and written extensively on contemporary Tibet at Case Western Reserve University in the United States, as saying that the crux of the issue is how to allow more Tibetans to benefit from the modernization drive, while still preserving religious traditions.

"There is change going on in Tibet, some of it positive, but it is a complicated process and it is not all in black or white," Goldstein told AFP. "Tibetans are more knowledgeable, they want change, and they are very materialistic. Many people are leaving the rural areas and going out to look for work. The Tibetans are trying to compete, but it is difficult."

If this is the general mood of native Tibetans, the prospects of an armed rebellion are dim. However, the Tibetan exile community, which sees Goldstein as a collaborator with the Chinese plans, say that information they receive through their own network paints a completely different picture—that of a community itching to take control of their destiny through any means. For their part, the Chinese government has taken the view that their adversary lacks the numerical, economic, and political strength to emerge as a serious threat to their control over Tibet.

The one clear conclusion out of all the ifs and buts of Tibet's future seems to be pointing to the wisdom of pursuing the Dalai Lama's idea of autonomy within China. A fair amount of work has been done in studying the structure and nature of the autonomy that China and the Dalai Lama should negotiate.

27

·

MODELS
OF AUTONOMY

Short of divine intervention or a catastrophe of staggering proportions, China is unlikely to give up Tibet. While there are Tibetans in exile who sincerely believe one of the two is always within the realm of possibilities, the more discerning among the Tibetan government-in-exile, and most certainly the Dalai Lama himself, recognize the need to be realistic about what can and should happen now.

The international community's interest in the Tibetan cause is peripheral at best. The Tibetan cause is of no consequence to those countries, more specifically the United States, that are known to intervene militarily or through economic sanctions in regions they perceive to be of economic or strategic importance to them. If Tibet had vast quantities of oil reserves, its fate would have been markedly different. Since it is nothing more than 471,700 square miles (1,221,600 square kilometers) of permafrost-covered plateau without any strategic importance to the West, Tibet captures hardly any imagination anymore among the Western capitals. The U.S. government's Tibetan Policy Act of 2002 could not be clearer on Washington's official position.

"The United States recognizes the Tibet Autonomous Region—hereinafter referred to as 'Tibet'—to be part of the People's Republic of China. This long-standing policy is consistent with the view of the international community. In addition, the Dalai Lama has expressly disclaimed any intention to seek sovereignty or independence for Tibet and has stated that his goal is greater autonomy for Tibetans in China.

"Because we do not recognize Tibet as an independent state, the United States does not conduct official diplomatic relations with the Tibetan 'government-in-exile' in Dharamshala. However, we maintain contact with representatives of a wide variety of political and other groups inside and outside of China, including with Tibetans in the United States, China, and around the world. Our contacts include meeting with the Dalai Lama in his capacity as an important world spiritual leader and Nobel laureate. It is a sign of our country's respect for the Dalai Lama that the President, the Secretary, and other senior administration officials have met with him on several occasions.

"We have consistently urged China to respect the unique religious, linguistic, and cultural heritage of its Tibetan people and to respect fully their human rights and civil liberties," the U.S. document says.

After its early involvement in arming Tibetan rebels through the Central Intelligence Agency in the 1950s, the United States has essentially maintained a policy of noninterference in Tibet. The United States sees Tibet as a question of human rights and civil liberties and in the context of preserving a unique heritage. But none of those concerns are compelling enough for the United States to mount a campaign to free Tibet. Apart from the United States, India has been the only power capable of making a difference in favor of what the Dalai Lama has stood for. Since India too has moved on to strike friendly relations with China, the Tibetan cause has become practically orphaned. New Delhi has never considered a military option. If its inability to do so in the decades between the 1960s and 1980s could be explained by India's having a decidedly weaker military than China, its reluctance to get any more involved in the last twenty years could be attributed to economic and strategic expediencies. The concept that Tibet could act as a buffer state, too, has long been overtaken by advances in India's military and weapons technologies and strike capabilities. Both India and China are nuclear powers, so the reassurance that an independent Tibet could keep them at safe distance from each other is no longer valid. Long-range missiles have made the concept of a buffer state outdated.

Since 1987 the Dalai Lama has been carefully preparing to build popular opinion among the Tibetans in exile as well as those in Tibet in favor of autonomy rather than independence. In an address to members of the U.S. Congress in September of that year, he said, "The world is increasingly interdependent, so that lasting peace—national, regional, and global—can only be achieved if we think in terms of broader interest rather than parochial needs.

"The Tibetan people are eager to contribute to regional and world peace, and I believe they are in a unique position to do so. Traditionally, Tibetans are a peace-loving and nonviolent people. Since Buddhism was introduced to Tibet over one thousand years ago, Tibetans have practiced nonviolence with respect to all forms of life. This attitude has also been extended to our country's international relations. Tibet's highly strategic position in the heart of Asia, separating the continent's great powers—India, China, and the USSR—has throughout history endowed it with an essential role in the maintenance of peace and stability. This is precisely why, in the past, Asia's empires went to great lengths to keep one another out of Tibet. Tibet's value as an independent buffer state was integral to the region's stability," he said.

Even as he spoke of the "illegal occupation" of Tibet by China he went on to propose a five-point peace plan:

1. Transformation of the whole of Tibet into a zone of peace;
2. Abandonment of China's population transfer policy which threatens the very existence of the Tibetans as a people;
3. Respect for the Tibetan people's fundamental human rights and democratic freedoms;
4. Restoration and protection of Tibet's natural environment and the abandonment of China's use of Tibet for the production of nuclear weapons and dumping of nuclear waste;

5. Commencement of earnest negotiations on the future
   status of Tibet and of relations between the Tibetan and
   Chinese peoples.

The Dalai Lama maintains that these five points are still the foundation of any settlement of the Tibetan question. The essential element of the peace plan was and still is self-governance of Tibet by Tibetans. Since his departure from Tibet, frequent attempts have been made to revive negotiations between the Dalai Lama and the Chinese government. In 1980, when the Chinese government began "liberalization" in the Tibet Autonomous Region (TAR), the Dalai Lama was invited to send delegations to monitor for himself the changes taking place in the region. Between 1979 and 1985 four high-level Tibetan delegations visited Tibet. After those visits the contact between the two sides practically died out despite the promise of those visits. For the next seventeen years the contact remained sporadic at best.

Contact was reestablished with a visit by Thubten Jigme Norbu in July 2002 during which he went to Beijing and Lhasa. Although he reported many changes in Tibet since the Dalai Lama's family had fled, he did not come back very convinced about prospects for fruitful future talks. Notwithstanding that in September 2002 Lodi Gyari, the Dalai Lama's special envoy to the United States, and Kelsang Gyaltsen, his envoy to Europe, visited Beijing. The two went again in May 2003. Their third visit took place in September 2004. That visit produced what Gyari officially called "so far the most extensive and serious exchange of views on matters relating to Tibet." But the statement by China's assistant foreign minister Shen Guofang, while acknowledging the "useful and beneficial" nature of the contact, remained less upbeat overall. The statement said China would consider discussing the Dalai Lama's "personal future" only if he was willing to give up his "splittist activities," recognize that Tibet and Taiwan were part of China, and admit that the government of China was "the sole legitimate government representing all of China."

The Dalai Lama does not view his activities in exile as anywhere close to being "splittist." "I am fighting for the survival of Tibetan culture. In that campaign I have to focus on the role China has played in destroying our way of life. Without its unique heritage Tibet loses its value," he said.

The idea of self-governance through autonomy has been around for quite some time, but it is only in the past six years that legal scholars have seriously examined various models that could be applied to Tibet. Eva Herzer, a Berkeley, California, lawyer specializing in mediation and international human rights law, has been intimately involved in the cause. As a founding member and former president of the Tibetan Justice Center, formerly known as the International Committee of Lawyers for Tibet, she has been working with exiled Tibetans on evolving a model of self-governance.

"The legal case of Tibet rests on two pillars. The first is its historical claim based on past independence, known as the right to territorial integrity. The second pillar is the right to self-determination, which allows a people to choose how to govern themselves. Both of them separately give the Tibetans an ability to determine their political status, which could be complete independence, an autonomous arrangement, or, in theory at least, total merger into the Chinese state. But one must remember here that the right to self-determination is not an option for Tibet's political status such as independence and autonomy. It is their legal right to choose independence or autonomy. It is an underlying right to choose a political status," Herzer said.

She said that while historical claims were always open to interpretation and therefore susceptible to dispute, the right to self-determination is separate from Tibet's territorial or historical claim. "Even if for the sake of argument one says China is correct in asserting that Tibet was not independent in the past, Tibetans still have the right to self-determination. And hence they have the legal right to decide their political status," she said. There is no dispute that Tibetans are a distinct people and that that qualifies them to exercise this right, as endorsed twice, in 1961 and 1965, by the United Nations General Assembly. Herzer said the Tibetans would be well advised to take the route of the right to self-determination since it avoids the uncertainties of history and helps internationalize the issue. It is possible that while exercising the right to self-determination Tibetans may in fact choose independence over autonomy and create complications. However, given the fact that the Dalai Lama has consistently supported autonomy over independence in recent times, the prospects of such an eventuality arising are not very strong.

Herzer said that during the twentieth century well over forty autonomous arrangements have been reached even though the term "autonomy" has no specific meaning in international law. While the dictionary meaning is "independence, freedom and the right to self-government," in practice the term has predominantly meant a form of self-government within a larger sovereign state. Typically authority over areas such as cultural affairs, education, official language, health and social services, economy, taxation, natural resources, environmental policy, transportation, law and order, telecommunications, judiciary, currency and monetary policy, citizenship, defense, foreign policy and customs, and border control and immigration come into play while discussing any autonomous arrangement. Under that definition, Herzer argued, the TAR as it exists today is an example of "negligible self-rule." "The TAR has very few governmental powers and whatever it has are really controlled by the Communist Party. So that is not the model to follow at all. I would cite the examples of Liechtenstein, which has an autonomous arrangement with Switzerland, and Greenland, which is a similar arrangement with Denmark, as two possible models. I also think the Dalai Lama's own Strasbourg proposal, which would give almost all powers except defense and foreign affairs to the Tibetans, is also worth considering," she said.

Some of the most important elements of an autonomous arrangement are cultural affairs, education, and official language. In the case of Tibet, since cultural perseverance, education, and the official language are the bedrock of their struggle, those powers would have to rest with the Tibetans. "Those are very crucial but I think we should also talk about other powers. My Strasbourg proposal is still a valid framework for China to follow. After all, their biggest concern is that in matters of defense and foreign affairs Tibet should appear one with the mainland is favorably addressed in that proposal," the Dalai Lama said.

At nearly 507,000 square miles (1.3 million square kilometers), the TAR is only about 50 percent of the entire area historically known as Tibet. It borders India, Nepal, Bhutan, Burma, and China and is home to over two million people. Any autonomous arrangement will also have to address the remaining 50 percent of the Tibetan territory, an area that both Tibet and China claim as their own. "It would be impossible not to address the issue of the whole of Tibet. But as we know, China is not willing to discuss any autonomy . . . of the TAR [let alone] the whole of Tibet," Herzer said.

In a sign of China's unassailable hold over Tibet, beginning September 6, 2005, Beijing decided to hold worldwide celebrations of the fortieth anniversary of the establishment of the TAR. The celebrations were scheduled to be organized at Chinese embassies in various world capitals. The most glaring of these would be in New Delhi, where Beijing was scheduling such a celebration for the first time. Experts said the fact that China was planning to celebrate the anniversary in India as well underscored how emboldened China has become.

The September 2004 visit of the two Tibetan envoys to Beijing was fruitful insomuch as it illustrated that the Chinese have not completely shut the door on holding talks. There is tacit recognition within the Chinese leadership that as long as Tibet remains an outstanding issue and as long as the Dalai Lama champions the cause with the vigor and conviction that he has done for decades, Beijing can never really pursue its larger ambitions of being a world power that could rival the United States. One Indian diplomat who has followed the conflict closely for years said, "Beijing may never publicly acknowledge it, but it would rather that Tibet was resolved in some way where the Dalai Lama is back, albeit on its terms but with some recognizable outcome that his struggle has not been entirely worthless. Contrary to the popular notion that China is waiting for him to die, I would argue that it would prefer an aging Dalai Lama with declining physical and mental faculties to be back in Lhasa. That way China can prove to the world that it made significant accommodation in the Dalai Lama's favor by letting him return but at the same time not really grant him much since death is always looming on the horizon."

The diplomat argued that at age seventy-one the Dalai Lama does not have too many effective years ahead of him. "If Beijing concedes some of the demands of the Dalai Lama and lets him return, it stands to gain even greater emotional control over the Tibetans in the long term. The Chinese leadership has accomplished the main task of making the Dalai Lama redundant among the younger Tibetans in Tibet. So what do they have to lose if they let him return before he finally dies? Nothing much, really," he said.

28

■

HAN CHINESE
TURN TO BUDDHISM

Nowhere was the Buddhist precept of impermanence more stunningly evident than in two
completely unrelated developments in Tibet in
August 2005. Both were reported by two international
wire services and together illustrated that things are
never as black-and-white, final, and as deeply entrenched as totalitarian regimes would have the world
believe. One was an Associated Press report from Lhasa
about how Han Chinese tourists are drawn to Bud-

dhism; the other was a Xinhua report about the continuing tectonic plate movement on the Tibet plateau.

LHASA (AP)—There's a new type of pilgrim spinning the prayer wheels at Tibet's holiest sites. Along with the Tibetans who prostrate themselves before the vacant throne of their exiled leader, the Dalai Lama, swarms of Chinese tourists rub crisp Chinese money on their foreheads and then cram the bills into collection boxes.

In matching tour group hats, the Chinese visitors bow at Tibetan shrines, light candles and ring temple bells. Style-conscious young women try the Tibetan look, weaving bright strips of cloth into their black hair.

"This is a mystical place, a bit of heaven on earth," said Tang Wei, a manager at a government-owned software company in Beijing. "Even though it's undeveloped, life here is good. People have their own peace in life and contentment in work."

As for the Dalai Lama, condemned by Beijing as a traitor, "he doesn't sound so bad to me," Tang said.

BEIJING (Xinhua): The Tibet plateau, also known as "roof of the world," is moving northward and eastward at seven to 30 millimeters a year, a Chinese researcher said here.

"The plateau is moving because it's being pushed by the Indian plate," Tan Kai, a researcher with China Seismological Bureau, was quoted by Xinhua as saying.

Tan and his colleagues found through a survey that Lhasa, on the southern end of the Tibet or Qinghai plateau, is moving 30 mm a year northeast at an angle of 38 degrees.

They said the Kunlum Mountains in the central plateau [are] moving 21 mm a year at 61 degrees while the Quilian Mountains

*further north [are] moving between seven and 14 mm a year, at an
angle of 80 degrees.*

*"Which means the entire plateau is moving 7 to 30 mm a year on
average," Tan told Xinhua. "Such moves are barely noticeable and will not
change the Chinese continental plate any time soon. But they're still
significant from the geological point of view."*

The great tectonic crunch operates on a geological timescale and
is not ordinarily perceptible, and hence it is of no significance to
an individual's life. But the changing profile of those drawn to Tibetan Buddhism in general and the Dalai Lama in particular in
China has a more immediate and comprehensible lesson somewhere. For quite some time the Tibetan government-in-exile has
claimed that many Han Chinese are increasingly drawn to Buddhism and the message of the Dalai Lama. But their claims have
been dismissed either as partisan drivel or wishful thinking. But
lately independent media reports have backed up these claims.
There is a realization that nearly five decades after the Dalai Lama
had to run out of Tibet to save his life, far from diminishing, his
stature has only grown within Tibet. As late as August 2005 the
Chinese authorities continued to arrest people and put them in
prison for up to four years for carrying images and pictures of the
Dalai Lama as well audiotapes of his teachings.

Those who understand the deliberate ways in which the Chinese leadership operates say that it is possible that Beijing has perhaps begun to understand that the problem of Tibet will remain
irrespective of whether a particular Dalai Lama, in this case Tenzin Gyatso, is around to advance it. At some level the battle of attrition between Beijing and the Dalai Lama, where the former
waits for the latter to die, could begin to lose its effectiveness.

While he is still alive Tenzin Gyatso continues to enjoy moral and spiritual authority over Tibetans inside and outside Tibet to make them accept a reasonable solution that is far short of independence. But once he is gone, which way the mood might swing is unpredictable. The accepted wisdom so far has been that once the current Dalai Lama passes, there will be no comparable figure in the next decade and a half to keep the issue alive with as much vigor, conviction, and persuasiveness as has Tenzin Gyatso. Therefore it makes sense for China to bide its time by creating a false impression that Beijing is interested in a negotiated settlement. The other less popular and barely articulated wisdom holds that the central leadership is not as much in control of popular mood as it has so far projected and that the people of China are interested in exploring options other than those handed down by Beijing, including whether they choose to follow any religious faith. Those who support this view cite news reports from Lhasa that speak of the changing mood among the Han Chinese about Tibetan Buddhism and its symbols, such as the Dalai Lama.

The Chinese population, although strictly controlled and regimented, remains considerably young. According to estimates, some 40 to 50 percent of its 1.2 billion people are in their twenties. By some projections in 2025 the median age in China will be forty. Those under twenty-five have no memory of the Cultural Revolution. They are also not as steadfast about socialist dogmas as their parents were. It is this huge segment of population that is expected to help shape many of China's future policies, including how Beijing deals with Tibet and the Dalai Lama. If the utterances by the young software engineer visiting Lhasa from Beijing are any measure, the Chinese leadership does have a lot to think about. Quite ironically, the Dalai Lama remains the most high-profile figure from that part of the world. The brand recognition of his name is so weighed in his favor that Beijing, despite its well-known aversion for building up personalities, will have to come up with a counter to it. If not, it will have to reconcile with him.

Partly, China has reasoned that with time the sanctity, power, and draw of the Dalai Lama over Tibetan life would erode to an extent where it would no longer matter. Developments in Tibet point to the contrary. More important for the Tibetans, as much as individual Dalai Lamas matter, what matters more is the institution of the Dalai Lama itself. It is hardly surprising that China's Communist establishment has had to disregard its institutional contempt for religion and allow the continuation of many of the traditions of Tibetan Buddhism, including the institution of the Panchen Lama. Some might argue that Beijing has made such an allowance out of political expediency and not because of any faith it has in the traditions themselves, since it understands the importance of using any means to retain its control over Tibet. If the latter is indeed the case, why would an ideological juggernaut as powerful as the Communist establishment even bother to keep the Dalai Lama and the traditions he represents in the loop while dealing with the issue of Tibet? They could easily treat the Dalai Lama and his institution as irrelevant in modern times and press on with whatever plans they have for Tibet. It would be stretching credulity to say that China has continued to engage the Dalai Lama purely under international pressure or for the sake of appearances or even as a political expedient. It is true that his death is much closer now than it was in 1959 and as a state China could afford to wait a decade or so before the inevitable happens to Tenzin Gyatso. However, there is something terribly flawed about a strategy that presumes that the Dalai Lama's demise would settle the question of Tibet for all practical intents and purposes.

Two factors could play a decisive role. One is the changing mood within China's young population and the other is the way the Tibetans themselves might deal with their problem if an effective Dalai Lama were no longer a part of the equation. Although there are no known reports of young Han Chinese demanding that their leaders resolve the issue of Tibet, signs such as recent media reports indicate that if nothing else, they don't see Tibet and Buddhism in the black-and-white terms that the leadership does. Since the Tiananmen Square uprising, there has been no serious report of a democracy movement led by the country's student leaders gaining more ground. Nevertheless, both Western and Tibetan sources speak of some profound changes taking place across China. They concede that these changes are not such that they would suddenly alter the course of history but at the same time they are strong enough that they could make a lasting impact over a period of time.

On the other hand, it is conceivable that nearly five decades of occupation have forced the Tibetans themselves into irreversible submission and that they are no longer interested in rising against the Chinese rule. On the contrary, exiled Tibetans and others say, the level of discontent within Tibet is so high it could explode into something uncontrollable were the Dalai Lama no longer around to cushion it. "It is His Holiness's uncompromising insistence on nonviolence and pacifism and his stature to ensure that it remains so that has stopped Tibet from going out of control. I don't think the Chinese recognize that fact at all and they should," Tempa Tsering said.

One way or the other the question of Tibet is now more ripe than ever before for resolution. For the Dalai Lama and the Tibetans the biggest danger is that their campaign could become ineffectual and irrelevant. For China the biggest danger is the outbreak of violence, which in turn could attract precisely the kind of international attention it wants to avoid at any cost. In theory, it makes perfect sense for the two parties to reach a negotiated settlement soon. In reality, though, animosities and suspicions, even though they have atrophied over the past five decades, are making any positive movement forward very difficult. There is a sinking feeling that if there is any party that could be forced to compromise more than the other, it would be the Tibetans. Other than the Dalai Lama's extraordinary campaign, these people have nothing going for them.

The latest example of how steadfastly committed China remains to keeping Tibet under its control were comments attributed to Zhang Qingli, Communist Party secretary of the Tibet Autonomous Region. According to a report on August 14, 2006, by Jane Macartney of the *Times* of London's Beijing correspondent, Zhang, a close ally of China's President Hu Jintao, was on a mission to "crush loyalty" to the Dalai Lama. In May, Zhang reportedly told senior party officials that Beijing was engaged in a "fight to the death" against the Dalai Lama. Among the many draconian measures that Zhang was enforcing on officials, one was peculiarly amusing. According to the *Times* report, senior civil servants were required to write ten-thousand-character essays condemning the Dalai Lama, while those in junior positions were asked to produce five-thousand-character essays. The utterances by Zhang was a classic instance of how quickly hopes of any resolution are belied in the Sino-Tibetan conflict.

29

WILL HE EVER
RETURN TO TIBET?

On June 20, 2005, only three months before
the fortieth anniversary of the establishment
of the TAR, Tibetan and Chinese interlocutors met for the first time outside China. The choice of
the Swiss capital, Berne, was not without symbolism.
These talks, the fourth in a series that began in 2002,
were taking place in a country that has professed neu-
trality to all major conflicts.

The Tibetan side was represented by Lodi Gyari,

special envoy to the United States, and Kelsang Gyaltsen, special envoy to Europe. Three other senior diplomats who accompanied them were Sonam Norbu Dagpo, secretary of the Department of Information and International Relations; Tsegyam Ngaba, the Dalai Lama's representative in Taiwan; and Bhuchung K. Tsering, a member of the Task Force on Negotiations of the Central Tibetan Administration. China was represented by Vice Minister Zhu Weigun, along with a six-member delegation.

In the China-Tibet context, it is not important what they really talk about. What is important is that they talk at all. Tibetan sources, not wanting to sound too upbeat and optimistic, said the talks were aimed at "exploring possibilities of what could be done" to prepare a ground for any possible solution. The sense one gets from talking to Tibetan sources who are privy to the bilateral talks is that China may be indirectly exploring what it might mean to allow the Dalai Lama to return. Although there are no official comments from either side on whether his return is on the table, China needs a dramatic breakthrough of that scale to convince the world of its intentions. On the sidelines of the talks the Dalai Lama was quoted by media reports as saying, "I wish to go on pilgrimage to prominent Buddhist sites in China."

In a striking new twist to the much talked about battle of attrition between China and the Dalai Lama, wherein Beijing would essentially wait it out until the frailties of life catch up with him, there are those who believe that it is possible that China in fact may have a lot to gain by letting him come back. A well-known Tibetan scholar who did not want to be identified said, "He is already seventy-one. His best years are behind him. As a state, China has no problem of life span compared to an individual. I would not be very surprised if the thinking in Beijing is that bringing him back could significantly blunt the sting of his campaign."

The scholar said that as long as the Dalai Lama remains outside Tibet he remains on a moral high ground and can push the cause with a great deal of conviction. But should he return, he might unwittingly lend himself to manipulation by the Chinese and make it easier for them to control his reach and cramp his style.

While this view is certainly interesting, it misses one basic point: that the Dalai Lama and his administration have enough intelligence and insight to know what returning at this stage could do to all that he has worked so hard for. Even though the Dalai Lama who fled Tibet in 1959 is no longer the same Dalai Lama who might return now, what would happen once he was inside China is impossible to predict. The Dalai Lama's return to Tibet would be unlike any other public figure returning to his or her homeland. Not only is his potential return loaded with the symbolism of the world's most respected refugee finally returning home, but it is fraught with enormous political, cultural, and religious consequences for both China and Tibet. In a political and ideological order that scoffs at personal celebrity, the presence of one of the most charismatic global leaders could seriously disrupt the equilibrium in the country. If the Dalai Lama living outside his domain can excite millions of people around the world, one can only speculate what he might do once he is surrounded by all the pomp and circumstance of his exalted life.

The speculation about the Dalai Lama's likely return has been in the air since at least 2003. It is anybody's guess whether it is bait that China is dangling as part of its ongoing negotiations with the

Tibetan envoys. In 2003 there were reports of "secret negotiations" wherein the Dalai Lama's envoys were preparing to cut a
major deal with the Chinese government under which he would return to Tibet.

At that time Thubten Samphel, a spokesman for Tibet's government-in-exile, had said, "The Dalai Lama wants to go back
very much. It is every Tibetan's hope that the Dalai Lama will return to Tibet sooner rather than later, under conditions which satisfy the majority will of the Tibetan people.

"The Chinese government has the mistaken conception that
the Dalai Lama is the problem rather than the solution to the issue of Tibet. We are trying to persuade them that if they want
long-term stability they must allow the Dalai Lama to play a useful role," he said.

During our conversations, the Dalai Lama's response was similar. "Now you see, it has been a long time since I have been out
of Tibet. Therefore I would very much like to return. But China
has to create conditions for that, conditions which satisfy most
people in Tibet. I like to think that my return can help matters and
help stability."

Over two years after those speculations there were still no
signs that China was close to allowing him to return. Nevertheless
fresh rounds of speculations began in August 2005. A Reuters report from Lhasa illustrated the equivocation on the subject. "The
channel for us to have dialogue with the Dalai Lama is open. I often have contact with his private representatives, for example his
family," Wu Yingjie, a vice governor of Tibet, told a news conference.

"We have never recognized the illegal government of Tibet
outside China so there is no such question of dialogue between

the central government and the [official] representatives of the Dalai Lama," Wu said.

The Dalai Lama has "taken advantage of religion to realize political goals," Wu said, adding that, to return, the spiritual leader would also have to recognize the self-governed island of Taiwan as a part of China.

"I think it is still too early to talk about this question," Wu said.

The last remark was particularly significant. Nearly fifty years after his exile the official Chinese thinking still is that it is too early for him to return.

The debate on whether China is better off with the Dalai Lama dead in exile rather than alive in Tibet has so many dimensions it is hard to keep track of them. There is a school of thought that holds that perhaps the biggest resistance to his return could come from the Tibetans themselves.

China scholar Geremie Barme, a professor at the Australian National University in Canberra, was quoted as saying in a news report, "Opposition could come from local Tibetans who have made money and local Chinese satraps. They are terrified of clean government, of the Dalai Lama and the expression of popular will.

"The Tibetans who for 50 years have sold out do not want a new Tibetan ruling class," he said. Barme did not buy the theory that China was waiting for the Dalai Lama to die. "There was a view that once he was dead the Tibet problem would be resolved because there would be no central figure to muster resistance," said Barme. The September 11, 2001, terror attacks on New York and Washington may have changed that logic. "With 9/11, they see that once the Dalai Lama is dead then many cells of resistance will abandon his message of a peaceful resolution of the Tibet question and become militarized," he said.

"I would be shocked if the Chinese are so crude and simple that they think this can be resolved by the death of this man in exile. I think they would love to get him back in Tibet before he dies," Barme said.

One major factor that is often not looked at seriously in discussions of the possible return of the Dalai Lama to Tibet is the 2008 Olympics that China will host. China's less than flattering human rights record could come under a harsh international glare during the run-up to the games. Allowing the Dalai Lama to return before the Olympic games could dramatically soften that glare and take away considerably from the demands of major human rights organizations. While his possible return would by no means be seen as an improvement in China's human rights situation, a gesture of that nature would be so grandly symbolic that it could generate quite a lot of appreciation.

However, no matter how keen the Dalai Lama may be to return to Lhasa, he is still not inclined to yield to the extent where he would just end up being a pawn in the great game that China might be playing in its quest for more global respect. China's economy has reached a level where it desperately needs political, ideological, and sociological respectability to gain the status of a world power that could rival the United States, a goal it has pursued so assiduously. The Chinese leadership may not articulate its aspirations in such clear terms, but China scholars say that it understands the inherent danger in just being an economic giant without the advantages of being a respectable power. To that end the Dalai Lama's early return is in China's interest.

In some ways, for the first time since his exile the Dalai Lama is now in a position to strike a reasonable deal with China that both parties would find acceptable. It is not clear how much opposition or resistance such a deal may encounter among the Tibetans in Tibet. Going by the respect, devotion, and admiration the Dalai Lama continues to enjoy among them, the question of Tibetan resistance is perhaps overstated. Those Tibetans who have gained in stature or wealth by supping with the Chinese have not risen so much as to feel threatened by the Dalai Lama's return. They know that they could never aspire to emerge as a rival power center to the Dalai Lama even under the Chinese tutelage—even the Dalai Lama hamstrung by Chinese dos and don'ts would still be a far more powerful figure than any native Tibetan leader who might have emerged with Chinese blessings.

"My return to Tibet is not just about myself. Attached to this is a larger question of all that we have fought for. We no longer insist on independence. But if the Chinese want us to give up autonomy as well I think it is not going to happen. If I wanted to give up even autonomy why should I have gone into exile in the first place?" the Dalai Lama said.

30

■

PERSONAL
IMPRESSIONS

With every step I take on the cobbled pathway awash in dew, the sky seems to light up a wee bit more. By the time I reach the Dalai Lama's bungalow the sun has managed to burn up some of the fog. In the forecourt of the bungalow some hundred young monks are chanting mantras through tiny clouds of vapor. Some of them are vigorously arguing Buddhist concepts, accompanied with well-orchestrated body movements. It is almost as if they are engaged in some divinely choreographed wrestling. Indian police guards, oblivious to the goings-on, are sipping cups of tea freshly plucked from the plantations in the nearby Kangra Valley.

As I enter the sparsely furnished living room I spot a silhouetted figure sitting cross-legged on the floor swaying back and forth; his pudgy babylike fingers are working the rosary with remarkable grace. The mauve glow of the sun lends the Dalai Lama's ochre robes an even deeper hue and gives his visage a touch of profound serenity. He smiles at me with a familiarity that far outweighs our acquaintance. After all, this is only my third meeting with him in a series of many more. He finishes with the rosary and bursts into uninhibited laughter.

"You enjoy laughing, don't you?" I ask.

He laughs again, this time even more vigorously, and replies, "You see, it keeps my . . . what do you call it . . . my soul clean."

If I were to sum up the Dalai Lama in one line, I think this would be it: Sitting before me is a man, monk, and mystic who has been deified or deferred to by just about everyone who has come in contact with him since he was three years old. Millions have fallen at his feet or bent in reverence over the years. His simple touch has sent many into paroxysms of devotion. Yet he remains self-effacing to the point of being ordinary in his personal dealings. I do not have an interview scheduled this morning. I am here to observe a general audience that the Dalai Lama grants frequently to hundreds of Tibetan exiles, Indians, and foreigners who line up outside his bungalow. On this particular morning, the police tell me the number is nearly five hundred. There is an assortment of Tibetans bent in utter reverence in anticipation of seeing the Dalai Lama, Westerners who seem like a throwback to the

1960s when the hippies dwelled in a world of enlightened care-
lessness, and curious and expectant Indians.

One of the Indians looks at my press badge and says, "You
must have met him already. Has he read your palm yet?" A German
"amateur Buddhist" bristles at the Indian's suggestion and says,
"His Holiness does not read palms. For that go to some roadside
charlatan." I sense tension in the air and make a quick getaway.

As the Dalai Lama emerges with one end of his robe draped
over his right forearm, the Tibetans in the line fall to the ground
as if hit by some mysterious force. The line begins to move.
Among the first devotees is Eric, a Swedish backpacker who has
"indulged in all sorts of Eastern practices but without much so-
lace" and who is wearing earrings. Eric says the Dalai Lama is his
last resort. "If he does not work, I go back to my decadent Western ways. I would conclude that Eastern mysticism is all bunkum,"
he says. As he approaches the Dalai Lama, Eric looks down. The
Dalai Lama notices his earrings and says, "They are pretty. You
like ornaments." Eric says, "I am looking for answers but I have
not found any yet. You are my last hope."

The Dalai Lama laughs for the umpteenth time that morning.
"I don't have answers. I have questions," he says and then becomes
reflective. "All I can tell you is that just as questions, answers too
come from within. If you look you find," he adds.

After more than two hours of blessing, reassuring, and occasionally regaling his audience, the Dalai Lama comes to the most
substantive part of the morning. He has to address a fresh batch
of Tibetan refugees who have crossed over into India from China
through Nepal.

"I admire your courage in somehow reaching India, a land that
has been like a mother to us. Our only wish is to live peacefully in

our land of Tibet and pursue progress and spiritual growth, but that seems unacceptable to our friends in Beijing. I have lived outside Tibet for more than forty years. I would like to go back home at the first possible opportunity. However, before I do that our friends in Beijing must understand that Tibet has always been an independent land. We have no desire to fight with anyone. Buddhism has always taught us the middle path. It has also taught us to stand for what is just and challenge what is not. I believe China has been unjust. I want to return to Tibet in my lifetime. If not, then . . ." the Dalai Lama pauses, thinks deeply, and says, "I don't know when. I cannot wait for the next birth. I do not want you to hate anyone. If you can, go back to Tibet and help your fellow Tibetans. If you cannot, stay here and help Tibetans in exile. Promise me never to betray India."

The refugees, all of whom were looking down throughout the discourse, look up for a brief moment at the Dalai Lama and then look down once again. He leaves the audience. As I walk to my hotel room I decide to take a detour around the narrow path that circles the mountain. With the temperature rising to a mild 62 degrees F and the sun now shining brightly, it is a perfect day to ruminate over one of the most remarkable figures of our time. In front of me walks an old but sprightly monk twirling his prayer wheel. He is about to step on an insect but stops himself. He picks up a leaf, scoops up the insect, and puts it on a tree.

"Is it not possible that you have unknowingly stepped on many insects before? Why save only this one?" I ask him. He stops twirling his prayer wheel and replies, "Because I saw it." I later found out that this particular monk has been regarded as one of the most learned.

About a year later as I walk around the same mountain and

greet an occasional monk, I begin thinking about whether and how my many meetings with the Dalai Lama have affected me. I sit on a rock overlooking the Dharamshala valley and begin going through my notes. One entry strikes me particularly for its complete lack of critical edge. It says, "June 6 . . . it must be quite an accomplishment being the Dalai Lama . . . he seems so pure and equanimous. . . ." Another one dated August 7 is more skeptical: "How credible all this talk about reincarnation really is! It seems a bit excessive to say that you are in your fourteenth reincarnation. But then who knows about life and after it?" The most striking, though, is the one I recorded on December 3. "When you first meet him you don't know what all the fuss is about. As you meet him more frequently and observe him more closely you are still intrigued by the aura surrounding the man. Eventually you just reconcile to the fact of him as someone inexplicably gifted."

As with most gifted figures, it is perhaps futile to try to analyze or unravel or demystify the Dalai Lama. The reason they stand out in any crowd is because they have that indefinable quality. One cannot analyze charisma without simultaneously destroying it. It is most likely that a rational scrutiny would turn up an ordinary result or conclusion. Nevertheless, there are seemingly ordinary attributes that add up to create an extraordinary persona. All people of consequence have something ephemeral about their personality. In the Dalai Lama's case the ephemeral is compounded by his complete lack of guile. It is possible that I am inaccurate in my assessment. Having observed him for a considerable length of time I am quite certain that the private Dalai Lama is perhaps totally inaccessible to anyone. A lot of Westerners who have had the opportunity to know him closely make the common mistake of claiming to be his close friend.

Tempa Tsering once told me, "After his formal initiation as the Dalai Lama decades ago, even his immediate family would hesitate to claim any proximity to him. It might seem oddly reverential to you, but the Dalai Lama is not a figure you strike a friendship with."

I suspect, though, that the Dalai Lama himself finds it awkward to stand apart as a sort of divinity among lesser mortals. His repeated description of himself as "just an ordinary monk" might sound like contrived humility or feigned self-effacement. I know for a fact that it comes from genuine conviction and profound knowledge about an individual's station in this vast and bewitching universe. I once asked him if he took all the devotion and worship seriously. He contemplated deeply and said, "Everyone has that special quality that the people find so much in someone like me. They just have to know how to find it within oneself and project it. I truly am an ordinary monk keen on learning about everything that surrounds me."

During my seven years working on the biography, I spent considerable time watching the Dalai Lama from close quarters in many different situations. From giving discourses on metaphysics to presiding over initiation ceremonies, from visiting Tibetan settlements to granting his morning audiences, from conducting exclusive teaching sessions for the chosen few to offering a word of advice to a fresh batch of refugees, and from participating in Tibetan New Year festivities to instructing novice monks—everything I saw had some common themes. The Dalai Lama remained remarkably free from striking a single discordant note. If he were a singer he would never be off-key. If he were a juggler he would never drop a ball. If he were a funambulist, he would never take a wrong step. He never looks anything but calm. He never fails to laugh at least once, even while talking to a fresh batch of despairing Tibetan refugees. He always appears restfully aware and never shows any degree of anxiety either on his face or in his body language. He is always curious without being prying, and demonstrative without being overbearing. He is always in complete control of his surroundings no matter where he is. Most important, he has a sense of detachment about everything he does without appearing to be indifferent to even the smallest of detail.

One instance that brought to the fore all his attributes was a lecture the Dalai Lama gave at a popular college in New Delhi. The lecture was yet again about *shunyata*, or nothingness. To most people this is esoteric nonsense, but it is really quite profound and has sound intellectual foundation. The hall was overflowing with thousands of students and others. The Dalai Lama sat unobtrusively against a black backdrop. The ochre in his robes contrasted stunningly against the black of the backdrop and made him look like a dancing flame from a distance. The effect was cinematic because of the way he swayed back and forth. He knew the people in the audience were waiting for him to begin his discourse. He suddenly looked up at the corrugated tin roof. "When I last came here there was a family of pigeons. I wonder whether it is still here," he said and laughed. Right on cue a pigeon fluttered across the hall. I could see that his opening remark had the audience completely under his spell for the next hour and a half, during which he dwelt upon metaphysical aspects of Buddhism. The discourse's brilliance was not lost in the translation from Tibetan to English.

This memory has stayed with me for many reasons. In a sense the Dalai Lama's entire life played out in front of me that evening. Here was someone born in a nondescript village in one of the world's most inaccessible regions to a family of no significant standing, both materially and in terms of learning. He is a person who has no trappings of power or material success that might draw people to him. The subject of his choice and the language of his communication were not such that they would captivate an audience. Yet he was capturing an eclectic audience with such consummate ease about a subject as abstract as nothingness in a language that few understood without the aid of a translator. That he began his discourse reminiscing about a flock of pigeons merely added to his effectiveness. Distill this down and one is left with a simple explanation—some people are inexplicably gifted.

Another incident that brilliantly illustrates what the Dalai Lama is all about took place during my travels with him to Bylakuppe, the largest Tibetan refugee settlement on the edge of the famous coffee gardens of Karnataka state in South India, where close to 40,000 Tibetan refugees live. The Dalai Lama's visits to Tibetan settlements are always full of pomp and pageantry no matter how frequently they take place. The Tibetans never seem to get enough of him. The nearly five-mile stretch leading up to the Sera Je monastery, where the Dalai Lama was offering Kalchakra teachings, was lined with thousands of Tibetans and others. The cool air of the region seemed still as not a single one of them made any sound while the Dalai Lama's entourage drove past. Many of them waited with white silk scarves in the hope they might get personally blessed by him. The convoy of cars was traveling at a deliberately slow speed, giving the faithful a chance to see the Dalai Lama. Then suddenly the Dalai Lama asked to stop his car. He seemed to have spotted something. He got out of the car, much to the anxiety of his security detail, and walked toward a throng of people. For a moment everybody thought he had recognized someone he knew. There was a Tibetan child, who was probably four or five years old, playing with a dog, which was about two years old. As the Dalai Lama approached the throng, many thought he had come to bless them. Instead he reached out to the child and the puppy, stroked them both, laughed out loud, and said, "Both look so happy. They don't care that the Dalai Lama is nearby, you see," and returned to his vehicle.

A few hours later the Dalai Lama was sitting atop an ornate throne in front of a few thousand people, taking them through the maze of Buddhist teachings. The contrast between a man who has not lost touch with the simple joys of life, a monk who is always aware of his religious obligations, and a mystic who seldom reveals what lies behind the obvious is quite telling in the Dalai Lama.

The burden of expectations that he will say something enchantingly clever or stunningly profound every time he opens his mouth has steadily grown on the Dalai Lama over the past twenty years. In a sense he is like an enormously successful stand-up comic who has to update his material constantly lest in his next show his jokes bomb. However, the Dalai Lama has steadfastly avoided positioning himself to please the gallery. His biggest success has been to refashion and reinvent the relevancy of his institution during a period of human history most regard as the most scientifically, technologically, and rationally driven. He has made his message nondenominational and nonreligious without compromising the enduring mystique of his life. He has successfully presented a version of Buddhism that is palatable to the modern and increasingly secularized Western mind.

The example of how he has repositioned his message was on display during his twenty-day visit to the United States in September 2005. Addressing a gathering at the Rutgers stadium in

New Jersey, the Dalai Lama began his speech in his characteristic self-effacing manner. "I have nothing to offer, no new ideas or new views," he said.

"We are living things, like trees and grass," he said surveying the green football field, and added a rider, "I don't know if this grass is true grass."

Just as the audience might have begun to wonder if he would ever say anything out of the ordinary, he called war "out of date." He then said, "Eventually the whole world should be free of nuclear weapons." The idea seemed quite trite and ordinary until then. But he elevated it, saying that before the world could achieve "external disarmament" it needed to achieve "internal disarmament."

In the same address he made a distinction between attachment and compassion. This is one of his favorite themes. Attachment, he said, is like a selective connection shared by friends or family. Compassion, on the other hand, is an "unbiased and selfless" act. He wrapped up his speech on that note, leaving the audience deeply reflective.

It is unlikely that the Dalai Lama or those around him would acknowledge it, but perhaps in his own mind he is conscious that as an individual he has reached beyond the cause he has come to embody. His campaign for Tibet's independence is at a crossroads to say the least and could be in danger of losing its relevance. Tibet could not have found a more arresting articulator of its plight. But therein lies the problem. Tibet is so closely identified with the Dalai Lama that sometimes the connection between the two could be counterproductive. In Tibet's case the nation is indeed the man. He has done for Tibet all that he could do as a man without a state, as a monk wedded to nonviolence, and as a mystic in search of deeper truths. In any cause of any scale and complexity it would generally be naïve to attribute success to a single individual. But Tibet has essentially been one man's relentless campaign spanning nearly five decades. It is to the Dalai Lama's credit that China is willing to even talk about Tibet as an outstanding issue. Left to the Chinese leadership, the issue would have been treated as settled in 1950 when the Red Army marched into Tibet practically unaccosted. Nonviolent and morally sharpened campaigns necessarily take a long time to make an impact, as was so powerfully underscored by Mahatma Gandhi's campaign against the British Raj.

As the Dalai Lama says, it is still possible that he would return to an autonomous, if not independent, Tibet in his lifetime. In many ways the question of Tibet has never been as ready for resolution to the general satisfaction of both sides as it is now. The realization that one individual, and that too an unarmed monk, stands in the way of a mighty nation is supremely inspiring.

The journey from Tengster to Lhasa and from Lhasa to the rest of the world has been an epic one. When twenty-four-year-old Tenzin Gyatso shed his robes and dressed up as a soldier to flee to India, little did he know that he would emerge as the world's conscience keeper. At seventy-one as he looks back on his life, divided between enormous personal growth and a virtually lost battle for his homeland, there could not be a more apt conclusion than the Sanskrit maxim *yatha bhutam*, or "the way it is."

ACKNOWLEDGMENTS

I want to acknowledge with utter and unequivocal gratitude a few people whose contributions to this book are remarkable.

I have dedicated the book to my wife, Kesumi, our son, Jashn, and our daughter, Hayaa. During the long hours that I spent writing this book they stood by me with the unquestioning faith that only one's immediate family can demonstrate. This book is as much theirs as it is mine. The book is also for my late father, Manharray, and my mother, Snehalata, and for the entire extended Chhaya family.

My agent and friend Lynn Franklin has been associated with the book from the get-go. I was first referred to Lynn by a common friend, Mallika Sarabhai. Lynn has been exceptionally supportive of me, often beyond the call of professional courtesy. Talk about life coming full circle—the book's Indian edition is being published by Mapin, a publishing house run by Sarabhai and her business partner, Bipin Shah.

There have been many friends and well-wishers who have wittingly or unwittingly become part of the project.

Chief among these is Harikrishna Majmundar, whose generosity of spirit and clarity of thought I cherish a great deal. Through him I would like to thank Kanubhai Gandhi for stepping in when I needed help.

I would also like to specially thank well-known Silicon Valley venture capitalist Raj Singh, who supported my media company, Literate World, with the detachment of a yogi.

My friends CPA Neeraj Bhatia and attorney Alex Reichl deserve particular gratitude for their time and support throughout this project. It is also important that I mention my friends and fellow journalists Preeti Verma Lal and Amit Kumar, both of whom were among the first to read the manuscript. My former colleagues Rajesh Ranjan, Sangeeta Singh, and Dharampal deserve to be applauded for their strength in the face of some difficult times. I would also like to thank my former personal assistant, Naresh Kumar, for his services. Friends such as Dr. Prakash Desai, Harsh Mehta, Nitin Karnik, George Albert, Sudhir Gupta, Sheri Flister, Ashok Easwaran, and Sunita Chopra also deserve a special mention here for their generosity.

I want to thank the editors at Random House, led by Trace Murphy, for their meticulous work. Trace in particular drove this project with quiet resolve. I also want to record my appreciation for Sean Mills, for his excellent production work.

From among two hundred people I interviewed for the book,

I would like to single out Dr. Orville Schell, Professor Robert Thurman, and Richard Gere, and thank them for their time. Each of these accomplished individuals generously shared his unique perspective with me.

Most important, I am particularly grateful to the Fourteenth Dalai Lama for granting me unfettered access to his time and his world, and in the process elevating the book's content to a whole new level. The Dalai Lama's elder brother Thubten Jigme Norbu opened his heart to me about his family as well as about Tibet, and for that I am forever indebted to him. I cannot thank the Dalai Lama's private secretary and my friend Tenzin Geyche Tethong enough for obtaining the authorization for this book. Without his unwavering support and trust, and that of former press secretary Tsering Tashi, this book would simply not exist.

In conclusion, I want to express gratitude to my friend Sam Pitroda, whose obsessive insistence on "physically touching" the manuscript helped propel the book to fruition. He has stood by me every step of the way, and I am grateful to him.

BIBLIOGRAPHICAL
REFERENCES

Chapter 1: Continental Cataclysm

- The formation of Tibet—based on widespread references from books including *Tibetan Nation* by Warren W. Smith, Jr. (Boulder Colo.: Westview Press, 1996); *Evolution of the Chinese Environment* by Robert Orr Whyte (Berkeley: University of California Press, 1983); "Project INDEPTH" (International Deep Profiling of Tibet and the Himalaya) by Simon Klemper, Professor of Geophysics; "Geology and Geography of Tibet and Western China" by Pete Winn, Science Director Earth Science Expeditions, <http://www.shangri-la-river-expeditions. com/wchinageo/wchinageo.html> (2002).
- History of Tibet—based on references from several books by the Dalai Lama, Warren W. Smith, Jr., Sir Charles Bell, Tibetan government-in-exile archives, as well as conversations with historians and

Buddhist scholars. Also *Inner Asian Frontiers of China* by Owen Lattimore (New York: Oxford University Press, 1988); *A Study of the Early Medieval Chinese, Latin, and Tibetan Historical Sources in Pre-imperial Tibet* by Christopher Beckwith, Ph.D. work, Indiana University, Bloomington, Indiana.

Chapter 2: Buddhism Comes to Tibet

- *Scriptures of the East*, edited by James Fieser and John Powers (Boston: McGraw-Hill, 2004).
- *Buddhism: The Light of Asia* by Kenneth K. S. Chen (Hauppauge, NY: Barron's Educational Series, Inc., 1977).
- *What the Buddha Taught* by Walpola Rahula (New York: Grove Press, 1959; repr. 1974).
- *The Buddha and Gospel of Buddhism* by Ananda K. Coomaraswamy (New York: Harper Torchbooks, 1916; repr. 1964).

Chapter 3: Clucking Like a Hen and Breaking Up Fights

- Based on extensive personal conversations with Thubten Jigme Norbu, the Dalai Lama's elder brother, in Bloomington, Indiana.
- *Kundun* by Mary Craig (Washington D.C.: Counterpoint, 1997); *The Last Dalai Lama* by Michael Harris Goodman (London: Sidgwick and Jackson, LTD., 1986).
- *Tibet Is My Country* by Thubten Jigme Norbu (London: Wisdom Tibet Book, Yellow Press, 1986).

Chapter 4: From a Prankster to the Dalai Lama Reincarnate

- *Tibetan Nation* by Warren W. Smith, Jr., especially for details related to events before the Thirteenth Dalai Lama's death.

- Conversations with the Dalai Lama and his aides.
- Tibetan archives and chronicles at the Norbulingka Library, Dharamshala.
- *Tibet Past and Present* by Sir Charles Bell (Delhi: Faith India, 1998).
- Sir Basil Gould was the political officer of Sikkim who represented the colonial British government in India at the enthronement of the Fourteenth Dalai Lama.

Chapter 5: Farewell to the Worldly World

- Jawaharlal Nehru's address at the Sino-Indian Cultural Society General Body Meeting at Santiniketan on December 23, 1945, India's National Archives.
- Jawaharlal Nehru and Sardar Patel perspectives on China: http://www.sinoindianwar.50megs.com/index.html and http://www.centurychina.com/plaboard/uploads/1962war.htm.

Chapter 6: Lhasa in Turmoil

- *Tibet Past and Present* by Sir Charles Bell.

Chapter 7: Tibet's New Ruler Is Not All of Five Years Old

- *Tibet Past and Present* by Sir Charles Bell.

Chapter 8: India, China, and Tibet

- Jawaharlal Nehru and Sardar Patel perspectives on China: http://sinoindianwar.50megs.com/index.html and http://www.centurychina.com/plaboard/uploads/1962war.htm.

- Government of India archives, as well as Tibetan chronicles.
- Jyotindra Nath Dixit, India's former Foreign Secretary and National Security Advisor, who died in 2005: quotes from him are based on personal interviews with the author.

Chapter 10: New Gods in Tibet

- "Reflections on Tibet" by Wang Lixiong, *New Left Review*, March–April 2002.

Chapter 12: Mao, Buddhism, and Tantra

- *Kundun* by Mary Craig.
- *The Dalai Lama* by Claude B. Levenson, translated by Stephen Cox (New York: Oxford University Press, 1999).

Chapter 13: To Talk or Not to Talk

- *Tibetan Nation* by Warren W. Smith, Jr.
- Tibetan government-in-exile Information Department.
- Quotes from two Tibetan experts Tashi Rabgey and Tseten Wangchuk Sharlho taken from www.phayul.com, a Tibetan news Web site on July 11, 2005.
- The Five-Point Proposal is based on official Tibetan government-in-exile documents.
- *Buddhist Logic* by Theodore Stcherbatsky (New Delhi, India: Motilal Banarsidass Pub., 2000).
- Material from Human Rights Watch Web site http://www.hrw.org/ as well as press releases.

Chapter 14: The Nobel Laureate: Gandhi's Successor

- The Dalai Lama's Nobel Prize acceptance speech: the Tibetan Government-in-exile Information Department.
- Excerpts from Egil Aarvik's speech, excerpts from official Web site of the Norwegian Nobel Committee in Stockholm, Sweden.

Chapter 15: Life After Nobel

- "Guidelines for Future Tibet's Polity and the Basic Features of Its Constitution" is taken from official Tibetan government-in-exile record.

Chapter 16: Unyielding Chinese and Uncompromising Tibetans

- White Paper: "Tibet: Its Ownership and Human Rights Situation" by the Information Office of the State Council of the People's Republic of China, 1992.
- Official rebuttal to "Tibet: Its Ownership and Human Rights Situation" from Tibetan government-in-exile.
- Report by the International Commission of Jurists' Legal Enquiry Committee on Tibet, 1966.

Chapter 17: Murders in the Monastery

- Official document of the Tibetan government-in-exile on the practice of Shugden followers, June 1996.
- Dharamshala/McLeod Ganj Police.
- "Did an obscure Tibetan sect murder three monks close to the Dalai Lama?" by Tony Clifton, *Newsweek*, April 28, 1997.
- Official documents from the Kashag, or the Tibetan cabinet.

Chapter 19: The Dalai Lama: The Monk

- Information about the controversy over the Dalai Lama's participation in Neuroscience 2005, the Society for Neuroscience's annual conference held in November 2005, is based on the author's personal research for a news story he wrote.

Chapter 20: The Dalai Lama: the Mystic

- *The Concealed Essence of the Hevajra Tantra* by G. W. Farrow and I. Menon, translated by G. W. Farrow, First ed. (Delhi: Motilal Banarsidass, 1992).

Chapter 21: Part Socratic, Part Rock Star, Part Eastern Wise Man, Mostly Buddhist Monk

- Author Jeffery Paine's quotes were culled from http://www.boston.com/ae/books/articles/2004/02/29/awakenings/, and other sites.

Chapter 26: Hotheads Versus Middle Way

- *State Growth and Social Exclusion in Tibet* by Andrew Fischer (Copenhagen: Nordic Institute of Asian Studies Press, 2005).
- "Options for Tibet's Future Political Status: Self-Governance Through an Autonomous Arrangement," by Tibet Justice Center, Eva Herzer (New Delhi, India: Tibetan Parliamentary & Policy Research Centre, 2002).
- Quotes of Khedroob Thondup, a former parliament member of the Tibetan government-in-exile were taken from www.phayul.com, a popular Web site on Tibetan affairs.
- The Dalai Lama's official address to the U.S. Congress was taken from the Tibetan government-in-exile archives.

Chapter 27: Models of Autonomy

- The U.S. government's Tibetan Policy Act of 2002 quotes were taken from the official State Department site www.state.gov.
- Comments by Eva Herzer were made to the author in an interview.

Chapter 29: Will He Ever Return to Tibet?

- Thubten Samphel's quotes are based on comments made to the author in an interview.
- Quotes by Wu Yingjie, a vice governor of Tibet, have been attributed to a news report by Reuters.
- Geremie Barme quoted in "Dalai Lama Return to Tibet May Be Simpler for China" by Jane Macartney, Reuters, September 24, 2003, http://www.tibet.ca/en/wtnarchive/2003/9/24_4.html.

Suggestions for Further Reading

"The Art and Politics of Tibet," lecture by Kasur Tenzin N. Tethong at the Asian Art Museum, San Francisco, June 2, 2005. Available online (http://www.phayul.com/news/article.aspx?id=10034&t=1&c=1).

Dalai Lama, My Son: A Mother's Story by Diki Tsering (New York: Viking Arkana, 2000).

Evolution of the Chinese Environment by Robert Orr Whyte (Berkeley: University of California Press, 1983).

India's China War by Maxwell Neville (Garden City, NY: Anchor Books, 1972).

In Exile from the Land of Snows by John Avedon (New York: Vintage, 1986).

My Land and My People: Memoirs of the Dalai Lama of Tibet (New York: McGraw Hill, 1962).

"The Myth of China's Modernization of Tibet and the Tibetan Language" by Jamyang Norbu, www.phayul.com.

Orphans of the Cold War: America and the Tibetan Struggle for Survival by John Kenneth Knaus (New York: Public Affairs, 1999). Knaus is an associate at the Fairbank Center for East Asian Research at Harvard University.

Re-enchantment: Tibetan Buddhism Comes to the West by Jeffery Paine (New York: W. W. Norton & Company, 2004).

"Reflections on Tibet" by Wang Lixiong (*New Left Review* 14, March–April 2002).

"Report on Tibet Negotiations," April 2005, U.S. Department of State, www.state.gov/p/eap/rls/rpt/45015.htm.

"Sino-Tibetan Dialogue in the Post-Mao Era" by Tashi Rabgey and Tseten Wangchuck Sharlho, www.phayul.com.

Tibet and the Tibetans by Tsung-lieu Shên and Shên-chi Liu. Foreword by George E. Taylor (Stanford, Calif.: Stanford University Press, 1953).

"Tibetan Policy Act of 2002," U.S. State Department, www.state.gov/p/eap/rls/rpt/20699.htm.

Tibet in Sino-Indian Relations 1899–1914 by Suchita Ghosh (New Delhi: Sterling Publishers, 1977).

Younghusband: The Last Great Imperial Adventurer by Patrick French (New York: Harper Collins, 1994).

INDEX